PRAISE FOR
The Monstrosity of Our Century

"Today more than ever, Arabs and Muslims must become aware of the terrible maneuvers and plots being hatched against them by lighting the fires of discord and sedition among the members of the Ummah, between Sunnis and Shiites, Arabs and Kurds, Arabs and Berbers and Muslims and Christians. Proof of this are the turpitudes suffered by the central cause of the Arabs and Muslims, that of plundered Palestine. I highly recommend reading Amir Nour's book because of the judicious choice of carefully documented writings by authoritative authors and studies, the sagacity of the analysis and the clairvoyance of the foresight."

DR. AHMED TALEB-IBRAHIMI
former Minister of Foreign Affairs of Algeria (1982–1988)

"The Monstrosity of Our Century is a deeply informed and meticulously researched work by a brilliant Arab intellectual familiar with both the Western and Islamic scholarly traditions. Uniquely, it draws on both traditions to dissect the factors that made both the October 7, 2023, attack on Israel by Hamas and other Palestinian resistance movements inevitable, and Western support for the genocidal reaction of the Israelis to this predictable. The author, Amir Nour, eloquently and unflinchingly shows how the course of events in Palestine has discredited the moral authority of the West and devalued international law, while changing the world order and isolating Israel, making its survival increasingly doubtful."

DR. CHAS W. FREEMAN JR.
formerly U.S. Assistant Secretary of Defense for International
Security Affairs and Ambassador to Saudi Arabia

"Amir Nour has made his bold and insightful book a prominent document exposing the Zionist settlement project, for which Palestinians and Arabs have paid a heavy price. Yet, the signs of the project's failure are becoming clear, just as its racist foundations and intentions have been revealed over the past seventy years, and as exemplified in the ongoing genocidal war on Palestine."

HASSAN JANABI
former Iraqi Minister and former Ambassador to Japan and Turkey

"A bold and refreshing critique of Western imperialism, centered on Israel's settler colonialism in Palestine and its genocidal war on Gaza, Amir Nour's book challenges many erroneous notions about the roots of global conflict, the binary narrative of the "war on terror," and the dangerous "us vs. them" mentality espoused by Washington and its Western allies. By situating the Israeli war on the Palestinian people within a global context, Nour helps liberate the history of the so-called "conflict" from the provisional, often short-sighted approach to history. Additionally, the book brilliantly demonstrates the need for an alternative form of history—one that shifts from the ethno-centric, dominant Western approach to a more equitable "global history." Strongly needed and highly recommended."

DR. RAMZY BAROUD
author of *My Father Was a Freedom Fighter* and *The Last Earth*

"Neither to accuse the West, nor to defend the East, Amir Nour's book brings back the human in us to the center, after having been, for so long, pushed to the margins of his own story. Nour strips this age of its borrowed virtues and moral disguises, revealing it as it truly is.

"No reader of these pages should look away. Because truth, as the book demonstates persuasively, has never been what we think we see; it is what the powers that be can no longer conceal."

LAALA BECHETOULA
Algerian journalist and writer, author of *The Book of Gaza Hashem: A Testament Written in Olive Wood and Ash*

THE MONSTROSITY OF OUR CENTURY

THE WAR ON PALESTINE AND THE LAST WESTERN MAN

AMIR NOUR

Clarity Press, Inc.

ISBN: 978-1-963892-28-4
EBOOK ISBN: 978-1-963892-29-1

Book design: Becky Luening Book Arts

Library of Congress Control Number: 2025950774

Clarity Press, Inc.
2625 Piedmont Rd. NE, Ste. 56
Atlanta, GA 30324, USA
https://www.claritypress.com

TABLE OF CONTENTS

FOREWORD

Richard Forer

Amir Nour's *The War on Palestine* takes readers on a comprehensive tour of Israel's ongoing offensive against Gaza, while documenting historical events that set the stage for this tragedy to unfold. In doing so, Nour does not shy away from implicating the West for its role in contributing to the conditions that all but made Hamas's October 7, 2023 invasion of Israel inevitable and Israel's genocidal reaction predictable.

For logistical reasons, if its goal was the extermination of Hamas and the dismemberment of Gazan society, Israel could not act alone. It needed both the blessing and the military assistance not only of the U.S., but of other nations, Britain and Germany in particular, whose leaders routinely congratulate themselves on their democratic values and respect for human life and international law. Answering every criticism of their acquiescence to what the International Court of Justice calls a "plausible genocide"—*plausible* in this case being a legal term so as not to prejudge the outcome of proceedings—with Israel's "need for security" and "right to defend itself," the representatives of those nations never explain how killing children by the thousands makes Israel more secure, nor do they consider the possibility that the killings will motivate a future generation of fighters to seek revenge in honor of their relatives and friends, whose lives were so brutally and even gleefully snuffed out by the Israeli war machine and its western facilitators.

Clearly, in its unrestrained codependency with Israel, hypocrisy plays a major role. An example of American hypocrisy, and the confusion and dissembling that occurs when a nation acts contrary to its publicly stated values, is the U.S. administration's National Security spokesperson's statement that "The United States condemns the bombing of an UNRWA school in Gaza that reportedly left Palestinians dead and injured innocent people—including children—and UN employees," followed a few hours later by a Pentagon spokesperson's announcement that the U.S. had supplied Israel with weapons and that "The United States is committed to ensuring the security of Israel, and it is crucial to American national interests to help Israel develop and maintain a strong and responsive self-defense capability (. . .) This arms sale is consistent with these goals." In deference to Israel's malevolent intentions, the Pentagon omitted reference to the rhetoric of virtually every notable member of Israel's military, political and religious establishments that their objective was to eradicate Hamas and that all Gazans, children included, were indeed Hamas.

Goals? Self-defense capabilities? American national interests? Pulling the plugs on incubators, murdering doctors and journalists, torturing and imprisoning Palestinians by the thousands, bombing ambulances, killing humanitarian aid workers, sexually abusing men and women, denying medical care, baiting starving Palestinians with food so Israel's soldiers can open fire and mow them down, distributing cans that children mistake for food only for the cans to explode when picked up? Those are Israel's immediate goals and means of self-defense, and I have no idea how the West's myopia to any of that contributes to America's stated national interests. Painfully, as I write this Foreword, that is what Israel is doing. In short, the American Israeli alliance has produced what Francesca Albanese, the United Nations Special Rapporteur on Human Rights in the Occupied Palestinian Territories, calls "the monstrosity of our century."

In addition to its hypocrisy and hubris, Nour exposes the West's incompetence and bewildered judgment in waging its so-called wars on terror, pointing out that "since the United States ramped up its counter-terrorism operations in Africa, terrorism has spiked 75,000%." Yet, even in the midst of a "textbook case of genocide," the West continues "to shield and thus bolster the actions of Israel." The West has abandoned its responsibility to the world order and made a mockery of its alleged respect for international law.

Traveling through history, *The Monstrosity of Our Century: The War on Palestine and the Last Western Man* contains a litany of factors that built upon one another to form the worldview of Israeli society, from *The Jewish State,* Theodor Herzl's dissertation on Zionism, published in 1896, to the 1917 Balfour Declaration, the 1936 Arab Revolt, the 1937 Peel commission, 1947 UN Partition Plan, 1948 Arab Israeli war, 1967

Six-Day War, up to the present-day horrors. Nour even references the Old Testament and, among other figures of Jewish history, Moses and the Amalekites.

Nour does not ignore the Jewish state's perverse redefining of antisemitism from authentic and historical hatred of Jews to the "embrace of egalitarian values," egalitarianism being a mortal threat to Jewish supremacy in an Arab-Muslim corner of earth. Critically, Nour points out how Israel, which could not have become a reality if not for the Holocaust, the greatest explosion of antisemitism the world has ever known, went from being "a cure for anti-Semitism to its cause when it was faced by the reality of Palestinian resistance." As anyone who has studied the history of Israel-Palestine knows, Israel's leaders, principally David Ben-Gurion and Vladimir Jabotinsky, were well aware that an indigenous people would not passively accept another people's theft of their homes and land and the slaughter of their people. In order to deceive the world, Israel's leaders had the foresight to conflate the Jewish religion with the nationalistic ideology of Zionism, the latter of which the vast majority of religious Jews considered heresy to the Torah because only the Moshiach (Messiah from the House of David), can establish a Jewish nation.

An avowed atheist who detested religious Jews, Theodor Herzl, who died in 1904, predicted, "the anti-Semites will become our most dependable friends, the anti-Semitic countries our allies." A few years ago, Israeli prime minister Benjamin Netanyahu, frustrated with criticism of his crimes against the Palestinians by the American Jewish community, especially its younger generation, said, "We have no better friends in the world than the Evangelical community." A significant number of evangelicals believe the Jews are guilty of the one unpardonable sin: the murder of Christ. In years past that assertion would instantly have been condemned as antisemitism. Evangelical Reverend John Hagee, who has millions of followers and has raised millions of dollars for Israel's illegal settlement enterprise, has said that Adolf Hitler, who was born from a lineage of "accursed, genocidally murderous half-breed Jews," was tasked with expediting God's will of having the Jews re-establish the State of Israel. That too would have been condemned as antisemitism, yet Ariel settlement, one of the largest in the West Bank, has honored the reverend with its John Hagee Building, part of its sports and recreational complex.

Finally, although I could write a book about Nour's book, I end with the following: Nour asks perhaps the fundamental question of our time, possibly for all of time with regard to one group's relationship to another's, a question that must always and necessarily be asked, a question that would come to the minds of rational and humane leaders: "Isn't it insane to believe that our civilized world is unable to find a path other than the one leading toward Mutually Agreed Destruction (MAD)?"

Richard Forer is the author of *Breakthrough: Transforming Fear into Compassion—A New Perspective on the Israel-Palestine Conflict* and *Wake Up and Reclaim Your Humanity: Essays on the Tragedy of Israel-Palestine.*

THE INSANITY OF WESTERN POLITICAL DISCOURSE

"In the emerging world of ethnic conflict and civilizational clash, Western belief in the universality of Western culture suffers three problems: it is false; it is immoral; and it is dangerous."
—SAMUEL PHILLIPS HUNTINGTON[1]

Often misattributed to Albert Einstein, the famous adage that "Insanity is doing the same thing over and over again and expecting different results" has rarely been more apt than in the case of the traditionally biased Western governments' position vis-à-vis the Israeli-Arab and Israeli-Palestinian conflict.

Remarkably unanimous as far as the core of the problem is concerned—even though occasionally divergent on trivial details—these governments, as well as their powerful relays among the globalist elites and mainstream media, have invariably supported and defended loud and clear the theses and objectives of the Israeli occupation, giving themselves a clear conscience by making false promises and failed commitments to the Palestinians, who in the process have steadily been uprooted from their ancestral lands.

Because of their customary hypocritical posturing and morally bankrupt duplicity, double-standard and variable geometry language and actions,[2] tantamount to Orwellian "double-think," they are incapable of

---

1 Samuel Phillips Huntington, *The Clash of Civilizations and the Remaking of World Order* (Simon & Schuster, 1998).

2 Epitomizing this deliberate and longstanding policy is—among many other documents—a U.S. State Department's secret cable under the title "Cashless in Gaza?," dated November 3, 2008, and released by Wikileaks. It informs that ". . . Israeli officials have confirmed to Embassy officials on multiple occasions that they intend to keep the Gazan economy functioning at the lowest

applying evenhandedly the law and justice in which they pride themselves whenever these do not suit their narrow interests. With such a sole compass in mind, they have thus culpably contributed to the perpetuation of both the plight of the Palestinians and a conflict that colonial Great Britain and France in particular and Nazi Germany created during the past century, and which the United States of America constantly feeds[3] in order to serve its strategic interests in a world it has relentlessly striven to dominate and control exclusively since the end of the Second World War.

As a result, the Israeli-Palestinian conflict has today become explosive, while its solution on a just and lasting basis seems to be moving further and further away, giving rise to an unprecedented degree of despair, mutual hatred and violence in an historically volatile region. The ongoing horrendous Israeli onslaught on the besieged Gaza Strip— the fifth of its kind in just 15 years—is further destabilizing the whole region. It is also gravely jeopardizing international peace and security and seriously undermining the credibility and durability of the entire international order put in place in 1945.

In this respect, as early as 2018, I asserted that "Epochal developments in nearly all areas of human activity have triggered increasing concern about the sustainability of an international order conceived, shaped and erected in large measure by the United States of America in the wake of World War II, thanks to its overwhelming economic and military power. But this so-called U.S.-led 'liberal' order has been witnessing steady erosion and is today brutally called into question, to say the least. And surprisingly enough, its very foundations have been subjected to incessant assaults carried out by those who have constructed it (...) As John Ikenberry stated, 'the world's most powerful state has begun to sabotage the order it created. A hostile revisionist power has indeed arrived on the scene, but it sits in the Oval Office, the beating heart of the Free world'.[4] The conjunction of such realities as illegal wars waged by self-proclaimed global policemen against weaker 'disobedient' albeit sovereign states, and unparalleled economic inequality stemming from the contradictions of capitalist globalization and the

---

level possible consistent with avoiding a humanitarian crisis. . . ."

3 During his July 18, 2003, meeting with his Israeli counterpart in the Oval Office of the White House in Washington D.C., President Joe Biden repeated a line he famously said in 1986: "If there were not an Israel, we'd have to invent one." *The Conversation,* July 25, 2023.

4 G. John Ikenberry, "The Plot Against American Foreign Policy: Can the Liberal Order Survive?," *Foreign Affairs,* May/June 2017.

behavior of unfettered corporate expansion exploiting almost every area of public and private life, has generated a growing global authoritarianism and social Darwinism. Pankaj Mishra[5] aptly captured and eloquently summed up the big picture and the choreography of this *danse macabre* entrapping the whole world in his observation that 'future historians may well see such uncoordinated mayhem as commencing the third—and the longest and the strangest—of all world wars, one that approximates, in its ubiquity, a global civil war.'"

Alas, in its annual report 2023/2024, *The State of the World's Human Rights,* Amnesty International is painting a similar gloomy picture. Indeed, the UK-based non-governmental organization that campaigns to end abuses of human rights worldwide is sounding an alarm on what it says is a watershed moment for international law amid flagrant rule-breaking by governments and corporate actors, which are abandoning the founding values of humanity and universality enshrined in the Universal Declaration of Human Rights. Powerful governments, Amnesty explains, cast humanity into an era devoid of effective international rule of law, with civilians in conflicts paying the highest price, while rapidly developing artificial intelligence is left to create fertile ground for racism, discrimination and division in a landmark year for public elections. Standing against these abuses, people the world over have mobilized in unprecedented numbers, demanding human rights protection and respect for our common humanity. All of this is occurring "in the midst of deepening global inequality, superpowers vying for supremacy and an escalating climate crisis" said Amnesty International's Secretary General, Agnès Callamard. But where many governments have failed to abide by international law, she goes on to say, "we have also seen others calling on international institutions to implement the rule of law. And where leaders the world over have failed to stand up for human rights, we have seen people galvanized to march, protest and petition for a more hopeful future ... People have made it abundantly clear that they want human rights; the onus is on governments to show that they are listening."

With regard to the genocidal war on Gaza, Callamard stated that "Israel's flagrant disregard for international law is compounded by the failures of its allies to stop the indescribable civilian bloodshed meted out in Gaza. Many of those allies were the very architects of that post-World

---

5 Pankaj Mishra, *Age of Anger: A History of the Present* (Farrar, Straus and Giroux, 2017).

War Two system of law ... In particular, over the last six months, the United States has shielded and protected the Israeli authorities against scrutiny for the multiple violations committed in Gaza ... By using its veto against a much-needed ceasefire, the United States has emptied out the [United Nations] Security Council of what it should be doing."

The blind and ironclad U.S. support for Israel once again manifested itself when its Deputy Ambassador to the UN, Robert Wood, was the only representative of a UN Security Council member country to vote against an Algerian-proposed draft resolution[6] recommending granting the state of Palestine full membership at the United Nations Organization. In a vote of 12 in favor to one against, with two abstentions (UK and Switzerland), the Council thus rejected Palestine's request, which, had it been adopted, would have recommended the General Assembly to hold a vote with the broader UN membership to allow Palestine to join as a full member state.

In so doing, the U.S. administration has doubled down on its almost visceral hostility to such a membership, which it had already opposed in 2012 when the General Assembly adopted—with a vast majority of 138 votes in favor and only 9 against—resolution 67/19 granting Palestine "non-member state" status, as a state on the 1967 borders with East Jerusalem as its capital. Washington's proclaimed "strong support for a two-state solution" has thus revealed itself to be singularly hollow and contradictory.

Commenting on that issue on X (formerly Twitter), Trita Parsi, founder of the National Iranian American Council and co-founder and executive vice-president of the Quincy Institute for Responsible Statecraft, said "Take a moment to ponder how isolated Biden has made the U.S. Biden lobbied Japan, South Korea & Ecuador HARD to oppose the Palestine resolution so that the U.S. wouldn't have to veto. They refused. So Biden cast his 4th veto in 7 months (!!). This is the opposite of leadership." By the same token, Washington has failed to use its diplomatic weight to accomplish its face-saving goal before the Security Council, has laid bare the contradictions between its words and deeds,

---

6 See United Nations News, "U.S. vetoes Palestine's request for full UN membership," April 18, 2024. The draft resolution is among the shortest in the Council's history: "The Security Council, having examined the application of the State of Palestine for admission to the United Nations (S/2011/592), recommends to the General Assembly that the State of Palestine be admitted to membership in the United Nations." Palestine has been a "Permanent Observer" at the UN since 2012, before which it was an observer in the UN General Assembly.

and has shown it cannot formulate a coherent strategy that aligns with its own stated values, thereby further exposing its gradual loss of soft power.[7]

Amnesty International has also finger-pointed several other Western countries for their "grotesque double standards," including the UK and Germany, for continuing to shield and thus bolster the actions of Israel, given those states' well-founded protests over war crimes by Russia and Hamas. The report specifically condemns the UK for failing to use its leadership role within the UN to prevent human rights violations in Gaza and its weak support for the International Criminal Court (ICC) investigation into human rights violations in Israel and Palestine. It also highlights Britain's unbridled involvement in arming Israel and warns Britain will be "judged harshly by history for its failure to help prevent civilian slaughter in Gaza."[8]

Yet, and fortunately enough, the wheel turns and the lines are starting to move in a changing global geostrategic context, chiefly under the combined effect of the end of the dismal brief era of American unipolar dominance, the resurgence of Russia and China on the global stage, and the gradual emergence of a Global South, which legitimately claims the right to participate in the management of the affairs of our increasingly interconnected "planetary village," most conspicuously under the aegis of the BRICS nations.

It is hoped therefore that there will soon be an end to the plunge into the abyss of lawlessness, unaccountability and impunity, lest the disenchanted peoples of the planet, starting with those of the Arab-Muslim world, irreparably lose faith in the so-called Western liberal values and norms of freedom, equality, human rights, democracy, and rule of law.

The government of South Africa courageously showed the way by dragging Israel into the International Court of Justice, and Chief Prosecutor of the ICC Karim Khan followed in its footsteps by filing applications for warrants of arrest for Benjamin Netanyahu and his defense minister Yoav Gallant, notwithstanding the scandalous letter[9] sent by 12 U.S. senators threatening to take action against him and his staff if the ICC were to issue international arrest warrants against Israeli officials. In

---

7 Bradley Blankenship, "The Middle East crisis has made one thing clear about the US," *RT,* April 22, 2024.

8 Karen McVeigh, "UK accused by Amnesty of 'deliberately destabilizing' human rights globally," *The Guardian,* April 24, 2024.

9 To download the letter: https://www.politico.com/f/?id=0000018f-4e0e-d759-a9ff-ff4ee9420000

this letter, which blatantly violates international law, the U.S. lawmakers told Khan: "If you issue a warrant for the arrest of the Israeli leadership, we will interpret this not only as a threat to Israel's sovereignty but to the sovereignty of the United States ... Target Israel and we will target you [and] will move to end all American support for the ICC, sanction your employees and associates, and bar you and your families from the United States. You have been warned."

Also worthy of special mention here is the resounding rise of the *Vox Populi* across the world. It's increasingly becoming a powerful force in modern political communication, from global popular street protests and demonstrations to smartphones, digital platforms and social media networks like Facebook a decade ago and TikTok today. The potent emergence of social media has undoubtedly changed the game in many important ways. It is in the process of seriously challenging the powerful control and influence the mainstream media once held almost exclusively with respect to setting the narrative for policymakers in the executive and legislative branches and public opinion alike. Its impact on political authority, participation and representation is therefore far from negligible.

The textbook case of genocide that Israel is carrying out against the Palestinian people, with the murderous complicity of most Western governments, has inflamed public opinion across the whole world as shown by the millions of pro-Palestinian protesters marching almost daily in rallies on the streets of major world cities. These multitudes are united in one overarching demand: end the Israeli bombardment of Gaza and Israeli occupation of Palestinian territories. Even in the United States, the staunchest supporter of Israel no matter how gravely damaging this blind support has been to the United States' national and global interests, growing numbers of protesters have taken to the streets of New York City, Washington D.C., Los Angeles and Dallas, among others.

This is particularly true in the case of young people who, in large numbers, are turning off the mainstream media and to alternative sources of information. Having meditated on the lessons of the past and taken stock of the change that is coming, they no longer take seriously or give credence to the illusions, embarrassingly sloppy lies and betrayals put forward by those who seek to rise or maintain themselves in power.[10] This was powerfully and cogently expressed by actor and environmental

---

10 Daniel Vanhove, "Faced with the moral bankruptcy of the West, what future for Palestine?," *Réseau International,* May 24, 2024.

activist Harrison Ford: "There's a new force of nature at hand, stirring all over the world. They are the young people whom frankly we have failed, who are angry, who are organized, who are capable of making a difference. They are a moral army. And the most important thing that we can do for them is to get the hell out of their way."[11]

One cannot but notice, however, that this advice has yet to be heeded by the powers that be. There has been violent repression of the ongoing student protests—reminiscent of opposition to the Vietnam War in the 1960s and 1970s, the anti-capitalist *Occupy Wall Street* guerilla war of 2011, and the *Black Lives Matter* international social movement formed in the U.S. in 2013 and dedicated to fighting racism and anti-Black violence—especially in the United States and in a growing number of Western countries, including but not limited to the UK, Canada, France, Germany, Belgium, Australia and New Zealand.

Furthermore, as observed by Chris Hedges,[12] not one university president has denounced Israel's destruction of every university in Gaza; not one has called for an immediate and unconditional ceasefire; not one has used the words "apartheid" or "genocide," or called for sanctions on and divestment from Israel. Instead, Hedges says, "heads of these academic institutions grovel supinely before wealthy donors, corporations—including weapons manufacturers—and rabid right-wing politicians. They reframe the debate around harm to Jews rather than the daily slaughter of Palestinians, including thousands of children. They have allowed the abusers—the Zionist state and its supporters—to paint themselves as victims.[13] This false narrative, which focuses on anti-Semitism,

---

11 Harrison Ford, statement on the importance of rainforests during the UN Climate Action Summit 2019, September 23, 2019.

12 Chris Hedges, "Revolt in the Universities," *ScheerPost,* April 25, 2024.

13 Read in this respect: Robert Tait, "Sanders hits back at Netanyahu: 'It is not antisemitic to hold you accountable'," *The Guardian,* April 27, 2024. In a two-and-a-half-minute video, Sanders—who sponsored an unsuccessful Senate bill in January to make U.S. aid to Israel conditional on its observance of human rights and international law—listed a catalogue of Israeli crimes in Gaza, including the destruction of infrastructure, hospitals, universities and schools, along with the killing of more than 400 health workers. The progressive Senator from Vermont—who is Jewish—accused Netanyahu of "insulting the intelligence of the American people" by using antisemitism to distract attention from the policies of his "extremist government" in the military offensive in Gaza, in particular Netanyahu's claim that U.S. universities were being overrun by antisemitism on a scale comparable to the rise of Nazism in Germany.

allows the centers of power, including the media, to block out the real issue—genocide."

Thus, for instance, during four hours of grueling testimony before the Republican-led Committee on Education and the Workforce, president of Columbia University Minouche Shafik was ruthlessly grilled about allegations of antisemitism on her campus. In a surreal moment during that congressional hearing, Republican Georgia Congressmember Rick Allen brought up the Bible in his questioning of Shafik. He cited the Old and New Testament and asked Shafik if she wanted Columbia University to be cursed by God![14]

For his part, Gilad Erdan, the Israeli Ambassador to the UN in New York took that point to a ridiculous extreme by declaring publicly that the pro-Palestine and pro-peace protesters in U.S. campuses are ideologically the same as Hamas. At a meeting of the UN General Assembly on Palestinian statehood, he claimed that the chants of the pro-Palestinian "rioters" on campuses are calls for Israel's destruction, adding: "We always knew that Hamas hides in schools. We just didn't realize that it's not only schools in Gaza; it's also Harvard, Columbia and many elite universities"![15]

Also speaking about the protests which sprang up at lightning speed on dozens of American campuses covering two-thirds of U.S. states, and were taking center stage on the international political and media theatre, Shahid King Bolsen argued[16] that the students were protesting against the ongoing genocide, the crime of crimes; a genocide for which the entire collective West is culpable, but of which America is the key enabler, sponsor, defender, protector, funder, armer, and in many ways, the architect. The crackdown on the students, he goes on to say, is for disavowing

---

14 Excerpt from the dialogue: Rep. Rick Allen: "Are you familiar with Genesis 12:3?" Minouche Shafik: "Probably not as well as you are, Congressman." Allen: "Well, it's pretty clear. It was the covenant that God made with Abraham. And that covenant was real clear: 'If you bless Israel, I will bless you. If you curse Israel, I will curse you.' And then, in the New Testament, it was confirmed that all nations would be blessed through you (. . .) Do you consider that a serious issue? I mean, do you want Columbia University to be cursed by God, of the Bible?" "Definitely not," answered Shafik. The Congressman then concluded by saying: "OK. Well, that's good."

15 *Voice of America News,* "More US campus unrest erupts over war in Gaza," May 1, 2024.

16 Shahid King Bolsen, "University Protests for Palestine | Campus Protests Signaling Significant Change in America," *Middle Nation,* April 27, 2024. https://youtu.be/-zAvTEBLme8

and disassociating themselves and their educational institutions from the crimes that their country is perpetuating in Palestine. He pointed out that these protests, which are by no means the first of their kind as they have been ongoing since October 2023, have now reached the ivy league, that is the *crème de la crème* of the institutions of the ruling class, the soil from which the ruling class grow their next generation of leaders. Some cop on the Harvard campus, he added, "probably just zip tied the future President of the United States, a future Secretary of State, a future diplomat, a future dignitary." Bolson rightly reminds us that on those same campuses, there have been demonstrations against Russia and in favor of Ukraine as well as protests against China over Xinjiang, and there were no zip ties, no arrests, and no young students going to jail; but the moment they start demanding that their institutions "stop partnering with Israel over a genocide and all hell breaks loose." He also quite appropriately reminded us that in 2020 this same generation was going around knocking down statues of slave owners and colonizers. This generation, he remarked, "didn't have a chance to try to oppose slavery and colonization a century ago or two centuries ago, so they just pulled down all the icons of slavery and colonization. Everything that they could find, they tore it down. But right now, today they have the opportunity to actively oppose and fight against present day colonization in Palestine, and that's what they're doing." These young people, Bolson concludes, "have been primed to take over the system, and instead of taking over the system they're taking the system down (...) America's most prestigious campuses have become occupied territories. This is a total system breakdown (...) It's a tectonic shift. The epicenter is in Gaza but the shock waves are shaking the foundation of American power."

While it's true that American opinion continues to vigorously support Israelis rather than Palestinians[17] and overwhelmingly believes that Hamas's attack on October 7 lit the fuse that set the region on fire, the current war on Gaza is precipitating the steady decline in Israel's popularity over the past decade among Democrats and young people, including among the Jews, signaling a yawning political and generational divide.

---

17 Jeffrey M. Jones, "Americans' Views of Both Israel, Palestinian Authority Down," March 4, 2024. According to Gallup figures, young adults show the biggest decline in ratings of Israel, dropping from 64% favorable among 18- to 34-year-olds in 2023 to 38%. Middle-aged adults (those aged 35 to 54) show a smaller but still significant drop, from 66% to 55%, while there has been no meaningful change among adults aged 55 and older.

As a consequence of this momentous historical evolution, there are clear signs of a revolt brewing both in the West and among Global South nations and peoples. And after more than three centuries of complete Western domination, a process of de-Westernization of the world coupled with a wrenching transition from a unipolar world where the U.S. was the undisputed global hegemon to a multipolar system where power is more distributed across states, companies, and non-state actors is dawning. To properly describe this grand transformation of world order shaped by Western colonialism's legacy, which today essentially manifests itself in the deep crisis of the U.S.-dominated "liberal international order," there still are no better words, it seems, than those uttered by late Italian philosopher Antonio Gramsci when the world was undergoing a similar transition in the early twentieth century: "The crisis consists precisely in the fact that the old is dying and the new cannot be born; in this interregnum, a great variety of morbid symptoms emerge."[18] One such symptom is a long-standing assumption that bipolarity and unipolarity are safer for the United States than multipolarity. That would imply that the United States should try to resist a multipolar world that defies its much-preferred "rules-based" order, whose rules it has itself written, imposed on others and ignored whenever convenient. Even for some Western scholars, that's simply yet another misleading assumption. They press the argument that multipolarity "does not render the United States powerless. In fact, it could be a boon to U.S. policymakers. By focusing on leveraging multipolarity to its advantage, the Biden administration can advance U.S. security and sustain America's global role. Multipolarity should not be feared; it should be embraced."[19]

To be sure, there is, for once, a silver lining in this new environment for the innocent, dispossessed and oppressed Palestinian people, and for the endlessly and purposefully divided and tormented part of the world they belong to, which the European colonizers once called the "Near East" until the Americans, pursuant to strategist Alfred Thayer Mahan's determination, decided it should rather be known as the "Middle East."[20] Thanks to their steadfast resistance, boundless courage and indescribable

---

18 Antonio Gramsci, *Selections from the Prison Notebooks* (New York: International Publishers, 1971).

19 Emma Ashford and Evan Cooper, "Yes, the World Is Multipolar," *Foreign Policy,* October 5, 2023.

20 Read the brilliant analysis of Chas W. Freeman Jr., "The Middle East is Once Again West Asia," Remarks to the Middle East Forum at Falmouth, August 6, 2023.

sacrifices, Palestinians, who have been fighting for more than a century for their land, rights and dignity in the name of justice—have at last, and against all odds, succeeded in having their just cause front and center at the global stage. No doubt, their fight will be hard, costly, and will give no quarter. But the countdown to the Zionist colonial rule in Palestine has begun, and the Palestinians have already decidedly paved the way for a long-awaited independence and a dignified life on their stolen ancestral land.

CHAPTER ONE

BEFORE THE FLOOD: FROM THE NAKBA TO AN APARTHEID STATE

"The Palestinian struggle is not just a cry for justice. It's a blistering battle for the most fundamental human rights that every living soul on this planet should inherit by birthright."
—MALCOLM X

Mowing the Lawn No More!

In my book *L'Orient et l'Occident à l'heure d'un nouveau Sykes-Picot*[1] published in 2014, following the bloody military operation launched by Israel on the caged population in the Gaza Strip, I dedicated an entire chapter to "Palestine: The new/old face of an eternal conflict?" in which I wrote:

> While the occupied West Bank is on the verge of explosion, perhaps a prelude to a third Intifada that the Israeli government fears above all else, the Gaza Strip is already in ruins. For a month, aerial bombardments and shelling, by land and sea, by the "fourth most powerful army in the world" spared neither the civilian populations, nor the homes, nor the hospitals, nor the mosques, nor Gaza's only power plant, nor other scarce vital infrastructure like universities and schools, including those run by UNRWA.
>
> The main aim of this deluge of fire was to defeat the government of national unity which had only just

---

1 Amir Nour, *L'Orient et l'Occident à l'heure d'un nouveau Sykes-Picot,* Alem El Afkar, Alger, 2014.

been formed by the Palestinians[2] and to break any desire for resistance in this overpopulated enclave transformed into an open-air prison by an inhumane blockade imposed on a population that the "democratic West" had criticized for having democratically chosen its representatives during the 2006 legislative elections. And until the outbreak of this umpteenth Israeli aggression against the Arab States and against the Palestinians, the effects of the blockade on the people of Gaza did not seem to move most of the international community, including some neighboring Arab States.

And what about the deafening silence of the UN Security Council, usually so quick to wield the sword of Chapter VII of the Charter of the United Nations to severely punish Arab and Islamic "dictators" and "terrorist organizations," but so incredibly slow to move— if there is unanimity among its members of course, which is often not the case—and ultimately settle for adopting non-binding presidential declarations calling on Israel to "exercise restraint"? This, even though it is a question of reacting to Israel's state terrorism and the war crimes and crimes against humanity perpetrated by its very misnamed "IDF" (Israel Defense Forces), according to the very admission of some of its members disgusted by what they see in the daily reality of colonization.[3] And what about the reaction

---

2 Read: Ari Shavit, "Top PM aide: Gaza plan aims to freeze the peace process," *Haaretz,* October 6, 2004. In this interview Dov Weisglass, a senior adviser to Israeli Prime Minister Ariel Sharon, revealed in clear terms the true and malevolent intentions of the Israeli government in the presentation of its so-called "disengagement plan" approved in June 2004. He said that Mr. Sharon devised the disengagement plan as a means of "freezing" the peace process and ensuring that there would be no political process with the Palestinians. Weisglass further explained that "when you freeze that process, you prevent the establishment of a Palestinian state, and you prevent a discussion on the refugees, the borders and Jerusalem. Effectively, this whole package called the Palestinian state, with all that it entails, has been removed indefinitely from our agenda. And all of this with authority and permission. All with a presidential blessing and the ratification of both houses of Congress."

3 "How an army of defense became an army of vengeance"; Avner

of the moribund League of Arab States, if not to join without hesitation in the appeal recently launched by Dr Ahmed Taleb Ibrahimi, former Algerian Minister of Foreign Affairs (1982–1988),[4] to Arab leaders with a view to its pure and simple dissolution and replacement by a new institution more in line with the demands of current times and, above all, with the real aspirations of the Arab peoples?

This genocidal and particularly destructive war,[5] whose authors thought they could wage smoothly and with impunity, is in fact transforming into a real strategic and moral rout for Israel and its accomplices in the region and elsewhere, and into a victory for Palestinian resistance.[6]

Even *Foreign Policy* and *The Economist*—which are far from being sympathetic to Hamas or hostile to Israel—have espoused this view. Thus, in an editorial with the revealing title "Winning the Battle, Losing the War,"[7] the British magazine, after having paid the requisite obeisance to Israel—noted that

---

Gvaryahu, "I've seen how shockingly we treat Palestinians"; Yehuda Shaul, "Un ancien officier israélien: Notre but était de semer la peur," in *Le Monde*, July 22, 2014 [http://www.lemonde.fr/idees/article/2014/07/22/un-ancien-officier-israelien-notre-but-etait-de-semer-la-peur_4460857_3232.html] as well as the poignant testimony of Eran Efrati, "On The Wrong Side Of History: Ex-Israeli Soldier Speaks Out" [http://www.informationclearinghouse.info/article39261.html].

4 Interview with the Algerian newspaper *El Khabar*, July 23, 2014. http://www.elkhabar.com/ar/politique/416135.html

5 Read to that effect:

−An opinion titled "Lever la voix face au massacre perpétré à Gaza," by former French Prime minister and minister of foreign affairs, Dominique de Villepin, in *Le Figaro*, July 31, 2014.

−Jess Rosenfeld: "Israel's Campaign to Send Gaza Back to the Stone Age," *The Daily Beast*, July 29, 2014.

−Amos Regev: "Return Gaza to the Stone Age," *Israel Hayom*, July 9, 2014.

6 Ariel Ilan Roth, "How Hamas Won: Israel's Tactical Success and Strategic Failure," *Foreign Affairs*, July 20, 2014; Brent Sasle, "Israel's Hollow Victory over Hamas," *Haaretz*, July 22, 2014; Jeffrey Goldberg, "Israel Is Winning Battles But Losing The War," *Business Insider*, July 28, 2014.

7 *The Economist*, "Winning the battle, losing the war," August 2–8, 2014.

it is not surprising that many Israelis have the feeling that the world is against them and believe that criticism of Israel often masks antipathy towards Jews. But they would be wrong to ignore them completely. This is partly because public opinion matters. For a trading nation built on the idea of freedom, delegitimization is, in the words of an Israeli think tank, "a strategic threat." But also, because certain criticisms coming from abroad are well-founded ... Time is not on Israel's side. Palestinians would already outnumber Israelis in places where they live together ... Without the two-state solution, the risk for Israel would be either a permanent and undemocratic occupation depriving Palestinians of the right to vote, or a democracy where Jews constitute a minority. Neither option would correspond to the Jewish homeland with equal rights for all that Israel's founding fathers aspired to.

Foreign Policy considers, for its part, that

ultimately, Israel lost, notwithstanding the power of its army and its resources, because the Palestinians have a secret weapon which constitutes an asset compared to the Iron Dome: time is in their favor. With each passing day, their population and the injustice they suffer increase. With each passing day, Israel's arguments for delaying the establishment of this (Palestinian) state diminish.

The Gazans are providing proof, if it were still needed, that only armed resistance can make law and justice triumph in the face of an occupier who has always made brutal force the supreme virtue. The growing Arab and international public opinion disapproval of Israel; the certainly still too timid inflection of the major Western mainstream media, until now almost entirely committed to Zionist theses; the courageous positions taken by a number of elected officials, politicians, academic circles, artists, renowned Western and Israeli authors and even survivors and descendants of victims of Nazism,[8] added to the indiscre-

8 –Noam Chomsky, "A Hideous Atrocity: on Israel's Assault on Gaza," *Democracy Now!* August 8, 2014.

tions of the American Secretary of State, John Kerry, recently revealed by the international press,[9] are the harbingers of a global awareness that is long overdue. We can only sincerely hope for it and rejoice just as much if it were to be finally confirmed. Perhaps we will then witness the beginnings of a salutary change in the attitude of those, among Western governments, who support Israel unconditionally and thereby continue to bear a heavy responsibility for the perpetuation of the historical injustice that they did to the Palestinians.

For now, however, the powerful Israeli lobby[10] and its no less powerful media arm are keeping an eye on things, particularly in the United States. How else to explain that just hours after the National Security Council spokesperson's statement that "The United States condemns the bombing of an UNRWA school in Gaza that reportedly left Palestinians dead and injured innocent people—including children—and

---

–Gideon Levy, "Killing Arabs to restore quiet," *Haaretz,* July 13, 2014.

–Amira Haas, "Sans changement de politique, l'Etat d'Israël n'est pas viable," *Courrier international.*

–MSN News, "Outcry after British MP tweets he would fire rockets at Israel." http://news.in.msn.com/international/outcry-after-british-mp-tweets-he-would-fire-rockets-at-israel;

–*Democracy Now!* with Norman Finkelstein and Mouin Rabbani, "After Palestinian Unity Deal, Did Israel Spark Violence to Prevent a New 'Peace Offensive'?," July 15, 2014.

–Information Clearing House, "Israel Accused of War Crimes (UK Parliament)."

–Stop Mensonges, "Les médias mainstream sont sur le point de tomber, la vérité est surpuissante !," July 21, 2014.

–Global Research news, "Over 300 Survivors and Descendants of Survivors of Victims of the Nazi Genocide Condemn Israel's Assault on Gaza," August 16, 2014.

9 –Courrier International, "Pour John Kerry, Israël risque de devenir un Etat d'apartheid," April 28, 2014.

–20minutes.fr, "Gaza : Kerry laisse filtrer son irritation devant un micro resté branché à son insu," July 21, 2014.

10 Read in this respect:

–John Mearsheimer and Stephen Walt, *The Israel Lobby and U.S. Foreign Policy* (Farrar, Straus and Giroux, 2007).

–Alison Weir, "Israeli Analyst Explains that the 'Special Relationship' Benefits Israel, NOT the U.S." Alison Weir is author of *Against Our Better Judgment: The Hidden History of How the U.S. Was Used to Create Israel* (CreateSpace Independent Publishing Platform, 2014).

–Paul Craig Roberts, "The Moral Failure of The West," Information Clearing House.

–See also: http://ifamericansknew.org/

UN employees," the Pentagon spokesperson confirmed for his part that Washington had resupplied Israel with munitions, the very ones which kill Palestinian children, declaring that "The United States is committed to ensuring the security of Israel, and it is crucial to American national interests to help Israel develop and maintain a strong and responsive self-defense capability ... This arms sale is consistent with these goals"?[11] And how else can we interpret the fact that Democratic and Republican members of Congress were working hard to finalize an agreement on an additional $225 million in funding for Israel's Iron Dome before their summer break?[12] And finally, how can we justify the presence in Gaza, alongside Israeli soldiers, of numerous American volunteers?[13]

The same influence of this Israeli lobby is true in other Western countries. In France, for example, the testimony recounted in Pascal Boniface's latest book *La France malade du conflit israélo-palestinien,*[14] concerning the risks run by those who dare to criticize Israel's policies, is overwhelming. He states that

> dealing with anti-Semitism, the Israeli-Palestinian conflict and its consequences on French society by departing from the agreed discourse, and above all by taking the opposite view of the dominant positions in the circles of political powers and media, is not without risk. I have already experienced this ... I know too many political leaders and too many journalists who do not dare to contradict the argument [of Jewish community authorities] for fear of being accused of antisemitism and suffering painful and serious consequences ... When in 2003 I published "Is it permissible to criticize Israel?,"[15] *l'Arche,* the major monthly magazine of the Jewish community, devoted

11 Le Monde.fr and AFP, "Les Etats-Unis réapprovisionnent Israël en munitions," July 31, 2014.

12 Arutz Sheva Israel National News, "Congress Scrambling to Approve Iron Dome Boost," July 30, 2014.

13 The Daily Beast, "1,000 Americans Are Serving in the Israeli Army and They Aren't Alone," July 23, 2014.

14 Pascal Boniface, *La France malade du conflit israélo-palestinien* (Editions Salvator, 2014).

15 The book was rejected by seven publishers before finally being accepted by Robert Laffont. The same goes for Michel Bôle-Ricard's book, *Israël, le nouvel apartheid,* which was rejected by ten publishers before its ultimate publication in 2013 by Les liens qui libèrent.

a file of several pages to me under the friendly title
"Is it allowed to be anti-Semitic?" As a result, some
of these personalities "are excessively harsh (towards
community organizations) off the microphone, while
totally approving of them in public"!

There is no doubt that what is currently happening in Gaza is closely linked to ongoing events in other parts of the Arab-Muslim world.
This is one facet, among others, of the long war—both overt and covert—which has continued to be waged against all Muslims for a very
long time. Questioned on this subject, Dr Ahmed Taleb Ibrahimi made
this reflection:

We must know that fifty years ago, we dreamed of
Arab unity and Islamic unity, whereas today, in a
strange irony, we have come to fear even for the preservation of the integrity of existing entities. Proof of
this is that we witnessed the official break-up of Sudan
without reacting in the slightest; proof of this is also
that we see a de facto partition of Iraq taking place before our eyes without us being able to move; proof of
this is also the process of partition and fragmentation
underway in Libya, in addition to other states waiting
their turn. The renewal of this nation is only possible
by being aware of these threats and making sure to
avoid them.[16]

Except for a few chronological details, these excerpts may be mistaken for a summary of the horrendous events presently taking place in
the occupied territories, whether it be for the industrial-scale atrocities
committed by Israel against the Palestinian population, epitomized by
the mass civilian casualties and the willful and systematic destruction of
their homes and infrastructure, the blatant violation of international humanitarian law, the inability of the international community represented
by the United Nations Security Council to impose a ceasefire, the active
complicity with and unconditional support for Israel on the part of the
overwhelming majority of Western governments, the betrayal of most of
the Arab and Muslim leaders, the scandalously biased coverage of the

---

16 Interview with El Khabar, op. cit.

war by the mainstream media in the United States and Europe, or for the way the Israeli-Palestinian conflict is affecting Western and non-Western public attitudes.

The big picture might even lead one to agree with French novelist Jean Baptiste Alphonse Karr's proverbial expression "the more things change, the more they stay the same." And yet, this war is different from the others in many important respects.

Contextualizing a Protracted Conflict: Self-Determination or Self-Defense?

What is of paramount importance to assert at the outset is that the ongoing assault on Gaza did not start when Hamas militants launched the "Al-Aqsa Flood" military operation on October 7, 2023. In this regard, a formidable parallel information warfare is raging, pitting Israel's backers in the West against the Palestinians and their supporters across the world. To see through this battle of narratives and help navigate its treacherous waters, an understanding of the conflict's history is critically important.

That's why United Nations Secretary-General António Guterres was perfectly right when, on October 24, 2023, he stated[17] before a special session of the Security Council convened to examine the situation in the Middle East that: "It is important to also recognize the attacks by Hamas did not happen in a vacuum. The Palestinian people have been subjected to 56 years of suffocating occupation. They have seen their land steadily devoured by settlements and plagued by violence; their economy stifled; their people displaced, and their homes demolished. Their hopes for a political solution to their plight have been vanishing." He uttered these undeniable facts after warning that "the situation in the Middle East is growing more dire by the hour. The war in Gaza is raging and risks spiraling throughout the region. Divisions are splintering societies. Tensions threaten to boil over. At a crucial moment like this, it is vital to be clear on principles—starting with the fundamental principle of respecting and protecting civilians." He also condemned unequivocally

---

17 https://www.un.org/sg/en/content/sg/statement/2023-10-24/secretary-generals-remarks-the-security-council-the-middle-east-delivered, October 2023. It is worth pointing out that this statement was delivered on the very same day the international community was celebrating the "United Nations Day," marking 78 years since the UN Charter entered into force. The Charter reflects the UN member states' shared commitment to advance peace, sustainable development and human rights.

"the horrifying and unprecedented 7 October acts of terror by Hamas in Israel. Nothing can justify the deliberate killing, injuring and kidnapping of civilians—or the launching of rockets against civilian targets. All hostages must be treated humanely and released immediately and without conditions."

Nonetheless, the Israeli government was quick to condemn this statement in the strongest terms, with Foreign Minister Eli Cohen disrespectfully lashing out at him publicly, saying: "Mr. Secretary General, in what world do you live? Definitely, this is not our world"; while his Permanent Representative to the United Nations in New York, Gilad Erdan, demanded the Secretary General's resignation for "ostensibly rationalizing terrorism and spreading pure blood libel," hence losing "all morality and impartiality." The Israeli media, jumped on the bandwagon, affirming that Mr. Guterres "has demonstrated a stunning degree of moral bankruptcy."

Such an unprecedented fury towards a serving U.N. Chief suggests that he, perhaps unwillingly, hit a sensitive nerve within Israel's establishment, and most probably also among their staunch defenders in the West, presaging a narrative change on the Israeli-Palestinian conflict they all fear to be a mortal threat to the continued existence of Israel as a "Jewish state."

Upholding the Human Right to Resist Occupation

In an eye-opening opinion,[18] Professor Ilan Pappé, a renowned Jewish historian and political scientist, provided a deep explanation for what prompted this wave of scathing Israeli criticism. He noted that Israel wants to erase context and history in the war on Gaza because so doing will "aid Israel and governments in the West in pursuing policies they shunned in the past due to either ethical, tactical, or strategic considerations" because now this "attack is used by Israel as a pretext to pursue genocidal policies in the Gaza Strip. It is also a pretext for the United States to try and reassert its presence in the Middle East. And it is a pretext for some European countries to violate and limit democratic freedoms in the name of a new 'war on terror'."

The wider historical context, Pappé added, goes back to the mid-19th century, when evangelical Christianity in the West turned the idea

---

18 Ilan Pappé, "Why Israel wants to erase context and history in the war on Gaza," *Al-Jazeera,* November 5, 2023.

of the "return of the Jews" into a religious millennial imperative and advocated the establishment of a Jewish state in Palestine as part of the steps that would lead to the resurrection of the dead, the return of the Messiah, and the end of time. That theology became policy toward the end of the 19th century and in the years leading up to World War I, for two main reasons: "First, it worked in the interest of those in Britain wishing to dismantle the Ottoman Empire and incorporate parts of it into the British Empire. Second, it resonated with those within the British aristocracy, both Jews and Christians, who became enchanted with the idea of Zionism as a panacea for the problem of anti-Semitism in Central and Eastern Europe, which had produced an unwelcome wave of Jewish immigration to Britain"; and when these two interests fused, "they propelled the British government to issue the famous—or infamous—Balfour Declaration in 1917." From that time on, Jewish thinkers and activists who redefined Judaism as nationalism hoped this definition would protect Jewish communities from existential danger in Europe by homing in on Palestine as the desired space for "rebirth of the Jewish nation." In the process, "the cultural and intellectual Zionist project transformed into a settler colonial one—which aimed at Judaizing historical Palestine, disregarding the fact that it was inhabited by an indigenous population."

Prof. Pappé then went on to lay out additional key historical context relevant to the present situation, consisting of: the 1948 ethnic cleansing of Palestine that included the forceful expulsion of 750,000 Palestinians into the Gaza Strip from villages on whose ruins some of the Israeli settlements attacked on October 7 were built; the expulsion of 300,000 Palestinians during and in the aftermath of the 1967 war and more than 600,000 from the West Bank, East Jerusalem and the Gaza Strip ever since; the Israeli persistent collective punishment inflicted by the occupational forces on the Palestinians in the West Bank and the Gaza Strip, exposing them to constant harassment by Israeli settlers and security forces and imprisoning hundreds of thousands of them, over the past 50 years; the increasingly aggressive Israeli policies towards Muslim and Christian holy places in Jerusalem; the 16-year-old siege on Gaza where almost half the population are children; and the encirclement of the Gaza Strip by barbed wire and its disconnection from the occupied West Bank and East Jerusalem in the aftermath of the Oslo Accords. Prof. Pappé draws the logical conclusion that "Hamas, in many ways, was the only Palestinian group that promised to avenge or respond to these policies."

Also, as early as 2006—just a few days before the first legislative elections were held in the Palestinian territories to elect the second Palestinian Legislative Council—following the publication of his book *"Palestine: Peace Not Apartheid,"*[19] former President Jimmy Carter (in office from 1977 to 1981) declared that:

> What is being done to the Palestinians now is horrendous in their own territory by the occupying power which is Israel. They have taken away all the basic human rights of the Palestinians, as was done in South Africa against the blacks, and I make it very plain in this book that the Apartheid is not based on racism as it was in South Africa but it is based on the desire of a minority of Israelis to acquire land that belongs to the Palestinians, and to retain that land, they need to exclude the Palestinians from their own property and subjugate them so they can't arise and demonstrate their disapproval of being robbed of their own property. That is what is happening in the West Bank, and the people in this country, in America, never know about this. They never discuss this, there is no debate about it, there is no criticism of Israel in this country. The basic cause of the conflict is a sustained occupation of other people's land by the Israelis, and this is a direct violation of the United Nations resolutions. It's a direct violation of the International Quartet's Road map. It is a direct violation of the commitments that leaders of Israel have made in the past at Camp David when I was President and in Oslo, promising that Israel will withdraw from occupied territories. They have failed to do so.

President Carter said that since the book was published, he had been branded an anti-Semite and a bigot.

Another Israeli writer and columnist who has for more than four decades recognized the dire plight of the Palestinian people and condemned Israeli occupation is Gideon Levy. In his book *The Punishment*

---

19 Jimmy Carter, *Palestine: Peace Not Apartheid* (Simon & Schuster, 2006).

of Gaza,[20] published in the aftermath of the first war on Gaza (December 27, 2008–January 18, 2009) he asserted that Israel's 2009 invasion of Gaza was an act of aggression that killed over a thousand Palestinians and devastated the infrastructure of an already impoverished enclave. Indeed, from 2005—the year of the so-called Gaza "liberation" that resulted from Israeli withdrawal—through to 2009, Levy tracks the development of Israel policy, which has abandoned the pretense of diplomacy in favor of raw military power, the ultimate aim of which being to deny Palestinians any chance of forming their own independent state. Punished by Israel and the Quartet (the United Nations, the United States, the European Union and Russia) for having democratically elected Hamas, Gaza has been transformed into the world's largest open-air prison. From Gazan families struggling to cope with the random violence of Israel's blockade and its targeted assassinations, to the machinations of legal experts and the continued connivance of the international community, every aspect of that tragedy is eloquently recorded and forensically analyzed.

Speaking at the National Press Club in Washington D.C., in March 2018, Levy indicated that across the mainstream Israeli political spectrum, there is no challenge to the occupation of Palestinian land. Discussion of the occupation is off the table in Israel, he said; nobody talks about it. He sees three sets of deep-rooted values as the core of Israeli society, which explain everything. The first is that: "We are the chosen people." The second is that "We are the victims—not only the biggest victims, but the only victims around … it enabled us to do whatever we want, and nobody is going to tell us what to do because we are the only victims." And the third is that "The Palestinians are not equal human beings like us." As a result of these entrenched attitudes, "the military occupation in the occupied territories is today one of the most brutal, cruel tyrannies on earth" and "there was never an Israeli statesman who really meant to put an end to the occupation—none of them." Levy concluded by saying: "the basis of Zionism is that there is one people which is privileged over the other. That's the core. This cannot go on. If it goes on, it has only one name. Here [in the United States] we call it apartheid."[21]

Regarding apartheid precisely, it is worth citing what Benjamin Pogrund had to say in an opinion published just a month before the 2023

---

20 Gideon Levy, *The Punishment of Gaza* (New York: Verso Books, 2010).
21 Gideon Levy, "The Zionist Tango: Step Left, Step Right." Read and watch: https://www.wrmea.org/2018-may/the-zionist-tango-step-left-step-right.html

war on Gaza.[22] In Israel, he said, "I am now witnessing the apartheid with which I grew up in South Africa. The Israeli government's fascist, racist power-grab is the gift Israel's enemies have long awaited. We deny Palestinians any hope of freedom and normal lives. We believe our own propaganda that a few million people will meekly accept perpetual inferiority and oppression. The government is driving Israel deeper and deeper into inhuman, cruel behavior beyond any defense. I've lived through it before: grabbing power, fascism and racism, destroying democracy. Israel is going where South Africa was 75 years ago." He confessed that he did not want to write that article: "It was torn out of me, addressed to Israelis because the right-wing government is taking the country into institutionalized discrimination and racism. This is apartheid."

Fulfilling the Divine Duty to Wipe Out the Amalekites

In his revelatory book,[23] David Livingstone Smith looked at why we dehumanize each other, with stunning examples from world history as well as today's headlines. "Brute," "Cockroach," "Lice," "Vermin," "Dog," "Beast," he writes, are among other monikers constantly in use to refer to other humans—for political, religious, ethnic, or sexist reasons. He pointed out that human beings tend to regard members of their own kind as less than human. This tendency has made atrocities like the Holocaust, the genocide in Rwanda, and the slave trade possible, and yet we still find it in phenomena such as xenophobia, military propaganda, and racism. The author draws on a rich mix of history, psychology, biology, anthropology and philosophy to document the pervasiveness of dehumanization, describes its forms, and explains why we so often resort to it.

Likewise, citing as an epigraph the well-known quote by German philosopher Friedrich Nietzsche "Whoever fights monsters should see to it that in the process he does not become a monster," the Chicago-based Family Institute at Northwestern University rightly observed that the

---

22 Benjamin Pogrund, "For Decades, I Defended Israel from Claims of Apartheid. I No Longer Can," *news24*, June 9, 2023. Benjamin Pogrund, born in Cape Town, was deputy editor of the *Rand Daily Mail* when it was closed in 1985. He moved to Jerusalem in Israel to start a dialogue center. South Africa awarded him the Order of Ikhamanga Silver for services to journalism and academia during apartheid.

23 David Livingstone Smith, *Less Than Human: Why We Demean, Enslave, and Exterminate Others* (St. Martin's Press, 2011).

atrocities throughout history—genocides, mass murders, incarcerations of large groups of people—have only been possible through the dehumanization of its victims, the gradual and widespread adoption of the view that those people are less than human. Words (like images) are an essential tool in the dehumanization process of those who are ethnically or racially different. When people are labelled monsters, it becomes easy over time to think of them as inhuman, as not like us. In the same vein, once we perceive others as inhuman, we create an opening that allows us to circumvent our hard-wired social feeling (the foundation of morality) that impedes us from causing them harm. It's the loophole that enabled the Nazis to perpetrate the Holocaust, that made the horrors of slavery possible for hundreds of years; it's the same loophole underlying today's persecution of the Muslim Rohingya by the Buddhist majority in Myanmar.

For her part, as a historian who studies colonial pasts, University of Victoria historian Elizabeth Vibert argues[24] that the dismissal of Palestinians as "barbaric" or somehow "less human" is rooted in a long history of colonizing narratives. Referring to renowned Palestinian-American literary scholar Edward Said's 1978 classic book *Orientalism*—in which he explained how British colonizers wielded the "power to narrate"—she recalled that already by the 18th century, the binary of East versus West or "us" versus "them" had grown into a vast archive of western-produced "knowledge," the relationship being cemented in the West as "superior" versus "inferior," "civilized" versus "uncivilized," "rational" versus "depraved" in all arenas of life: politics, culture, religion.

Israelis have for long adopted such a discourse. It only got worse in the aftermath of "Operation Al-Aqsa," revolving around the same recurring themes, namely: the October 7 attack is a terrorist attack against innocent civilians; was unprovoked; is likened to 9/11 attacks; is compared to the Russian aggression in Ukraine and portraying both as part of the conflict between the "forces of good" represented by the U.S. and other democratic Western countries and the "forces of evil" represented by the likes of Russia, China, Iran and Hezbollah; is depicted as a war between the Democratic state of Israel and Hamas (not all Palestinians), which is an extremist Islamic group resembling or even worse than ISIS or Al-Qaeda; the Gaza Strip is no longer occupied since 2005. All the above

---

24 Elizabeth Vibert, "How colonialist depictions of Palestinians feed western ideas of eastern 'barbarism'," *The Conversation,* November 16, 2023.

means that justice and legality are on the side of Israel, which therefore deserves empathy and solidarity and has the full right to retaliate, in the name of self-defense.[25]

From that point onward—shocked by the enormity of its most disastrous military and intelligence failure in decades if not in its entire history since 1948 and the ensuing lasting effect on the army's morale and the population's psyche—a process of extreme demonization of Hamas and dehumanization of the Palestinians in general, with explicit statements of intent by leaders in the Israeli government and military, started to build up, the obvious objective of which being to obtain an internally and internationally accepted justification for what was soon to become documented vengeful and large-scale war crimes and crimes against humanity in the besieged enclave of Gaza, coupled with increased repression and purging rooted in ethnonationalist settler colonial ideology in the occupied West Bank and East Jerusalem.

When Israel's defense minister, Yoav Gallant, ordered a complete siege of the Gaza Strip with "no electricity, no food, no fuel, everything is closed," he said: "We are fighting human animals, and we are acting accordingly." Prime Minister Benjamin Netanyahu told German Chancellor Olaf Scholz that "Hamas are the new Nazis (...) and just as the world united to defeat the Nazis (...) the world has to stand united behind Israel to defeat Hamas." Commenting on these statements, Natasha Roth-Rowland said that the rhetorical value of "casting your enemies as Nazis—which the Israeli right and its supporters frequently do when discussing Palestinians writ large—is the way it suggests, implicitly or explicitly, that there is only one logical, even moral, course of action: the complete elimination of the Nazi-designates and anyone deemed to be affiliated with them. In addition, Nazi-like imagery has also been making the rounds among hasbarists on social media; in one drawing that could have come straight out of *Der Stürmer*, an IDF boot is pictured about to step on a cockroach with the head of a Hamas fighter. If the legacy of the Holocaust is interpreted to present Israel with carte blanche to cage, bomb, starve, dehydrate, and otherwise exert necropolitical power over the 2.3 million Palestinians in Gaza—almost half of them children—then 'never again' does not merely ring hollow. It becomes a

---

25 Dina Shehata, "Western media and public opinion and Israel's war on Gaza," October 25, 2023.

call for unchecked violence, a war cry in an eliminationist campaign of retaliation."[26]

To be sure, of this textbook of genocidal rhetoric and practices against the Palestinian population, two statements stand out as an unbelievable public call for an outright genocide. Firstly, when far-right Jerusalem Affairs and Heritage minister Amichai Eliyahu said in a radio interview that dropping a nuclear bomb on the Gaza Strip is "an option." And secondly, when in his press briefing on October 27, Netanyahu cited a biblical reference to "Amalek" in the Old Testament to justify killing Palestinians. He said the troops that he has met in the field are determined to make Hamas pay for its actions on October 7: "They are determined to eradicate this evil from the world, for our existence and, I add, for all of humanity," before insisting: "You must remember what Amalek has done to you, says our Holy Bible. And we do remember."[27] The reference to "eternal enmity" between the Amalekites and the Jewish people is found in the Book of Exodus (17:8–16): "Because hands were lifted up against the throne of the Lord, the Lord will be at war against the Amalekites from generation to generation"[28] and in 1 Samuel (15:1-35): "Samuel said to Saul, I am the one the Lord sent to anoint you king over his people Israel; so listen now to the message from the Lord. This is what the Lord Almighty says: 'I will punish the Amalekites for what they did to Israel when they waylaid them as they came up from Egypt. Now go, attack the Amalekites and totally destroy all that belongs to them. Do not spare them; put to death men and women, children and infants, cattle and sheep, camels and donkeys.'"[29]

Jeffrey Goldberg points out that tradition holds that the Amalekites are the undying enemy of the Jews, and the rabbis teach that successive generations of Jews have been forced to confront the Amalekites. Nebuchadnezzar, the Crusaders, Torquemada, Hitler and Stalin are all manifestations of Amalek's malevolent spirit.[30] For his part, rabbi Jill Jacobs—the head of *T'ruah,* a rabbinical human rights organization—said that it remains common for Israeli extremists to view Palestinians as

---

26 Natasha Roth-Rowland, "When 'Never Again' Becomes a War Cry," October 28, 2023.

27 Noah Lanard, "The Dangerous History Behind Netanyahu's Amalek Rhetoric," November 3, 2023.

28 "The Amalekites Defeated," in Bible Gateway.

29 "The Lord Rejects Saul as King," in Bible Gateway.

30 Jeffrey Goldberg, "Israel's Fears, Amalek's Arsenal," *The New York Times,* May 19, 2009.

modern-day Amalekites. In 1980, rabbi Israel Hess wrote an article that used the story of Amalek to justify wiping out Palestinians. Its title has been translated as *Genocide: A Commandment of the Torah,* as well as *The Mitzvah of Genocide in the Torah.*[31]

Finally, Donald Wagner thinks that the "annihilate Amalek" theme invokes support from the divine in this modern crusade to exterminate the Amalekites, interpreted today as every Palestinian. He explained that Netanyahu's base of political support among militant settlers finds inspiration from these violent biblical texts. Another base of Netanyahu's support is the international Christian Zionist movement. Wagner informs that shortly after the October 7 attacks, a letter of support for Israel's war on Gaza was issued by 60 conservative evangelical leaders in the United States, including two former presidents of the Ethics and Religious Liberty Commission—Russell Moore, now editor of *Christianity Today,* and Richard Land. The letter was delivered to the White House and every Congressional office on Capitol Hill, lending support for the Israeli aggression on Gaza.[32]

Israeli politicians have helped drive their "Holocaustization" narrative, and the sentiment that the Palestinians are collectively responsible for the actions of Hamas has been echoed far beyond Israel's borders, more so in the U.S. Indeed, Deborah Lipstadt, President Biden's antisemitism envoy, for example, tweeted the day after the attack that it was the most lethal assault against Jews since the Holocaust. Not long after, in a 60 Minutes interview less than a week after Hamas' attack on southern Israel, President Joe Biden himself said that the Palestinian Islamist movement had "engaged in barbarism that is as consequential as the Holocaust," and U.S. Senator Lindsey Graham went as far as calling for the wholesale destruction of Gaza, saying: "We are in a religious war here. I'm with Israel. Do whatever the hell you have to do to defend yourself. Level the place."[33]

The support to the Israeli discourse has become so strong and pervasive that in a 2002 interview, Shulamit Aloni, a former Israeli government minister was asked: "Often when there is dissent expressed in the United States against policies of the Israeli government, people here are called antisemitic. What is your response to that as an Israeli Jew?"

---

31 Noah Lanard, op cit.

32 Donald Wagner, "Netanyahu abuses Bible to impress US evangelicals," *The Electronic Intifada,* November 7, 2023.

33 Chris McGreal, "The language being used to describe Palestinians is genocidal," October 16, 2023.

Aloni replied: "Well, it's a trick, we always use it. When from Europe somebody is criticizing Israel, then we bring up the Holocaust. When in this country [the U.S.] people are criticizing Israel, then they are antisemitic." She explained that there was an "Israel, my country right or wrong" attitude and "they're not ready to hear criticism." Antisemitism, the Holocaust and "the suffering of the Jewish people" were used to "justify everything we do to the Palestinians."[34]

From Oslo to Onslaught

A recent Frontline documentary[35] provided a sweeping examination of the most critical moments leading to the ongoing war on Gaza. Starting with the Oslo Accords and continuing through to the current predicament, it draws on years of reporting and takes an incisive look at the long history of failed peace efforts and violent conflict in the region. It also looked at the increasing tensions between Israel and its ally, the U.S., over the war's catastrophic toll and what comes next.

On September 13, 1993, an historic and hopeful moment in the century-long Israeli-Palestinian conflict took place in Washington D.C. Israeli Prime Minister Yitzhak Rabin and Palestine Liberation Organization (PLO) negotiator Mahmoud Abbas signed a *Declaration of Principles on Interim Self-Government Arrangements* (The Oslo I Accord) at the White House, under the aegis of U.S. President Bill Clinton. The agreement was the fruit of secret negotiations that began in January 1993 between representatives of Israel led by Shimon Peres and representatives of the PLO led by Mahmoud Abbas in the Norwegian capital, Oslo. Israel accepted the PLO as the representative of the Palestinians, and the PLO renounced armed struggle and recognized Israel's right to exist in peace. Both sides agreed that a Palestinian Authority (PA) would be established and assume governing responsibilities in the West Bank and the Gaza Strip over a five-year period. Then, permanent status talks on the issues of borders, refugees, and Jerusalem would be held. Two years later, on September 28, 1995, Yitzhak Rabin, Shimon Peres, and Yasser Arafat signed the Oslo II Accord, formally called *Israeli-Palestinian Interim Agreement on the West Bank and the*

---

34 Steve Cooke, "Is antisemitism a trick? A closer look at that Shulamit Aloni meme," June 6, 2019.

35 James Jacoby, *Netanyahu, America & the Road to War in Gaza,* FRONTLINE Production, December 20, 2023.

Gaza Strip, which detailed the expansion of Palestinian self-rule to population centers other than Gaza and Jericho.

But in Israel an outcry against the peace process had been building among the ultra-religious right-wing and security-minded conservatives. Leading the charge was Benjamin Netanyahu, the leader of the Likud party. He famously said that "The PLO, Islamic State, 15 minutes from Jerusalem or 5 minutes from Tel Aviv is a prescription not for peace but for dangerous and renewed conflict." Back then—and still today—he did not believe in the possibility of a deal with the Palestinians whom he has never trusted nor liked.

On November 4, 1995, at the end of a rally of his own Labor party in support of the Oslo peace process, Yitzhak Rabin was gunned down by Yigal Amir, a right-wing Israeli Jew. Rabin's widow blamed Netanyahu for contributing to her husband's death and said so on worldwide television. After Rabin's death, the peace process he had championed was in jeopardy. His successor, Shimon Peres, would now try to win an election to keep it alive. He had to face Netanyahu, who had railed against the Oslo Accords and promised security to the growing number of Israelis scarred by mounting violence.

Just over a month later, as the new prime minister of Israel, Netanyahu was in the White House where he reluctantly pledged to further implement the Oslo peace process. But close observers said he was slow walking it, and nobody was happy with him: the left was unhappy for what he was doing to undermine Oslo and the right didn't like what he was doing to keep Oslo. As a result, in 1999 Netanyahu lost his bid for re-election.

Netanyahu would spend the next several years working his way back into power. He watched with concern as President Clinton brought his left-wing successor Ehud Barak and Yasser Arafat together at Camp David for another peace effort that would have created a Palestinian state in the Gaza Strip and the West Bank. Eventually, the negotiations failed, stumbling on the highly sensitive and contentious issue of the control of Jerusalem. The failure to make a deal set in motion a new round of frustration and violence on both sides.

By 2005, Netanyahu was back at the center of the Israeli government. He was Finance Minister in the administration of prime minister Ariel Sharon, who had a new plan for dealing with the Palestinians: a unilateral withdrawal of Israeli settlements and troops from the Gaza Strip but no negotiations. Netanyahu grew uneasy about the implications of handing over Gaza to the Palestinians. A week before the pull out, he resigned in protest, declaring "I cannot be a partner to a move that I think compromises the security of Israel."

In Washington, President George W. Bush had been pushing the Palestinians to quickly take advantage of the moment and hold democratic elections in 2006. The Bush Administration threw its support behind the Palestinian leader Mahmoud Abbas, who'd taken over since the death of Yasser Arafat. Abbas and his Fatah party were unpopular among many Palestinians who saw them as corrupt and ineffective. The Islamic Resistance Movement (Hamas in short)—that was only established in 1987 during the first Intifada—decided to run against them in what was unanimously considered as open and free elections which were promoted by the U.S. but cautioned against by Israel. And, to the surprise of everyone, Hamas—which had been designated by Israel, the U.S. and many European countries as a terrorist organization a decade earlier because of its armed resistance against Israel—won the election in Gaza. In the wake of this electoral victory, Hamas took complete control of the Strip, Mahmoud Abbas's Fatah party retreated to the West Bank City of Ramallah, and the Israeli government imposed a blockade on the Gaza Strip.

By 2008, Netanyahu was once again running for prime minister with a campaign slogan of "strong against Hamas." But during the runup to his eventual victory, a new president, Barack H. Obama, had entered the White House. Netanyahu was concerned. From his first day in office, President Obama had set a new tone and signaled to the Palestinians and Israelis alike that he wanted to restart the peace process. In May 2009, he invited Netanyahu to the White House, pressing him to stop the construction of Israeli settlements in the West Bank on land captured in the 1967 war and claimed by the Palestinians. For Netanyahu, his first meeting with the president couldn't have gone worse.

But Obama's peace efforts over the next few years wouldn't be able to break the cycle of violence that had been raging between Israel and the Palestinians. He would send his veteran conflict negotiator, George Mitchell, to the region more than 20 times. Eventually Mitchell gave up. He submitted his letter of resignation in 2011. With his Middle East efforts in trouble, Obama doubled down. Amid the 2011 "Arab Spring," he delivered a speech at the State Department that lasted nearly an hour but would be remembered for just one line: "We believe the borders of Israel and Palestine should be based on the 1967 lines with mutually agreed swaps." That Israel should return land it captured in the 1967 war to form a Palestinian state was a familiar demand, but one never endorsed so publicly by a U.S. president. For Israel this was a major and perilous development.

The Palestinians who once cheered Obama's election, now watched with disappointment as the peace process not only faltered, but Israel continued to build settlements. Obama's approach has been to send signals, but to never follow up his signals with actual action. Netanyahu understood that and proved to the Israeli public that "when I defend you, even against the strongest person in the world, the president of the United States, we still get what we need in defense terms, and we still get this huge check from the United States." He managed to prove that Israel didn't pay a price.[36]

Netanyahu would capitalize on his defiance of Obama. As he ran for re-election in 2015, he publicly lashed out at the President over his deal with Iran to curtail its nuclear program. And it played well to his base on the Israeli right. He took an even harder line on the Palestinian issue, declaring

> I opposed, and I adamantly oppose, the division of Jerusalem. I adamantly oppose going back to the 67 borders. I adamantly oppose the right of return. And that's not all. Look at practical reality. I haven't pulled back a single centimeter. For years, we ... I have been facing this whole pressure campaign. I have continued to build in Jerusalem's neighborhoods. I have never agreed to divide Jerusalem. I have never agreed to pull back to the 67 borders and I never will.

Netanyahu's Likud party won what's been called a stunning re-election victory, one which emboldened Netanyahu's approach toward the Palestinians. He would take advantage of the fact that post Hamas' election victory and Abbas' rejection of same, they were divided between Hamas in Gaza and the Palestinian Authority in the West Bank. "He wanted to divide, and he wanted to make sure that he doesn't have to negotiate any deal where you would connect between the territories and Gaza,"[37] hence preventing a Palestinian State.

---

36 Diana Weiss, Israeli TV journalist.
37 Diana Weiss.

With the Palestinians divided and Netanyahu pursuing a strategy to keep it that way, a new U.S. President, Donald Trump, came to power with a new approach to the region. He boasted he'd be the first U.S. President to broker an Israeli-Palestinian peace deal. "I speak to you today as a lifelong supporter and true friend of Israel," he declared to an AIPAC audience. He surrounded himself with a team that included his son-in-law, Jared Kushner, who was a family friend of Netanyahu and David Friedman, who supported Israeli settlements. And so, "You had these advisers on Israel, all of them Jewish, all of them strong supporters of Israel, none of them with any particular background in negotiation in the region in terms of peace talks, but with very, very developed positions and points of view."[38]

Just one month into his term, Trump invited Netanyahu to the White House to discuss the possibilities of his approach to the Israel/ Palestine conflict, and gave Netanyahu an early nod in his favor, saying he would be open to something other than a two-state solution: "I'm looking at two states and one state and I like the one that both parties like. I'm very happy with the one that both parties like, I can live with either one." That was a sea change in American policy, because going back for multiple Presidents, the idea of an independent Palestinian State as part of an ultimate resolution of this conflict was thus thrown out the window. Trump would soon follow that up with an even more surprising announcement, fulfilling a longtime wish of Netanyahu: "Today we finally acknowledge the obvious: that Jerusalem is Israel's capital. I am also directing the State Department to begin preparation to move the American Embassy from Tel Aviv to Jerusalem." Quite understandably, Palestinians took to the streets to protest.

In May 2018, Friedman, Kushner, Netanyahu and nearly a thousand guests gathered in Jerusalem for the official ceremony marking the move of the U.S. Embassy. That same day, around 50 miles south, at the border with Gaza, tens of thousands of Palestinians gathered to protest the embassy move and Israel's blockade. Hamas urged protesters to break through the border fence. Israeli soldiers responded with rifle fire, killing more than 60 people. "What the embassy move symbolized to Palestinians was that they were not going to have a state with its capital in Jerusalem, because now the President of the United States had said

---

38 Peter Baker, *The Divider: Trump in the White House* (Knopf Doubleday Publishing Group, September 19, 2023).

that only Israel had a legitimate claim to Jerusalem, and that it would remain eternally Israel's capital."[39]

Soon afterwards, Netanyahu's government began a rapid expansion of settlements in the West Bank, the very move Obama had personally warned against. The Trump administration backed it, reversing the U.S.'s 40-year position that the settlements were illegal. Palestinian ambassador Husam Zomlot had this to say about it: "Seeing the U.S. performing, behaving, acting this way to the majority of the Palestinian people was definitely a source of hopelessness. And you know, hopelessness is a very dangerous feeling, and when hopelessness accumulates over decades, it's no longer just dangerous, it's catastrophic."[40]

Adding insult to injury for the Palestinians, Trump and Netanyahu convened at the White House to announce what would be called the "Deal of the Century." On that occasion, Trump declared: "I was not elected to do small things or shy away from big problems (...) Under this Vision, Jerusalem will remain Israel's undivided—very important—undivided capital." Husam Zomlot said "That scene was the most vulgar expression of what the Trump Administration and the Netanyahu government were all about. They were about liquidating the two-state solution, liquidating the Palestinian issue and cause." The deal offered Netanyahu much of what he wanted. It was

> a fantastic blueprint from the perspective of Netanyahu's point of view. No settlements to be removed, a rump Palestinian entity that they might call a state but was not really a state, would have no control of its borders, no control even of its own water, no control of its airspace. It would not be able to function as a state. It would be a collection of municipalities.[41]

To try to lure the Palestinians into the deal, Trump promised international investment worth $50 billion. Commenting on that announcement, Husam Zomlot said: "An American President stands next to an Israeli Prime Minister and tells them we will buy you off with some money. That scene has hit the heart of every Palestinian, the heart of

---

39 Khaled Elgindy, *Blind Spot: America and the Palestinians, from Balfour to Trump* (Brookings Institution Press, April 2, 2019).

40 Husam Zomlot, Head of Palestinian Mission to the U.S., 2017–2018.

41 Natan Sachs, Center for Middle East Policy.

Palestinians who have been struggling for 100 years." Then Netanyahu took to the podium and went even further than the terms of the deal. He announced Israel was about to annex almost a third of the West Bank. "It's a unilateral claim on territory, and it really throws a lot of sand in the gears of what's going on here, because if you start unilaterally claiming sovereignty over sections of the West Bank without having made any concessions, what is the incentive for the Palestinians to come to the table?"[42]

The Palestinians were now effectively sidelined. Moreover, Trump's plan unexpectedly set the stage for yet another major shift in the Middle East. Indeed, in the summer of 2020, Yousef Al-Otaiba, a friend of Jared Kushner and the United Arab Emirates' ambassador to the U.S., saw an opportunity to propose a different kind of peace deal to Netanyahu. Not between Israel and the Palestinians, but between Israel and some of its Arab neighbors.

> By this time, many of the Arab governments are eager to have relations with Israel, and the Palestinian issue is a nuisance on the way. And for some of them, they felt that they were always putting their interest second to the Palestinian cause. And when Israel speaks of annexing parts of the West Bank, the Emiratis in particular, the United Arab Emirates, see an opportunity to prevent that annexation in exchange for a peace deal.[43]

Al Otaiba said that the UAE and other Arab nations would consider normalizing relations with Israel if Netanyahu stopped his planned annexations. The fact that the UAE would even consider signing a normalization deal with Israel, without consulting Palestinians, was pretty remarkable: "It's really a sign of just how much the region has changed in the past decade and how much lower the Palestinian issue was now on even the priorities of Arab states."[44]

At the White House, Trump's team jumped on the idea as "This was Netanyahu's theory of the case: that the world was moving on from the Palestinians, that in fact Israel could achieve meaningful and lasting stability without having to trade away land for peace to the Palestinians,

---

42 Peter Baker, *The New York Times.*
43 Natan Sachs, Center for Middle East Policy.
44 Khaled Elgindy. Middle East Institute.

which had always been the premise of the two-state solution." After talks facilitated by Trump's team, Israel and two Arab countries—the UAE and Bahrain—announced they would normalize relations, and Netanyahu dropped his annexation plans. It was the first peace treaty between Israel and any Arab country in almost 30 years. "The Abraham Accords were definitely seen as a betrayal by Palestinians. And the Palestinians in general felt that the Arab states had abandoned them."[45] The Palestinian Authority called the Accords despicable.

The Abraham Accords would incite Israel's enemies and seed the conflict to come.

> What you see if you're Hamas is the world is moving beyond you. They no longer care, it seems, about the plight of the Palestinians in Gaza. And this is a deal that is essentially marginalizing Hamas, marginalizing the Palestinians, marginalizing their grievance, and they're left to wonder: well, what becomes of us, you know, what do we do to get some attention to our cause again?[46]

Ambassador Zomlot responded by saying:

> You cannot ignore the Palestinian people, no matter how much you try by the power of the missiles and the tanks as we have seen throughout the years and now, or by the power of the complete capitulation of a U.S. Administration like a Trump or by the power of getting some Arab countries to normalize without a real solution. All this, all that does not work, and shall never, ever work.

In May 2021, violent protests erupted in Jerusalem over the potential evictions of Palestinians from their homes. The conflict further escalated when Israeli police raided the al-Aqsa mosque, one of Islam's holiest sites. From Gaza, Hamas retaliated, firing rockets toward Jerusalem, and in response, Netanyahu launched multiple air strikes. It was just

---

45 Khaled Elgindy, Middle East Institute.
46 Peter Baker, *The New York Times.*

four months into President Joe Biden's term and the Israeli-Palestinian conflict was suddenly front and center.

As the violence intensified, Biden pushed Netanyahu for a cease-fire, which "ended in a sort of a miserable draw. As usual, the Israeli leadership were saying we've won this round again, and Hamas is weakened and deterred. But for Hamas, the conflict was a breakthrough. They used it to tout themselves as fighting not just for Palestinians in Gaza, but in Jerusalem as well."[47] Khaled Elgindy added: "Hamas now is not just protecting its fiefdom in the Gaza Strip, but now vying for leadership of the Palestinian struggle as a whole by being the only party that is responding to events in Jerusalem, in contrast to the impotence and ineffectiveness of the Palestinian leadership in Ramallah."

In the wake of the conflict, a photo of Yahya Sinwar, Hamas's leader in Gaza, sent a foreboding message. "What Sinwar did, which was quite interesting, is take a picture of him sitting on an armchair. The destruction around him was quite clear. This was saying, okay you're maybe stronger right now, but I haven't lost anything. I'm willing to go for another round whenever I choose. At the same time, Hamas was also beginning to prepare its plan of attack."[48]

Netanyahu's go-to strategy toward Hamas—containment in Gaza—was beginning to crack, but his focus was elsewhere: he was em-broiled in scandal, facing charges of bribery and corruption. He and his coalition government were briefly toppled. To regain power, Netanyahu courted Israel's most extreme parties. And so, for Netanyahu, "he felt I have no chance but to go to the right, even the very far right. Even parties on the extreme far right that his own Likud party had always shunned. Recently re-elected, and now the head of a new far-right government, controversial plans to overhaul the justice system started pursuing a dramatic overhaul of Israel's judicial system that would weaken the court's power over the executive branch. Protests erupted across Israel. He needed to change Israel's legal system so he could somehow stop the trial."[49]

All the while, inside Netanyahu's government, intelligence offi-cials worried that the political unrest was leaving the country vulnerable to its enemies. "In many meetings, the chiefs of Israeli intelligence warned Netanyahu that the political crisis and its effect on the military

---

47 Amos Harel, *Haaretz*.
48 Amos Harel.
49 Natan Sachs, Center for Middle East Policy.

are perceived by the Israeli enemy as the time to take more aggressive initiative against Israel."[50]

In Washington, President Biden watched the situation with alarm and urged Netanyahu to reverse course. For Biden, the unrest in Israel threatened to disrupt a plan he'd been nurturing to take the UAE-initiated Abraham Accords to the next level in the Middle East. He and Netanyahu had been quietly courting Saudi Arabia. "They did push and try to expand on the Abraham Accords in particular with a vision of Israeli-Saudi normalization that would offer a dramatically different vision of the Middle East and one that would fit in well to their vision of creating alliances in particular in competition with China and Russia."[51]

By late September 2023, at the UN General Assembly in New York, a deal was taking shape. Netanyahu met with Biden for the first time since forming his far-right government. Biden used the meeting to discuss how to bring the Palestinians into the deal. "When he sat down with prime minister Netanyahu the main topic of that meeting which lasted almost two hours was about the Palestinians and how they fit into the Saudi deal. Now, I'll say Gaza was not a part of that process and that's because Hamas is in charge of Gaza."[52] And less than three weeks before the October 7 attacks, Netanyahu would make a fateful speech contending that: "I've long sought to make peace with the Palestinians, but I also believe that we must not give the Palestinians a veto over new peace treaties with Arab states."

The leaders of Hamas and other Palestinian resistance movements understood that this meant the Palestinian issue would be completely taken off the world agenda. They decided to react and had their combatants carry out the deadliest single assault in Israel's history, the military assault on Israel of October 7, 2023.

---

50 Ronen Bergman, *The New York Times.*
51 Natan Sachs, Center for Middle East Policy.
52 Brett McGurk, Biden's senior Middle East advisor.

CHAPTER TWO

OPERATION "AL-AQSA FLOOD"

"The most successful military raid of this century,"
—SCOTT RITTER

Neither a Surprise nor Unprovoked

First and foremost, and contrary to what the mainstream media in general and pro-Israel propaganda in particular has been stressing unremittingly, the "Al-Aqsa Flood" military operation of October 7 targeting the Gaza envelope was neither a "surprise" nor an "unprovoked" attack. Quite the contrary, what is astounding regarding those influential voices is the denial of the simple idea that the ultra-violent repression meted out to the Palestinians for so long, under a Zionist regime founded on occupation and apartheid, would backfire sooner or later.

Every lucid observer, whether in Israel or elsewhere, would have seen all this coming. As was put by Zehava Galon in *Haaretz* newspaper not long before the October 7 attack, "Israelis have learned to exact a price for every news report about the occupation, every hint that Palestinian blood is as red as theirs. We're not an occupying country, we're an occupation with a country. The occupation is our major national project, and it has gone on for so long that we can't imagine ourselves without it."[1] Such an admission objectively describing a despicable everyday reality could not have boded well for the Israelis themselves, let alone for the Palestinians.

Indeed, there were clear signs of gathering clouds, and surely the writing was on the wall for those monitoring the tense situation engendered both by the Israeli government's repressive policies and the settlers' provocations—mainly around the Muslim holy sites—during the preceding days, weeks and months in the West Bank and Al-Qods

---

1 Zehava Galon, "Israel Is an Occupation with a Country Attached to It," *Haaretz*, June 12, 2023.

(the Arabic name for Jerusalem, hence the operation's name Al-Aqsa "Flood" or "Deluge").

On April 27, Human Rights Watch (HRW) released a 213-page meticulously researched report[2] concluding that Israeli authorities are committing the crimes against humanity of apartheid and persecution. The finding was based on an overarching Israeli government policy to maintain domination by Jewish Israelis over Palestinians and by the grave abuses committed against Palestinians living in the occupied territory, including East Jerusalem. This unprecedented report by HRW further stated that

> The international community has for too long explained away and turned a blind eye to the increasingly transparent reality on the ground. Every day a person is born in Gaza into an open-air prison, in the West Bank without civil rights, in Israel with an inferior status by law, and in neighboring countries effectively condemned to lifelong refugee status, like their parents and grandparents before them, solely because they are Palestinian and not Jewish. A future rooted in the freedom, equality, and dignity of all people living in Israel and the OPT [Occupied Palestinian Territories] will remain elusive so long as Israel's abusive practices against Palestinians persist.

As for the situation in the Gaza strip, it could not be worse in the aftermath of the May 2023 brutal five-day-long Israeli offensive on the besieged enclave. On June 13, Amnesty International published its investigation on that offensive, stating:

> The root cause of this unspeakable violence is Israel's system of apartheid. This system must be dismantled, the blockade of the Gaza Strip immediately lifted, and those responsible for the crime of apartheid, war crimes and other crimes under international law must be held to account.

---

2 Human Rights Watch, "A Threshold Crossed: Israeli Authorities and the Crimes of Apartheid and Persecution."

Amnesty called on the international community to address the source of those repeated cycles of violence and to intervene to protect civilians and prevent further suffering as a matter of high urgency. This, the organization insisted, "requires upholding international law and ending Israel's 16-year-long illegal blockade on Gaza, and all other aspects of Israel's system of apartheid imposed on all Palestinians."[3] Once again unfortunately, that cry of alarm was not heeded and the call for an urgent action fell on deaf ears.

On August 2, far-right minister Amitai Eliyahu—the same warmonger who contemplated the option of dropping a nuclear bomb on Gaza—urged the government to annex the West Bank, calling the Green Line that separates Israel from the occupied territories "fictitious," saying:

> I don't really think there is a Green Line. It's a fictitious line. This is our homeland. This is where the Jewish people arose. The attitude of the State of Israel that there are two states here is a mistake. We should impose sovereignty on Judea and Samaria . . . We should advance this as quickly as possible, as smartly as possible. We should begin to say this everywhere, to create international recognition that this place is ours. In Judea and Samaria, everyone understands that our roots and history are there, and therefore, I think that the entire Green Line is just an abnormality. There is a distorted reality that we need to erase.[4]

On August 25, Abdel Bari Atwan, a Palestinian-born British journalist and editor-in-chief of Arab world digital news and opinion website *Rai al-Youm,* wrote a prescient piece,[5] which he concluded by saying:

> Finally, we reveal that the escalation of Israeli threats to launch an attack on the Gaza Strip, despite the state of calm it is currently in, comes because the occupation

---

3 Amnesty International, "Israel/OPT: Civilians on both sides paying the price of unprecedented escalation in hostilities between Israel and Gaza as death toll mounts," October 7, 2023.

4 TOI Staff, "Far-right minister says Green Line 'fictitious', urges annexation of West Bank," *The Times of Israel,* August 2, 2023.

5 Abdelbari Atwan, *Rai al-Youm,* August 25, 2023.

generals know that the Operations Management Office for the West Bank is based in the Gaza Strip. Israel is experiencing its most difficult and most dangerous predicaments these days, because the military and security threat comes from both inside and outside, and its leaders understand the next, and perhaps imminent war will be of a regional nature and will be conducted on several fronts. It seems that the end of the occupying state is much closer than ever before due to the presence of men wishing for martyrdom and praying to obtain it ... and time will tell.

On August 31, Yigal Carmon, a former adviser on counterterrorism to prime ministers Yitzhak Shamir and Yitzhak Rabin, published a report titled *Signs of Possible War in September-October.* The forecast, published by the Middle East Media Research Institute, a watchdog better known by the acronym MEMRI that Carmon heads, focused mainly on the possibility of an escalation from the West Bank or Lebanon. Gaza was mentioned only in the context of Palestinians in the West Bank adopting Gazan fighting methods.[6]

On September 6, Tamir Pardo, a former Mossad chief appointed by Netanyahu (2011–2016), told the Associated Press that "There is an apartheid state here. In a territory where two peoples are judged under two legal systems, that is an apartheid state." He also said that as Mossad chief, he had repeatedly warned Netanyahu that he needed to decide what Israel's borders were or risk the destruction of a state for the Jews. In reaction, Netanyahu's Likud party issued a statement, saying: "We firmly condemn the shameful and false remark by Tamir Pardo ... Instead of defending Israel and the IDF, Pardo is slandering Israel. Pardo, shame on you."[7]

But perhaps the most dangerous looming storm was the one coming from New York, just two weeks later. In effect, on September 22, addressing the delegates of all member states of the United Nations Organization during the 78th session of the General Assembly, Netanyahu brandished

---

6 Gianlucca Pacchiani, "The writing was on the wall, says counterterror expert who saw war looming," *The Times of Israel,* October 9, 2023.

7 AP and TOI Staff, "Former Mossad chief Pardo says Israel enforcing 'apartheid' system in West Bank," *The Times of Israel,* September 6, 2023.

a map of the "New Middle East" that showed the Gaza Strip, the West Bank and East Jerusalem as part of Israel. In his speech[8] he declared:

> A few years ago I stood here with a red marker to show the curse, a great curse, the curse of a nuclear Iran. But today, I bring this marker to show a great blessing. The blessing of a new Middle East, between Israel, Saudi Arabia and our other neighbors. We will not only bring down barriers between Israel and our neighbors. We'll build a new corridor of peace and prosperity that connects Asia through the UAE, Saudi Arabia, Jordan, Israel, to Europe.[9]

But, he added, "there's a caveat. It must be said here forcefully. Peace can only be achieved if it is based on truth. It cannot be based on lies. It cannot be based on endless vilification of the Jewish people." And, more significantly, he stated that for that peace to prevail "the Palestinians must stop spewing Jew-hatred and finally reconcile them-selves to the Jewish state. By that I mean not only to the existence of the Jewish state but to the right of the Jewish people to have a state of their own in their historic homeland, the Land of Israel."

What that means was explained by Palestinian Ambassador to Germany Laith Arafeh in a tweet:

> No greater insult to every foundational principle of the United Nations than seeing Netanyahu display before the UNGA a "map of Israel" that straddles the entire land from the river to the sea, negating Palestine and its people, then attempting to spin the audience with

---

8 To read the full speech: https://www.timesofisrael.com/full-text-of-netanyahus-un-address-on-the-cusp-of-historic-saudi-israel-peace/

9 Officially called the India-Middle East-Europe Economic Corridor (IMEC), this new project was agreed upon during the G20 meeting in New Delhi on September 10, 2023. It is a part of the Partnership for Global Infrastructure and Investment (PGII), a G7-led initiative for funding infrastructure projects across the world. It is commonly seen as a counter to China's Belt and Road Initiative (BRI). The Corridor will include a shipping route connecting Mumbai and Mundra (Gujarat) with the UAE and a rail network connecting the UAE, Saudi Arabia and Jordan with the Israeli port of Haifa to reach the shores of the Mediterranean Sea. Haifa will then be connected by sea to the port of Piraeus in Greece to eventually be connected to Europe.

rhetoric about "peace" in the region, all the while en-
trenching the longest ongoing belligerent occupation
in today's world.

What that means was also expressed, albeit more bluntly, by
Israel's UN ambassador to the United Nations Danny Danon in a *New
York Times* op-ed on June 24, 2019, in which he essentially urged the
Palestinians to surrender their struggle for a homeland in exchange for
economic benefits, as the United States prepared to roll out part of a
peace plan promising $50 billion in investment for Palestinians and their
Arab neighbors. He wrote: "I ask: What's wrong with Palestinian surrender? Surrender is the recognition that in a contest, staying the course will
prove costlier than submission. The Palestinians have little to lose and
everything to gain by putting down the sword and accepting the olive
branch."[10] In a later tweet he explained that Israel "awaits the emergence
of a Palestinian Anwar Sadat, a leader who is willing to do what is best
for his people—a leader who recognizes that building a bright future
requires surrendering a dark past."

To correctly put in perspective what Netanyahu and Danon said—
in particular with regard to their understanding of Israel's frontiers—one
has to keep in mind that according to the ruling Likud party's original
"platform": a) The right of the Jewish people to the land of Israel is eternal and indisputable and is linked with the right to security and peace;
therefore, Judea and Samaria will not be handed to any foreign administration; between the Sea and the Jordan there will only be Israeli sovereignty, and b) A plan which relinquishes parts of western Eretz Israel
(Greater Israel), undermines our right to the country, unavoidably leads
to the establishment of a "Palestinian State," jeopardizes the security of
the Jewish population, endangers the existence of the State of Israel, and
frustrates any prospect of peace.[11]

The clear message conveyed through such statements is the total
denial of the legitimate rights of the Palestinian people and the definitive
liquidation of their cause. It is nothing less than the completion of the
Nakba (catastrophe), the ethnic cleansing initiated in 1948, as was to
be confirmed in a later Israeli Intelligence Ministry document[12] recom-

---

10 AFP, "Israel's UN envoy: What's wrong with Palestinian surrender?,"
June 24, 2019.

11 *Jewish Virtual Library,* "Israel Political Parties: Likud Party."

12 Yuval Abraham, "Expel all Palestinians from Gaza, recommends Israeli
gov't ministry," October 30, 2023.

mending the forcible and permanent transfer of Gaza Strip's 2.3 million Palestinian residents to Egypt's Sinai Peninsula.

All the while, Israel's sprawling array of the 40-mile-long state-of-the-art chain of walls and fences at the Gaza border—which cost more than a billion dollars and was completed in 2021—were supposed to have left the country nearly invulnerable to anything Hamas or any other Palestinian faction, for that matter, was capable of throwing at them. Teeming with sensors and automated weapons, this defense system is supported by an electronic intelligence network that monitors every phone call, text message and email in the territory, in addition to a large, well-trained military standing ready with ultra-modern weaponry to respond rapidly to incoming threats.[13] When the Palestinian combatants attacked, what was presumed to be a vast technological advantage suddenly emerged as deeply flawed. This shocking predicament prompted Yossi Kuperwasser, director of research at IDSF—an Israeli defense think tank with close ties to the military—to observe "no technology can replace the soldier on the battlefield."[14]

The Israeli government characterized the attack on the various military bases and militarized settlements (Kibbutzim), which comprised an essential component of the Gaza barrier system, as a massive act of terrorism, likening it to the September 11 terror attacks against the U.S. The problem with this characterization, according to many military experts and investigative journalists, is that it is demonstrably false and misleading. Scott Ritter, for one, asserted that "Nearly a third of the Israeli casualties consisted of military, security, and police officers. Moreover, it turns out that the number one killer of Israelis on October 7 wasn't Hamas or other Palestinian factions, but the Israeli military itself, as later reports confirmed."

Ritter rightly observed that the reason why the Israeli government went out of its way to manufacture a narrative designed to support the false characterization of the attack is because what happened on that day "was not a terrorist attack, but a military raid. The difference between the two terms is night and day; by labelling the events of October 7 as acts of terrorism Israel transfers blame for the huge losses away from its military, security, and intelligence services, and onto Hamas." Conversely, if Israel were to acknowledge that what Hamas and the other Palestinian

---

13 David H. Freedman, "Disaster at the Border," *Newsweek,* November 24, 2023.

14 *Newsweek,* idem.

factions did was a raid, a military operation, then "the competency of the Israeli military, security, and intelligence services would be called into question, as would the political leadership responsible for overseeing and directing their operations. And if you are Israeli Prime Minister Benjamin Netanyahu, this is the last thing you want."[15]

The West's Lies and Distortions of the Events of October 7, 2023

In the wake of the monumental "technological collapse," another no less unexpected crumbling is taking place—the response of the once powerful Israeli propaganda machine commonly known as "hasbara" to the events of the flood of the Al-Aqsa military operation is being steadily washed away. This time though, Dr Frank Luntz's manual[16] that guides Israel's supporters on how best to speak to the media seems to be of little assistance. Patrick Cockburn called the manual "The secret report that helps Israel hide facts" and said that "On every occasion, the presentation of events by Israeli spokesmen is geared to giving Americans and Europeans the impression that Israel wants peace with the Palestinians and is prepared to compromise to achieve this, when all the evidence is that it does not."[17]

In retrospect, one can safely say that the war on Gaza has massively exposed the lies, distortions, and hypocrisies at the heart of most of the Western world's leading agenda-setting outlets, including CNN in the U.S. and the BBC in the UK.

Indeed, almost from the first hours of the October 7 attacks, Israel and its Western supporters started to spread claims about many atrocities purportedly committed by Palestinian fighters during their raid on

---

15 Scott Ritter, "The most successful military raid of this century: The October 7 Hamas assault on Israel," *Pearls and Irritations,* November 19, 2023.

16 Dr. Frank Luntz, "The Israel Project's 2009 Global Language Dictionary," *Transcend,* April 2009. https://www.transcend.org/tms/wp-content/uploads/2014/07/sf-israel-projects-2009-global-language-dictionary.pdf

17 Patrick Cockburn, "The secret report that helps Israel hide facts," *The Independent,* July 29, 2014. According to Cockburn, the report was written in the aftermath of Operation Cast Lead in December 2008 and January 2009, when 1,387 Palestinians and 9 Israelis were killed. Every one of the 112 pages in the booklet was marked "not for distribution or publication," but it was leaked almost immediately to *Newsweek Online.* It should be required reading for everybody, especially journalists, interested in any aspect of Israeli policy because of its "dos and don'ts" for Israeli spokespersons.

Israeli military posts and kibbutzim. In particular, three major issues have been the subject of false, misleading, unsubstantiated, or outright fabrications on the part of Israeli officials and media, namely claims that Hamas beheaded babies, raped women, and killed hundreds of people at an outdoor music festival.

These claims were subsequently amplified by the overwhelming majority of the mainstream Western news organizations. A case in point in this regard is the now infamous article by the *New York Times* titled "Screams Without Words: How Hamas Weaponized Sexual Violence on Oct. 7."[18] The main objective of this narrative was to dehumanize not only the "bloodthirsty Hamas terrorists," but all the Palestinians as well, hence creating an atmosphere in which the genocide, ethnic cleansing, and mass expulsion of Palestinians that were to follow would go unchecked and even seem somehow justifiable; all the more so since shortly after the attacks, Israel sealed off Gaza's borders, including to foreign reporters, who might have countered their narratives.

However, with the passage of time in the course of this nearly two-year-old genocidal war, these allegations have, wholly or partly, been exposed as baseless.[19] They have even provoked a backlash among Western governments and newsrooms, with some journalists, citing their consciences, resigning publicly, and others trying their best to change things from the inside.

Thus, among other rejections of said narratives, the White House walked back President Joe Biden's false suggestion that he had seen photographic evidence of children with their heads cut off; ICC's chief prosecutor Karim Khan did not include any allegations of rape when he applied for arrest warrants against senior Hamas leaders; two separate UN reports[20] could not verify any rape claims, and Israeli prosecutor

---

18 Authored by Jeffrey Gettleman, Anat Schwartz and Adam Sella; published on December 28, 2023.

19 Read: Arun Gupta, "American Media Keep Citing Zaka – Though Its October 7 Atrocity Stories Are Discredited in Israel," *The Intercept,* February 27, 2024; Jeremy Scahill, Ryan Grim, "Kibbutz Be'eri Rejects Story in *New York Times* October 7 Exposé: "They Were Not Sexually Abused," *The Intercept,* March 4, 2024; Richard Sanders and Al-Jazeera Investigative Unit, "October 7: Forensic analysis shows Hamas abuses, many false Israeli claims," *Al-Jazeera.* com, March 21, 2024; TRT World, "October 7 'rape claims' debunked as Israeli propaganda unravels," May 22, 2024.

20 To read the reports: https://www.un.org/sexualviolenceinconflict/ wp-content/uploads/2024/03/report/mission-report-official-visit-of-the-office-of-the-srsg-svc-to-israel-and-the-occupied-west-bank-29-january-14-february-

Moran Gez confirming that 15 months after the events of October 7, Israel still has not identified a single victim on behalf of whom a prosecution can be brought against an alleged perpetrator of a sexual attack.[21]

As senior political analyst Marwan Bishara rightly observed: "Fortunately, the lies have finally caught up with the liars, as more and more Western journalists, pundits and officials started to doubt the spin and question the Israeli spinners, even ridiculing them for their poor performances, doctored evidence, and vulgar lies. Soon, they will start to question the spinners' overall deception about the war, its conduct and root causes."[22]

2024/20240304-Israel-oWB-CRSV-report.pdf (March 4, 2024), and https://documents.un.org/doc/undoc/gen/g24/086/64/pdf/g2408664.pdf (June 14, 2024).

21 Ali Abunimah, "Rights and Accountability: Israel still can't find any 7 October rape victims, prosecutor admits," *The Electronic Intifada,* January 6, 2025; and Jean Shaoul, "Another set of Israeli lies collapses: Prosecutor admits no evidence of rape in October 7 attack," *World Socialist Web Site,* January 20, 2025.

22 Marwan Bishara, "Israel, Gaza, and the mass production of myths for mass media," November 20, 2023.

CHAPTER THREE

UNRAVELING THE UNFATHOMABLE PARADOX OF WESTERN BIAS

"The love of power is the demon of mankind."
—FRIEDRICH NIETZSCHE

The True Facts of the Genocide of the Palestinian People

Palestine's story at the United Nations began on November 29, 1947, with the UN General Assembly's (UNGA) adoption of resolution 181. The so-called *"Partition Resolution"* divided historic Palestine into two states, despite the fact that Resolution 181, a recommendation to the United Kingdom (the mandatory power) and other parties to implement the partition plan, was not a legally binding decision, as the General Assembly lacks the authority to unilaterally dispose of territory or enforce territorial divisions without the consent of the affected parties. Its legal authority was also contested due to the plan's perceived violation of the Palestinian right of self-determination

Seven decades later, full membership of Palestine in the universal organization has yet to be approved, although in 2012 it achieved an upgrading of its status in the organization through UNGA resolution 67/19, which granted Palestine *"non-member state"* status, based on it being a state on the 1967 borders with East Jerusalem as its capital. This resolution passed with a vast majority (138 votes in favor and only 9 against).[1] The Palestinian people, whether in exile or under occupation, have continued to suffer the consequences of the first UN infringement and later lack of international action to fulfill their inalienable rights—including resolution 2334 of the UN Security Council[2]—thereby enduring one of

---

1 Countries voting against: Canada, Czech Republic, Israel, Marshall Islands, Micronesia, Nauru, Palau, Panama and the U.S.

2 United Nations, "Five years after UNSC Resolution 2334, international accountability to end the Israeli occupation is more important than ever," December 23, 2021.

the greatest injustices seen within the Western-dominated international system.

Conversely, Israel became a member of the UN on May 11, 1949 through UNGA Resolution 273. It is important to mention that its membership, as established in the resolution, was conditional[3] upon honoring, *inter alia,* UNGA resolutions 181 (on two states) and 194 (on the right of return of Palestinian refugees). To this day, Israel continues to violate the conditions it accepted to become a full member of the UN, but the UN has not contested this failure.

On December 8, 2023, the UN Security Council gathered for an emergency meeting to discuss the catastrophic situation in Gaza. The meeting was convened after UN chief António Guterres invoked article 99 of the UN Charter[4]—an exceptionally important power conferred

---

3 Resolution 273 clearly stated that "Noting furthermore the declaration by the State of Israel that it 'unreservedly accepts the obligations of the United Nations Charter and undertakes to honor them from the day when it becomes a Member of the United Nations,' Recalling its resolutions of November 29, 1947 [Resolution 181] and December 11, 1948 [Resolution 194] and taking note of the declarations and explanations made by the representative of the Government of Israel before the ad hoc Political Committee in respect of the implementation of the said resolutions, The General Assembly (. . .) decides to admit Israel to membership in the United Nations."

4 Text of article 99: "The Secretary-General may bring to the attention of the Security Council any matter which in his opinion may threaten the maintenance of international peace and security." The nature of the powers conferred upon the Secretary-General under Article 99 has been described by the Preparatory Commission in its report to the General Assembly in the following terms: "Under Article 99 of the Charter, moreover, he has been given a quite special right which goes beyond any power previously accorded to the head of an international organization, viz: to bring to the attention of the Security Council any matter (not merely any dispute or situation /57) which, in his opinion, may threaten the maintenance of international peace and security. It is impossible to foresee how this Article will be applied; but the responsibility it confers upon the Secretary-General will require the exercise of the highest qualities of political judgment, tact and integrity." Under the terms of rule 3 of the Security Council's provisional rules of procedure, the President of the Security Council is under the obligation to call a meeting if the Secretary-General brings to its attention any matter under Article 99. Historically, the provision has been rarely invoked. It was first used by Trygve Lie, the first Secretary-General of the United Nations (1946–52), who resigned largely because of the Soviet Union's resentment of his support of UN military intervention in the Korean War. In addressing the General Assembly in 1950, he said: "I refer ... to my statement to the Security Council on 25 June last concerning the Korean conflict, when for the first time I invoked Article 99 of the Charter." Past examples include the upheaval in the Republic of the Congo in

upon the UN Secretary-General and exercised for the first time in decades—to warn the Security Council of an impending *"humanitarian catastrophe"* in Gaza, and to urge members to demand an immediate humanitarian ceasefire. Speaking at the meeting, he said he had invoked article 99 because

> We are at breaking point. There is a high risk of the total collapse of the humanitarian support system in Gaza, which would have devastating consequences. We anticipate that it would result in a complete breakdown of public order and increased pressure for mass displacement into Egypt. I fear the consequences could be devastating for the security of the entire region. We have already seen the spillover in the occupied West Bank, Lebanon, Syria, Iraq and Yemen. There is clearly, in my view, a serious risk of aggravating existing threats to the maintenance of international peace and security.

He added:

> All this takes place amid a spiraling humanitarian nightmare. First, there is no effective protection of civilians. More than 17,000 Palestinians have reportedly been killed since the start of Israel's military operations. This includes more than 4,000 women and 7,000 children. Tens of thousands are reported to have been injured, and many are missing, presumably under the rubble. All these numbers are increasing by the day. Attacks from air, land and sea are intense, continuous and widespread. So far, they have reportedly hit 339 education facilities, 26 hospitals, 56 health-care facilities, 88 mosques and three churches. Over 60 per cent of Gaza's housing has reportedly been destroyed or damaged—some 300,000 houses and apartments.

1960 following the end of Belgium's colonial rule and a complaint by Tunisia in 1961 against France's naval and air forces attack. The last time it was formally invoked was during fighting in 1971 that led to the creation of Bangladesh and its separation from Pakistan.

Some 85 per cent of the population have been forced from their homes. The people of Gaza are being told to move like human pinballs—ricocheting between ever-smaller slivers of the south, without any of the basics for survival. But nowhere in Gaza is safe . . . Second, Gazans are running out of food. According to the World Food Programme (WFP), there is a serious risk of starvation and famine . . . Third, Gaza's health system is collapsing while needs are escalating.

He concluded his statement by saying:

Everything I have just described represents an unprecedented situation that led to my unprecedented decision to invoke Article 99, urging the members of the Security Council to press to avert a humanitarian catastrophe, and appealing for a humanitarian ceasefire to be declared . . . International humanitarian law cannot be applied selectively. It is binding on all parties equally at all times, and the obligation to observe it does not depend on reciprocity . . . The people of Gaza are looking into the abyss . . . The international community must do everything possible to end their ordeal . . . I urge the Council to spare no effort to push for an immediate humanitarian ceasefire, for the protection of civilians, and for the urgent delivery of life-saving aid. The eyes of the world—and the eyes of history—are watching. It's time to act.

On December 12, after a long and thorough examination, the International Federation for Human Rights (FIDH)—the elected body of legal experts and human rights defenders from all over the world—adopted a resolution[5] recognizing that Israel's actions against the Palestinian people constitute an unfolding genocide; that states and individuals who

---

5 The International Federation for Human Rights, "The unfolding genocide against the Palestinians must stop immediately," December 12, 2023. To read the full resolution, "Resolution on Israel's unfolding crime of genocide and other crimes in Gaza and against the Palestinian People," go to: https://www.fidh. org/IMG/pdf/fidh_resolution_on_israel_s_unfolding_crime_of_genocide_and_ other_crimes_in_gaza_and_against_the_palestinian_people.pdf

provide assistance to Israel are hereby rendering themselves complicit; that an immediate ceasefire is imperative to save civilian lives and bring ongoing crimes to an end; and calling the International Criminal Court to immediately issue arrest warrants for Israeli officials who are responsible for international crimes against Palestinians. FIDH President, Alice Mogwe, declared that

> Palestinians have to endure thousands upon thousands of unimaginable tragedies, all intentional. This level of orchestrated violence by an occupying force is genocide[6] ... To say it is unfolding is also to say that it can, and indeed must be stopped. To political leaders and high officials, we must stress that support and assistance to Israel is complicity in this unfolding genocide. You have been warned.

The same day, the UN General Assembly voted overwhelmingly in favor of a resolution demanding an "immediate humanitarian ceasefire," the immediate and unconditional release of all hostages as well as *"ensuring humanitarian access."* It passed with a large majority of 153 votes in favor, 23 abstentions and 10 votes against including the United States, which vetoed a similar resolution put forward by the UAE at the Security Council only four days before, with 13 members voting in favor and the UK abstaining. The resolution, which failed to pass, took note of the Secretary-General's invocation of Article 99, expressed grave concern over the *"catastrophic situation"* in Gaza, and emphasized that both Palestinian and Israeli civilians must be protected. It demanded an immediate humanitarian ceasefire and the immediate and unconditional release of hostages as well as humanitarian access.

The following day, the Geneva-based Euro-Med Human Rights Monitor, an independent organization with regional offices across the MENA region and Europe, called for allowing the entry of investigation committees and specialized technical committees into Gaza to document

---

6 The genocide convention of 1948 defines genocide as "acts committed with the intent to destroy, in whole or in part, a national, ethnical, racial or religious group," in particular by "killing members of the group," and "deliberately inflicting on the group conditions of life calculated to bring about its physical destruction in whole or in part." For the crime to be qualified as such, it must meet two constitutive conditions: an action characterizing the crime and the intention to carry such crime.

and determine the extent of the horrific Israeli crimes in shelter schools, including field executions, torture, starvation, and the Israeli military's use of civilians as human shields. Israel, Euro-Med Monitor stated, "is determined to escalate its genocidal war against Palestinian civilians in order to push for their forced displacement, which is in violation of international law. This amounts to a war crime." The same rights group had said in a press release on November 2 that "Israel has dropped more than 25,000 tons of explosives on the Gaza Strip since the start of its large-scale war on 7 October, equivalent to two nuclear bombs," noting that the area of the Japanese city of Hiroshima is 900 square kilometers, while the area of Gaza does not exceed 360 square kilometers.[7]

Also, as reported by the *New York Times,* experts say that even a conservative reading of the casualty figures shows that the pace of death during Israel's campaign has few precedents in this century. They say that people are being killed in Gaza more quickly than in even the deadliest moments of U.S.-led attacks in Iraq, Syria and Afghanistan, which were themselves widely criticized by human rights groups. Marc Garlasco, a military advisor for the Dutch organization PAX and a former senior intelligence analyst at the Pentagon, told the newspaper "It's beyond anything that I've seen in my career." He said that to find a historical comparison for so many large bombs being used on such a small area, we may "have to go back to Vietnam, or the Second World War."[8]

Western Bias and Double Standards: Incurable Cognitive Dissonance?

Despite propaganda to the contrary, sold by legions of Zionist zealots and paid agents through a mighty disinformation machine depicting it as the "only democracy" in the region, Israel is today one of the world's worst pariah states. That said, why hasn't that understanding penetrated the minds of Western elites? Occupation and annexation of others' territories by force have been and continue to be legalized and legitimized; political, social, economic and religious discrimination is institutionalized; repressive and brutal policies and practices towards the Palestinians in the occupied territories and in the Gaza Strip continue unabated; and almost every major international law convention, treaty

---

7 Euro-Med Human Rights Monitor, "Israel hits Gaza Strip with the equivalent of two nuclear bombs," November 2, 2023.
8 Lauren Leatherby, "Gaza Civilians, Under Israeli Barrage, Are Being Killed at Historic Pace," *The New York Times*, November 25, 2023.

and UN resolution, including but not limited to, the UN Charter, the Geneva Conventions, the Oslo accords are willfully violated by Israel, immune as it is to any significant international pressure, accountability or sanctions.

Most Western governments continue to show an uncompromising alignment to Israel. They do not condemn its criminal behavior. They are not seeing the ongoing genocide in Gaza as how it is seen in the eyes of the United Nations, the human rights non-governmental organizations, and most of the peoples of the world. They are not even exerting the necessary pressure on Israel to accept an immediate ceasefire. Quite the contrary, some of those governments, like the U.S., continue to send money, arms and soldiers to Israel, hence perpetuating the relentless massacre of the innocent and defenseless Palestinian population.

Such an incoherent attitude in the West—in blatant contradiction with public statements as vain as they are useless—is perplexing to any rational, humane, and fair-minded person anywhere else in the world. Before trying to assess the whys and wherefores of this unfathomable Western stance, let's review the sequence of events.

Immediately on October 8, U.S. Secretary of Defense Lloyd J. Austin III announced that he had

> directed the movement of the USS *Gerald R. Ford* Carrier Strike Group to the Eastern Mediterranean. This includes the U.S. Navy aircraft carrier USS *Gerald R. Ford* (CVN-78), the Ticonderoga-class guided missile cruiser USS *Normandy* (CG 60), as well as the Arleigh-Burke-class guided missile destroyers USS *Thomas Hudner* (DDG 116), USS *Ramage* (DDG 61), USS *Carney* (DDG 64), and USS *Roosevelt* (DDG 80). We have also taken steps to augment U.S. Air Force F-35, F-15, F-16, and A-10 fighter aircraft squadrons in the region. The U.S. maintains ready forces globally to further reinforce this deterrence posture if required.[9]

The very next day, the "Quint" Group—an informal decision-making group consisting of the U.S., France, Germany, Italy and the United Kingdom—released a joint statement expressing "steadfast and united

---

9 U.S. Department of Defense, "Statement from Secretary Lloyd J. Austin III on U.S. Force Posture Changes in the Middle East," October 8, 2023.

support" for the state of Israel and "unequivocal condemnation" of Hamas. The five leaders said, "Our countries will support Israel in its efforts to defend itself and its people" emphasizing that "this is not a moment for any party hostile to Israel to exploit these attacks to seek advantage." And while making some concession to what they vaguely called the "legitimate aspirations of the Palestinian people," they hastened to add "But make no mistake: Hamas does not represent those aspirations, and it offers nothing for the Palestinian people other than more terror and bloodshed."[10]

The same discourse was then heard at the UN. In effect, on the one hand, pleading the cause of his people before the Security Council, the Palestinian ambassador Riyad Mansour, said Israeli strikes on Gaza had "placed every possible impediment on humanitarian aid and access." He said the aim of Israel's war was not security, but to prevent forever any prospect of Palestinian impudence and peace. "These intentions are clear in the Gaza Strip as well as in the West Bank, including East Jerusalem." He also noted the universality of international law, adding that

> Israeli exceptionalism has to end, and it has to end now. The Palestinian people will not die in vain, the Palestinian people deserve respect, we have earned it, we have paid the heaviest price to end it, show us respect, not in words but in deeds, show us respect for our lives and our rights.

On the other side of the spectrum, Israel's ambassador to the UN, Gilad Erdan, firmly rejected calls for a ceasefire. Erdan said regional stability in the Middle East could "only be achieved once Hamas is eliminated." Calling for a ceasefire would not achieve that end. He said Hamas's main weapon was terror and that it was seeking to "maximize civilian casualties" to put more and more pressure on Israel to relent. He added that calling for a ceasefire would ensure that the suffering and the fighting in Gaza would continue and that if Hamas was not destroyed, then atrocities would be carried out by the group "again and again." Israel, he concluded, would continue with its mission while supporting "every humanitarian initiative," but the destruction of Hamas was the only option.

---

10 The White House, "Joint Statement on Israel," October 9, 2023.

Echoing the Israeli discourse, U.S. ambassador Robert Wood said his country does not support an immediate ceasefire in Gaza. Wood said the Security Council's failure to condemn the Hamas October 7 attacks on Israel was a serious moral failure. Hamas continues to pose a threat to Israel, he said, before concluding, "For that reason, while the U.S. strongly supports a durable peace in which both Israel and Palestine can live in peace and security, we do not support calls for an immediate ceasefire. This would only plant the seeds for the next war, because Hamas has no desire to see a durable peace, to see a two-state solution." The ambassador later vetoed a draft resolution calling for a temporary ceasefire and a pause of the genocide.

Likewise, the UK's ambassador, Barbara Woodward, said Israel must be "targeted and precise" in achieving its goal "to defend itself against Hamas terrorism." She said the sheer scale of civilians killed in Gaza was "shocking," and civilians must be protected, then added that the world needed to "work to avoid escalation" in violence in the occupied West Bank, noting that Israel's announcements approving new settlements there was alarming and that it would only raise tensions. She emphasized: "Let us be clear, settlements are illegal under international law. They present an obstacle to peace, and they threaten the physical viability and delivery of a two-state solution." Having said that, she later abstained when voting on the U.S.-vetoed resolution!

More recently, Prime Minister Rishi Sunak said the UK "doesn't agree" with Israeli ambassador to the UK Ms. Hotovely's comments that there is "absolutely no" prospect of a Palestinian state. Our longstanding position, he declared, "remains the two-state solution. What is going on is incredibly concerning. I've said consistently, far too many innocent people have lost their lives. No one wants this conflict to go on for a moment longer than is necessary."[11] What exactly he meant by "longer than necessary" is far from clear.

As for France—whose famous national moto "Liberty, Equality, Fraternity" did not prevent the genocide of millions of Algerians throughout the French colonial rule between 1830 and 1962—a recent investigation by *Europe 1*[12] revealed that more than 4,000 soldiers of

---

11 Greg Heffer and James Tapsfield, "David Cameron ramps up the pressure on Israel with travel ban on 'extremist settlers' who are 'targeting and killing Palestinians'," *Mail Online,* December 14, 2023.

12 Sébastien Le Belzic (Special Envoy to Israel), "'Quelque chose d'irréel': le témoignage d'un Français engagé avec l'armée israélienne" ("Something unreal: The testimony of a Frenchman enlisted in the Israeli army"), *Europe 1,* October 30, 2023.

French or dual French-Israeli citizenship are currently enlisted in the Israeli army to fight against a subjugated and defenseless population caged in a tiny territory. Left-wing opposition *La France Insoumise* MP Thomas Portes published a statement demanding that these soldiers be tried in France for war crimes. This is "the largest contingent after the United States. France is dishonored," he wrote.

And what can be said about Germany, the country which bears a historical responsibility for the current plight of the Palestinians as a direct consequence of the Holocaust Nazi Germany committed against the Jews not that long ago? Well, it seems that the German leaders have failed to learn from their own history. They still think that some lives are more valuable than others. As recounted by Josephine Valeske,[13] amid the unfolding genocide in Gaza, they convened on November 9 in a Berlin synagogue to mark the 85th anniversary of the *Kristallnacht*—the 1938 November pogrom that formed part of the genocide perpetrated by Germany against Jews in Europe. In his memorial speech for the victims, Chancellor Olaf Scholz affirmed that "Germany's place is on Israel's side." Referring to pro-Palestine solidarity protests, he said: "Any form of antisemitism poisons our society, just like Islamist demonstrations and rallies" before going on to threaten participants with deportation if they exhibited antisemitic behavior. Only a week before, German President Frank-Walter Steinmeir apologized publicly for colonial-era atrocities committed by German forces in Tanzania.[14] During a visit to this country, he said "I bow before the victims of German colonial rule. And, as Germany's Federal President, I want to ask for forgiveness for what Germans did to your forefathers." Tanzania is not the only victim of German colonial-era atrocities in Africa. In 2021, the German government announced $1.3 billion support to descendants of the victims of the genocide committed against the Herero and Nama ethnic groups in Namibia[15] between 1904 and 1908. Also, during his visit to Sheba Medical Center near Tel Aviv on November 7, German Air Force Chief Commander General Ingo Gerhartz said: "I have done so much with the

---

13 Josephine Valeske, "In supporting Israel's genocide, Germany has learnt nothing from history," *Middle East Eye,* November 17, 2023.

14 Historians estimate that as many as 300,000 people were killed by German colonial troops during the Maji-Maji rebellion between 1905 and 1907.

15 Read Hamilton Wende, "Our Auschwitz, Our Dachau: Reckoning with Germany's genocide in Namibia," November 6, 2022, and Farouk Chothia, "Namibia pulls down German colonial officer's statue in Windhoek," *BBC,* November 23, 2022.

Israeli Air Force, and especially the people living here in the last years. Now as you fight a war with Hamas, it is an honor for me to be here and show solidarity with your country and people and donate blood in case you need it." So, when is the next visit of a German leader to Palestine to seek forgiveness for supporting the ongoing Israeli genocide in Gaza?

With respect to the European Union's position, the least one can say is that it has been all but clear, strong and efficient. As with several other international issues, its 27 members have long been divided in their approach to Israel and the Palestinians. Furthermore, some statements made in the early days of the war by German President of the European Commission Ursula von der Leyen and High Representative of the Union for Foreign Affairs and Security Policy Josep Borell, supposedly on behalf of the EU, were deemed ill-considered and outrageously biased toward Israel.[16] This EU position could not be better summed up than as done by Ireland's Prime Minister Leo Varadkar when he said "Lately, I think the European Union has lost credibility because of our inability to take a stronger and more united position on Israel and Palestine ... We've lost credibility at the global South, which actually is most of the world, because what is perceived to be double standards. And there's some truth in that, quite frankly."

Finally, addressing supporters during a private campaign fundraiser at a Washington D.C. reception, President Joe Biden said[17]

> I believe, without Israel as a freestanding state, not a Jew in the world is safe—not a Jew in the world is safe. It's up to what happens at the moment ... One of the things that Bibi understands, I think, now—but I'm not sure Ben-Gvir and his War Cabinet do, who I've spoken to several times—is that Israel's security can rest on the United States, but right now it has more than the United States. It has the European Union, it has Europe, it has most of the world supporting it. But

---

16 Raf Casert, "European Union reverses earlier announcement that it was suspending development aid to Palestinians," *AP,* October 9, 2023; and Liyana Kayali, "By condoning Israel's collective punishment of Gaza, Western powers are plunging Palestinians further into hopelessness," *ABC News,* October 16, 2023.

17 The White House, "Remarks by President Biden at a Campaign Reception," December 12, 2023.

they're starting to lose that support by the indiscrimi-
nate bombing that takes place.

Speaking about Hamas, he said "They're animals. They're animals. They exceeded anything that any other terrorist group has done of late." He also revealed—which has hardly been reported, let alone commented upon by the mainstream media—"It was pointed out to me—I'm being very blunt with you all—it was pointed out to me that—by Bibi—that 'Well, you carpet-bombed Germany. You dropped the atom bomb. A lot of civilians died.' I said, 'Yeah, that's why all these institutions were set up after World War Two to see to it that it didn't happen again'—it didn't happen again."

Why Does the "Free World" Condone Israel's Occupation, Apartheid, and Genocide?

Assuredly, occupation, apartheid and ethnic cleansing are among the worst violations of international law. They are not acceptable any-where in the world. So why do "civilized liberal democracies of the free world" condone them in the case of the Palestinians? Do they not contra-dict the great principles and very core values of life, freedom, pursuit of happiness, prosperity, equality, brotherhood, fairness, enshrined in such erudite and convoluted texts as the U.S. Declaration of Independence, the French Declaration of the Rights of Man and of the Citizen and the Universal Declaration of Human Rights?[18]

It is certainly true that most of the West has always colluded with Israel since the time of the infamous 1917 Balfour declaration. Indeed, most of the European countries, and more so the U.S., not only massive-ly and unconditionally supported Israel, but actively aided and abetted Israeli settler-colonialism as well. "Holocaust awareness" alone does not explain everything. As Israeli writer Boas Evron observes, it is "actually an official, propagandistic indoctrination, a churning out of slogans and a false view of the world, the real aim of which is not at all an understand-ing of the past, but a manipulation of the present." For his part, UK his-torian David Irving claims that the Jewish Holocaust Industry "silences its critics by a combination of terrorism and moral blackmail."[19]

18 Tomas Pueyo, "What Does the Free World Stand For?," December 6, 2023.
19 Norman Finkelstein, "The Holocaust Industry," *Sage Publications*, December 6, 2012.

Also, as pointed out by Avigail Abarbanel in an illuminating article,[20] the Holocaust

> is not an excuse for Jewish Zionist settler-colonialism. The Zionist movement began to consider fully populated Palestine as a future "national home" for the Jewish people in the late 19th century. Back then, it was not regarded as a crime by the international community. There was nothing unusual in yet another group of white people coveting the territory and resources of non-white others. Everyone was doing it.

It is also a fact that the Israeli-marketed narrative based on the biblical tale of David [Israel] and Goliath [the Arabs] prevailed in the West up until the June 1967 war. In much of the world Israel was seen as a "living example of historical reparation. A people who managed to rise from the ashes of Auschwitz and build their own state in adverse and hostile circumstances. A weak but resilient *people*."[21] But since then, this narrative has collapsed. Present-day belligerents living on the same holy land have turned the timeless parable upside down. Yesteryear's underdog and its powerful Philistine adversary have today seen their roles reversed. Thus, in the eyes of many people around the world, the strong and assertive Israeli democracy has mutated into an oppressor state serving the imperialist designs and interests of the West in general and the American empire more particularly, an empire to which Israel is joined at the hip.

But how about today? The sinister Western crimes of colonization, genocide, enslavement, racism, oppression of indigenous peoples and theft of their lands and resources—under the ill-named pretext of the "White Man's civilizing mission"—are a distant and fading memory for most of the modern human species. And the same presumably holds true for the six-day-war of 1967, were it not for the Arab and Palestinian peoples.

Isn't it sensible then to suppose that such a Western civilizational mindset is bygone forever, and that those Western countries, having

---

20 Avigail Abarbanel, "You Reap What You Sow," *Substack,* October 8, 2023.

21 Gustavo Surazski, "David and Goliath: A letter from Ashkelon," July 14, 2014.

repented for colonial-era crimes (albeit not having paid reparations for them) would quite logically now stand for the values and principles of the so-called "rules-based international order" they themselves conceived, set up and sold to the rest of the world in the aftermath of their two internecine wars—also known as World War I and II? Or should we rather come to terms with the evidence that when it comes to the Palestinian people, they are still stuck in the dark ages of the law of the jungle—in which case the short and brutal lesson would be that one life is not worth another, that human rights are not universal, and that international law is arbitrarily applied?

The latter contention is seemingly more in line with the current hardcore unthinking Western support for Israel, and Avigail Abarbanel is right to conjecture: "Does Israel seriously suggest that the Palestinians should just wait to be led like 'sheep to the slaughter'? The answer, of course, is 'yes'! This is precisely what Israel wants, and what its media reflect and indeed, had expected. They want the Palestinians to accept to die, to disappear quietly into the night, until everyone has forgotten about them, and Israel can live happily ever after in its exclusively Jewish home."[22] I would personally argue that the answer is also "yes" for the U.S., the UK and many other European countries. By siding blindly and unconditionally with Israel and condoning its collective punishment of the Gazans, they are, in the words of the International Federation of Human Rights, rendering themselves complicit in a crime of genocide.

In truth, the United States and the former European colonialist countries have not tired of their unrepentant commitment to defending "Israel's right to defend itself," which in reality boils down to the insane logic whereby the occupying Israeli power has the "right" to defend its regime of apartheid and Jewish supremacy against the indigenous people of Palestine. As columnist Nesrine Malik put it,[23] "It seems, for the first time that I can think of, Western powers are unable to credibly pretend that there is some global system of rules that they uphold. They seem to simply say: there are exceptions, and that's just the way it is." She was right to add: "One thing I can say with more certainty is that people have seen too much that will stay with them for a long time. Whatever happens with the fragile truce that has released a thin ray of light, a darkness

---

22 Avigail Abarbanel, op cit.

23 Nesrine Malik, "The war in Gaza has been an intense lesson in Western hypocrisy. It won't be forgotten," *The Guardian,* November 27, 2023.

has also been released into the world. Its final form is yet to take shape but take shape it will."

As a reliable report[24] reveals, Israel is the largest cumulative recipient of U.S. foreign assistance since World War II, despite constituting only 0.01% (9 million) of the world population and being classified as a high-income country. Successive administrations, working with Congress, have provided Israel with

> assistance reflective of robust domestic U.S. support for Israel and its security; shared strategic goals in the Middle East; a mutual avowed commitment to democratic values; and historical ties dating from U.S. support for the creation of Israel in 1948. To date, the United States has provided Israel $158 billion (current, or non-inflation-adjusted, dollars) in bilateral assistance and missile defense funding. At present, almost all U.S. bilateral aid to Israel is in the form of military assistance; from 1971 to 2007, Israel also received significant economic assistance. In 2016, the U.S. and Israeli governments signed their third 10-year Memorandum of Understanding (MOU) on military aid, covering FY2019 to FY2028. Under the terms of the MOU, the United States pledged to provide—subject to congressional appropriation—$38 billion in military aid ($33 billion in Foreign Military Financing (FMF) grants plus $5 billion in missile defense appropriations) to Israel.

According to a more recent analysis,[25] the United States has given Israel more than $260 billion (representing about 30% of all U.S. foreign aid) in combined military and economic aid since World War II, plus about $10 billion more in contributions for missile defense systems like the Iron Dome.[26]

---

24 Jeremy M. Sharp, *U.S. Foreign Aid to Israel,* Congressional Research Service, March 1, 2023. To download the full report: https://crsreports.congress.gov/product/pdf/RL/RL33222

25 https://www.foreignassistance.gov/aid-trends

26 Christopher Wolf, "How Much Aid Does the U.S. Give to Israel?," October 10, 2023. See also: Louis Jacobson, "U.S. aid to Israel: What to know," *Politifact,* October 18, 2023.

It is generally acknowledged that the main reasons for the long-standing and unwavering Western backing of successive Israeli governments and policies are based on obvious geostrategic and economic considerations, Israel having always been viewed as an indispensable Western beachhead in the heart of the politically volatile and energy-rich Middle East. In the special case of U.S. policy where the extremely close U.S.-Israeli relationship has played an outsized role for over five decades, this justification is supported by a cohort of the influential neoconservative establishment, an all-powerful Jewish lobby mainly represented by AIPAC, and an immense financial and media apparatus. All of this is often further rationalized on dubious moral grounds.

As Stephen Zunes explains in a well-thought and well-written analysis,[27] "the growing U.S. support for the Israeli government, like U.S. support for allies elsewhere in the world, is not motivated primarily by objective security needs or a strong moral commitment to the country. Rather, as elsewhere, U.S. foreign policy is motivated primarily to advance its own perceived strategic interests." Therefore, there is a broad bipartisan consensus among policymakers that Israel is a key partner in the quest to serve and promote U.S. interests in the Middle East and beyond. According to Zunes, those interests can be summed up in: preventing victories by radical nationalist movements in Lebanon, Jordan, and Palestine; providing battlefield testing for American arms, often against Soviet (Russian) weapons; serving as a conduit for U.S. arms to regimes and movements too unpopular in the United States; assisting the U.S. in intelligence gathering and covert operations; and cooperating with the U.S. military-industrial complex in the field of research and development for new jet fighters and anti-missile defense systems.

Nevertheless, in my opinion, there are three more essential reasons to consider seriously, as they might better explain not only the quasi-reflexive West's support for Israel, but also its contemptuous disregard for the Palestinian people and casual callous disdain for international law and obligations. And as always, history is the best and wisest of guides. Those reasons are to be found in the West's fervid adherence—albeit socially and psychologically repressed—to white supremacy and racial prejudice toward non-white others;[28] the deep-seated antisemitism in

---

27 Stephen Zunes, "Why the U.S. Supports Israel," *Foreign Policy in Focus,* May 1, 2002.

28 See Yousef Munayyer's eye-opening article: "It is time to admit that Arthur Balfour was a white supremacist—and anti-Semite, too," *Forward,* November 1, 2017. Munayyer is a political analyst and writer and Executive

the societal mindset and behavior of a non negligeable portion of the European peoples; and the powerful influence of the Christian-Zionists (the Christian Right) in the United States—all serving humankind's inherent love of power as demonstrative of one's superiority over the Other. Those elements are all the more pivotal as they were clearly or implicitly alluded to in the short paragraph I purposefully singled out from President Biden's aforementioned speech during the Washington D.C. private campaign fundraiser.

In fact, regarding the first two intertwined elements, in an article published by the Jewish publication *Forward,* Yousef Munayyer said that

> Though he may be most known for aiding the Zionist cause in 1917, it's crucial to remember that Arthur Balfour was a white supremacist. He made that much clear in his own words. In 1906, the British House of Commons was engaged in a debate about the native blacks in South Africa. "We have to face the facts," Lord Balfour said, "Men are not born equal, the white and black races are not born with equal capacities: they are born with different capacities which education cannot and will not change."

Munayyar added that Balfour saw in Zionism not just a blessing for Jews, but for the West as well. As he wrote in 1919 in his Introduction to Nahum Sokolow's *History of Zionism,* the Zionist movement would "mitigate the age-long miseries created for Western civilization by the presence in its midst of a Body which it too long regarded as alien and even hostile, but which it was equally unable to expel or to absorb." So, rather than solving the problem of how to handle a minority living in a white majority country, the Balfour Declaration just shifted the same problem to a different geography. Munayyar also recounted that Balfour was unabashedly aware of the hypocrisy of his stance. "The weak point of our position of course is that in the case of Palestine we deliberately and rightly decline to accept the principle of self-determination," he wrote in a letter to the British prime minister in 1919. "We do not propose even to go through the form of consulting the wishes of the present inhabitants of the country … the 700,000 Arabs who now inhabit that ancient land."

Director of the U.S. Campaign for Palestinian Rights.

Munayyer concluded his article by saying: "Therein lies the fundamental problem that continues through this day, 100 years later. Palestinians are denied the right to have rights because from the outset, their views, their human rights and by extension their very humanity, were consistently seen as inferior to those of others ... Rather than resolving this tension, Balfour's support for Zionism merely exported it to Palestine."

More recently, Chris Bambery argued[29] it's time to come to terms with the role of Scottish imperialist Arthur Balfour. He writes that "Understanding his racism, and the British state's role in the region, is part of resisting the assault on Gaza today." He, too, confirmed that "Balfour was an imperialist, true and blue. Like so many of his co-thinkers, he had a racialized view of the world, that justified European colonialism. He developed a theory of natural racial inferiority regarding the Arabs and other Muslim peoples. In his 1908 book *On Decadence,* Balfour wrote of the races: "They have been different and unequal since history began; different and unequal they are destined to remain." Bambery further informed that "From Czarist Russia, to France, Germany and elsewhere, antisemitism flourished in the first decades of the 20th century, as class and imperial tensions grew and bred paranoia among European elites. Britain was far from immune, and many leading imperialists like Balfour and Winston Churchill, readily took up the view of Jewish people as essentially 'alien' non-Europeans." Bambery concludes his article by saying: "Today, Israeli Defense Forces bombard Palestinian universities, hospitals, mosques, schools and homes. It is surely time to reckon with the history, which laid the basis for the policy our politicians still adhere to—unconditional support for Israel, regardless to the crimes committed."[30]

With respect to the third element related to the American influence of the Christian Zionists—of whom Christians United for Israel's Pastor

---

29 Chris Bambery, "Arthur Balfour: The Scot who Authored the Palestinian Tragedy," *Conter,* December 4, 2023. Chris Bambery is a Scottish writer, broadcaster, journalist, and author of *A People's History of Scotland* and *The Second World War: A Marxist History* and co-author of *Catalonia Reborn.*

30 As a matter of fact, both Munayyar and Bambery drew Lord Balfour's quotes from Gudrun Krämer's book, *A History of Palestine: From the Ottoman Conquest to the Founding of the State of Israel* (2002).

John Hagee[31] is one of the most prominent figures—Muslim public intellectual Sahid King Bolsen recently acerbically noted:[32]

> So, because you and your people are so self-admittedly antisemitic, that you can't be trusted to not commit another Holocaust, so the Jews need to be somewhere else for their own safety; and somehow this is regarded as the pro-Jewish, non-hateful position. And the Christian Zionists are even worse. We know that the only reason that they want the Jews to be gathered in Palestine is so that they can be wiped out in some apocalyptic Holocaust according to their twisted understanding of the Bible, and they think that this is going to bring back Nabi Issa [Prophet Jesus, peace be upon him] who as far as I know never advocated genocide against the Jews. But these Christians expect for Nabi Issa to be happy with them when he comes and they're going to explain to him apparently that they supported a genocide against the Palestinians in order to keep the Jews in Palestine so that they could all also be wiped out. So, they supported death and destruction

---

31 John Hagee is the founder and senior pastor of Cornerstone Church, a charismatic megachurch in San Antonio, Texas, a non-denominational evangelical church with more than 20,000 active members. He is also the CEO of his non-profit corporation, Global Evangelism Television (GETV). He is the President and CEO of John Hagee Ministries, which telecasts his national radio and television ministry carried in the United States on ten television networks, including 62 high-power stations aired to more than 150 million households. He is shown on networks around the globe, including The Inspiration Network (INSP), Trinity Broadcasting Network (TBN), and *Inspiration Now TV*. John Hagee Ministries is in Canada on the Miracle Channel and CTS and can be seen in places including Africa, Europe, Australia and New Zealand. Hagee is the founder and National Chairman of the Christian-Zionist organization, Christians United for Israel, incorporated on February 7, 2006. On November 14, Hagee addressed a pro-Israel rally in Washington D.C. during which he affirmed the need for Israel to decide the contours of the war on Gaza and to not cave into international pressure. "You, the leaders of Israel, and you alone, should determine how this war is going to be conducted and concluded" Hagee says. "You decide—no one else."

32 Shahid King Bolsen, "Unraveling the Paradox: U.S. Foreign Policy, Zionism, and the Call for Global Accountability," *Middle Nation Podcasts*, December 18, 2023.

of two peoples in order to bring back the prince of
peace and this all makes sense to them somehow.

It is important to underline that while not all Christians support
Zionism,[33] most evangelical, Baptist, Pentecostal, and megachurch
Christians do based on their belief in dispensational premillennialism.[34] By contrast, practicing the nonviolence that Jesus Christ demonstrated in the Gospels, Protestant, Roman Catholic, Eastern Orthodox,
and Peace churches do not support Christian Zionism in their biblical
interpretations of the End Times. One of them is Dr Chuck Baldwin, a
prominent American evangelical pastor, who was the presidential nom-
inee of the Constitution Party for the 2008 U.S. presidential election. In
an interview[35] he gave in 2018, he said he preached Christian Zionism
for more than 30 years before rejecting it, revealing his step-by-step
account of his long journey of change to put aside the distorted view of
history required to believe the teachings of "Christian Zionism."

In a similar way, there are Jews who oppose Zionism. Among them
are the Ultra-Orthodox Jews who believe Jews must wait for the coming
Messiah to lead them back to the land of Israel. In rabbinic thought, the
Messiah (Moshiach in Hebrew, meaning literally "the anointed one") is
the king who will redeem and rule Israel at the climax of human history
and is the instrument by which the kingdom of God will be established.
Jewish tradition affirms at least five things about the Messiah: He will
be a descendant of King David; gain sovereignty over the land of Israel;
gather the Jews there from the four corners of the earth; restore them to
full observance of Torah law, and, as a grand finale, bring peace to the
whole world.[36]

In 2017[37] I wrote that:

---

33 Read Stephen R. Sizer, *Christian Zionism: Justifying Apartheid in the
Name of God* (Churchman, 2001).

34 See Got Questions Ministries, "What is dispensational premillennialism?"
https://www.gotquestions.org/dispensational-premillennialism.html

35 Listen to his very insightful 47-minute podcast with Chuck Carlson and
Craig Hanson of *We Hold These Truths:* https://whtt.podbean.com/e/what-made-
pastor-dr-chuck-baldwin-reject-christian-zionism/

36 See definition of "The Messiah," *Jewish Virtual Library.*

37 Amir Nour, "The Neoconservatives and the 'Coming World': A
Response to the Questions of a Virtual Friend," *Algérie Network,* August 1, 2017.
https://algerienetwork.com/blog/the-neoconservatives-and-the-coming-world-a-
response-to-the-questions-of-a-virtual-friend/

Stephen Green affirms[38] that since 9/11, a small group of neoconservatives, many of whom are senior officials in the Defense Department, National Security Council and Office of the Vice President, have effectively gutted—they would say reformed—traditional American foreign and security policy. After reviewing the internal security backgrounds of some of the best known among them, he concluded that they had dual agendas, while professing to work for the internal security of the United States against its terrorist enemies.

Bill Christison[39] and Kathleen Christison reach the same conclusion.[40] They say that since the long-forgotten days when the State Department's Middle East policy was run by a group of so-called Arabists, U.S. policy on Israel and the Arab world "has increasingly become the purview of officials well-known for tilting toward Israel." These people, "who can fairly be called Israeli loyalists, are now at all levels of government, from desk officers at the Defense Department to the deputy Secretary level at both State and Defense, as well as on the National Security Council staff and in the vice president's office."

According to the Christisons, Elliott Abrams is "another unabashed supporter of the Israeli right, now bringing his links with Israel into the service of the U.S," after his appointment as Middle East director on the NSC staff.

Interestingly, the Christisons were of the view that the dual loyalists in the Bush administration "have given added impetus to the growth of a messianic strain of Christian fundamentalism that has allied itself with Israel in preparation for the so-called End of Days." These crazed fundamentalists, they say, see Israel's

---

38 Stephen Green, "Neo-Cons, Israel and the Bush Administration," *Counterpunch,* February 28, 2004.

39 Bill Christison was a senior official of the CIA. He served as a National Intelligence Officer and as Director of the CIA's Office of Regional and Political Analysis.

40 Bill Christison and Kathleen Christison, "The Bush Neocons and Israel," *Counterpunch,* September 6, 2004.

domination over all of Palestine as a "necessary step toward fulfillment of the biblical Millennium, consider any Israeli relinquishment of territory in Palestine as a sacrilege, and view warfare between Jews and Arabs as a divinely ordained prelude to Armageddon"; which raises the horrifying albeit real prospect of an apocalyptic "Christian-Islamic war."

And in a subsequent 2017 article[41] whose conclusion I reiterate forcefully today—with all due respect to Ayaan Hirsi Ali[42]—I wrote:

We would like to invite the public to ponder the wisdom of a thinker who once said that in the past, weapons were manufactured to wage wars, but today wars are manufactured to sell weapons.

Yet unfortunately, it must be recognized that the rhetoric on the "clash of civilizations," constantly and tirelessly repeated by some since the end of the Cold War and the subsequent disappearance of the "indispensable enemy," seems to have achieved the objective assigned to it, chiefly by those who benefit from and pull the strings of the perpetuation of conflicts all over the world. This rhetoric has thus produced a dangerous "clash of fundamentalisms," which is updating the notions of "revenge of God," "Crusades" and "Jihad," and adding new ones such as "Islamofascism." The consequence of this dramatic turn of events is illustrated, on the sought and obtained

41 Amir Nour, "The Western roots of 'Middle-Eastern' terrorism," *Algérie Network,* August 10, 2017. https://algerienetwork.com/blog/the-western-roots-of-middle-eastern-terrorism/

42 In a recent article, Ayaan Hirsi Ali explained why she moved from being a native Muslim to embracing atheism, to (finally?) settling for Christianity. Part of the explanation, she wrote, is because: "Western civilization is under threat from three different but related forces: the resurgence of great-power authoritarianism and expansionism in the forms of the Chinese Communist Party and Vladimir Putin's Russia; the rise of global Islamism, which threatens to mobilize a vast population against the West; and the viral spread of woke ideology, which is eating into the moral fiber of the next generation." To read her article: "Why I am now a Christian: Atheism can't equip us for civilizational war," *UnHerd,* November 11, 2023.

ground of confrontation, by a "clash of barbarities." In today's increasing international turmoil, nobody should be blind to the fact that the biggest danger associated with this change is that since the end of World War II, the world has entered the age of the "supreme weapon"—the atomic bomb—and other weapons of mass destruction, and that extremists on all sides are promising and fervently promoting a "Cosmic War"[43] for "the triumph of Good over Evil." For some of them, it is a religious war, the ultimate war prior to the Apocalypse or the end times, whose theatre of operations one party sets in "Armageddon" and the other in "Dabiq," both places being situated in the Levant, comprising Syria which is itself being today put to fire and sword.

Isn't it insane to believe that our civilized world is unable to find a path other than the one leading toward Mutually Agreed Destruction (MAD)?

---

43 Read Reza Aslan's excellent book, *How to Win a Cosmic War: God, Globalization, and the End of the War on Terror* (Random House, 2009), as well as the following book review by Jason Burke in *The Guardian* of August 16, 2009: https://www.theguardian.com/books/2009/aug/16/win-cosmic-war-reza-aslan

CHAPTER FOUR

HOW WE GOT TO THE "MONSTROSITY OF OUR CENTURY"

"I am not willing to see anybody associated with those misled and criminal people."
—ALBERT EINSTEIN[1]

The Hamas military attack of October 7, 2023 was all the more significant as it happened on Benjamin Netanyahu's watch. Netanyahu "saw himself as the greatest protector of the state of Israel, and persuaded himself and his supporters that Israel was safe and that he could handle everything."[2] He reacted to what he viewed as a supreme personal humiliation by saying "Israel will win this war, and when Israel wins, the entire civilized world wins," a thinly veiled appeal to the U.S. in particular and the West in general.

---

1 Albert Einstein supported Jewish migration to Palestine but stood strongly against the creation of a Jewish nation-state. In 1948, the American Friends of the Fighters for the Freedom of Israel (AFFFI), which represented the terrorist Stern Gang/LEHI, sought Einstein's help in raising funds for their Jewish fighters. AFFFI Executive Director Shepard Rifkin explained in the letter that when Stern Gang commander Benjamin Gepner asked him to reach out to Albert Einstein for the purposes of gaining propaganda and fundraising assistance, he responded: "Are you crazy? He is completely against violence!" Still, Rifkin wrote a letter to Albert Einstein asking for his help raising funds in America for arms. Einstein refused with this letter: https://www.deiryassin.org/images/EinsteinLetter041048.jpg

Also, on December 4, 1948, Einstein co-wrote a letter to the *New York Times* that described one of Israel's founding political parties (future Israeli Prime Minister Menachem Begin's Freedom Party) as "closely akin in its organization, methods, political philosophy and social appeal to the Nazi and Fascist parties." https://archive.org/details/AlbertEinsteinLetterToTheNewYorkTimes. December41948/page/n1/mode/2up

2 Amos Harel, *Haaretz.*

72

Unsurprisingly, President Biden was visibly shaken by the killing and taking of hostages: "Let there be no doubt. The United States has Israel's back. We will make sure the Jewish and democratic state of Israel can defend itself today, tomorrow, as we always have. It's as simple as that." But despite his full-throated public support, as Israel began air strikes in Gaza, behind the scenes, Biden was concerned and within days, he arrived in Tel Aviv, in what constituted the first ever visit of a U.S. president during wartime.

The humanitarian crisis from Israel's military response has brought widespread condemnation. In the U.S., there has been increasing pressure on President Biden to do more to restrain Israel's response. In the face of the criticism, the president has been trying to turn attention to the day after. "What Biden seemed to want is to use this tragic moment for something bigger, for two-state solution, for negotiation, and this is where he and Netanyahu are like in totally different worlds."[3] Indeed, Netanyahu staked out his own hard line: "I wish to clarify my position. I won't allow Israel to repeat the mistake of Oslo."

In the strong and meaningful words of Khaled Elgindy, "There is no going back. Everyone agrees. Israelis, Americans, Palestinians, Gaza, West Bank, anywhere you ask, everyone agrees, there's no going back to the October 6 status quo. The question is: where do we go from here? Is it a pathway to something less awful? Or is it more destruction and death and something considerably worse than what we've had before? Those are still open questions."

Unprecedented Carnage and Devastation in Gaza

To be sure, from day one of the war on Gaza, Israel has been waging a war of genocide with thousands of innocent lives being sacrificed live before our eyes via social media all over the world. United Nations experts have been sounding the alarm in reaction to the Israeli military campaign, which resulted in crimes against humanity and the threat of genocide against the Palestinian population. They decried an ever-expanding catalogue of blatant violations of international humanitarian and criminal law, including willful and systematic destruction of civilian homes and infrastructures, known as "domicide," cutting off drinking water, essential food, medicine, fuel and electricity, within a complete

---

3 Ronen Bergman, *The New York Times.*

siege of Gaza, coupled with unfeasible evacuation orders and forcible population transfers.

The IDF's vengeful killing spree continues unabated. It took a turn for the worse with the deliberate destruction of Gaza's hospitals. As Chris Hedges explained, the IDF "is not attacking hospitals in Gaza because they are 'Hamas command centers.' Israel is systematically and deliberately destroying Gaza's medical infrastructure as part of a scorched earth campaign to make Gaza uninhabitable and escalate a humanitarian crisis. It intends to force 2.3 million Palestinians over the border into Egypt where they will never return."

This observation quite perfectly echoes what many at the heart of Israel's establishment now want to impose. Israeli Major General Ghassan Alian, coordinator of Government Activities in the Territories, warned Gazans: "You wanted hell, you will get hell."[4] As recounted by Jonathan Ofir,[5] there has been no shortage of genocidal calls from Israeli leaders, as well as clear plans, also at ministerial level, for the complete ethnic cleansing of Gaza. And while the usage of biblical euphemisms like Prime Minister Netanyahu's *Amalek* reference may appear too vague for some, even if the story suggests killing infants, on November 19, 2023, ret. Major General Giora Eiland, former head of the National Security Council and current advisor to the defense minister decided to spell out genocide more explicitly.

In effect, in a Hebrew article on the printed edition of the centrist *Yedioth Ahronoth* newspaper titled "Let's not be intimidated by the world," Eiland clarified that the whole Gazan civilian population was a legitimate target: "Israel is not fighting a terrorist organization but against the State of Gaza ... Israel must not provide the other side with any capability that prolongs its life ... Who are the 'poor' women of Gaza? They are all the mothers, sisters or wives of Hamas murderers." The formulation about the Palestinian women is reminiscent of the far-right former Justice Minister Ayelet Shaked, who, during the 2014 onslaught, suggested that Israel's enemy was the entire Palestinian people: "including its elderly and its women, its cities and its villages, its property and its infrastructure."[6] As for Palestinian women, she believes that:

---

4 Gianluca Pacchiani, "COGAT chief addresses Gazans: 'You wanted hell, you will get hell'," *The Times of Israel,* October 10, 2023.

5 Jonathan Ofir, "Influential Israeli national security leader makes the case for genocide in Gaza," *Mondoweiss,* November 20, 2023.

6 Ali Abunimah, "Israeli lawmaker's call for genocide of Palestinians gets thousands of Facebook likes," *The Electronic Intifada,* July 7, 2014.

> Behind every terrorist stand dozens of men and wom-
> en, without whom he could not engage in terrorism.
> Now, this also includes the mothers of the martyrs who
> send them to hell with flowers and kisses. They should
> follow their sons; nothing would be more just. They
> should go, as should the physical homes in which they
> raised the snakes. Otherwise, more little snakes will
> be raised there.

Regarding the "humanitarian concern" of the international community, Eiland is of the opinion that it must be resisted:

> The international community warns us of a humani-
> tarian disaster in Gaza and of severe epidemics. We
> must not shy away from this, as difficult as that may
> be. After all, severe epidemics in the south of the Gaza
> Strip will bring victory closer and reduce casualties
> among IDF soldiers ... Israel needs to create a human-
> itarian crisis in Gaza, compelling tens of thousands or
> even hundreds of thousands to seek refuge in Egypt or
> the Gulf ... Gaza will become a place where no human
> being can exist.[7]

It is worth recalling in this respect that back in 2004, in his capacity as head of the National Security Council, he regarded the Gaza
Strip as "a huge concentration camp" and advocated for the U.S. to force
Palestinians into the Sinai desert as part of a "two-state solution. This
was reported in the following U.S. diplomatic cable leaked to Wikileaks:[8]

> Repeating a personal view that he had previously
> expressed to other USG visitors, NSC Director
> Eiland laid out for Ambassador Djerejian a different
> end-game solution than that which is commonly envi-
> sioned as the two-state solution. Eiland's view, he said,

---

7 Kenan Malik, "'There is no alternative' is the last resort of those
defending morally wrong acts," *The Guardian,* November 19, 2023.
8 Wikileaks, "Israeli Officials Brief Djerejian on Improved Regional
Security Situation; Unilateral Disengagement plans," Public Library of U.S.
Diplomacy, March 31, 2004. To read full document: https://wikileaks.org/plusd/
cables/04TELAVIV1952_a.html

was prefaced on the assumption that demographic and other considerations make the prospect for a two-state solution between the Jordan and the Mediterranean unviable. Currently, he said, there are 11 million people in Israel, the West Bank, and Gaza Strip, and that number will increase to 36 million in 50 years. The area between Beer Sheva and the northern tip of Israel (including the West Bank and Gaza) has the highest population density in the world. Gaza alone, he said, is already "a huge concentration camp" with 1.3 million Palestinians. Moreover, the land is surrounded on three sides by deserts. Palestinians need more land and Israel can ill-afford to cede it. The solution, he argued, lies in the Sinai desert.

Specifically, Eiland proposed that Egypt be persuaded to contribute a 600 square kilometer parcel of land that would be annexed to a future Palestinian state as compensation for the 11 percent of the West Bank that Israel would seek to annex in a final status agreement. This Sinai block, 20 kms of which would be along the Mediterranean coast, would be adjacent to the Gaza Strip. A land corridor would be constructed connecting Egypt and this block to Jordan. [Note: Presumably under Egyptian sovereignty.] In addition, Israel would provide Egypt a 200 square km block of land from further south in the Negev. Eiland laid out the following advantages to his proposed solution:

- For the Palestinians: The additional land would make Gaza viable. It would be big enough to support a new port and airport, and to allow for the construction of a new city, all of which would help make Gaza economically viable. It would provide sufficient space to support the return of Palestinian refugees. In addition, the 20 km along the sea would increase fishing rights and would allow for the exploration of natural gas reserves. Eiland argued that the benefits offered by this parcel of land are far more favorable to the Palestinians than would be parcels Israel could offer from the land-locked Negev.

- For Egypt: Israel would compensate Egypt with a parcel of land on a 1:3 ratio, which is the ratio of the size of Israel to the Sinai. Egypt would enjoy the land corridor to Jordan, hereby controlling the shortest distance between Jordan and Saudi Arabia to Europe.

- For Jordan: The greater the capacity of the Gaza Strip to absorb Palestinian refugees, the fewer the number of refugees who would "return" to settle in the West Bank, thereby resulting in less pressure on Jordan. Jordan would also benefit economically from the land bridge.

Eiland, having previously debated the merits of this proposal with Ambassador Kurtzer, conceded the point that Egyptian President Mubarak "would never agree" to it, and he also took the point that in negotiating the Israel-Egypt peace treaty Israel had foregone the entire Sinai and accepted the Palestinian issue as an "Israeli" problem. He nonetheless refused to be dissuaded from exploring the idea, noting that he had reason to believe that Prime Minister Sharon would support such a proposal, if it were tabled by a third party.

Eiland's call for genocide was endorsed by Israelis in positions of the highest responsibility, including finance minister Bezalel Smotrich, who tweeted the full article and said he "agreed with every word."[9] He and his far-right partner in the government, Ben Gvir, also endorsed the rebuilding of settlements in the Gaza Strip and the encouraging of "voluntary emigration" of Palestinians. Speaking during their parties' respective faction meetings in the Knesset, they presented the migration of Palestinian civilians as a solution to the long-running conflict and as a prerequisite for securing the stability necessary to allow residents of southern Israel to return to their homes. The war presents an "opportunity to concentrate on encouraging the migration of the residents of Gaza,"

9 https://twitter.com/bezalelsm/status/1726198721946480911

Ben Gvir told reporters and members of his far-right Otzma Yehudit party, calling such a policy "a correct, just, moral and humane solution."[10] Reacting to those remarks, Arab Israeli lawmaker MK Ahmad Tibi condemned Smotrich and Ben Gvir, comparing their statements to Nazi calls for "Lebensraum" (living space) and declaring that such rhetoric was "inciting genocide." A day will come, he said, when "these two senior ministers in the Israeli government will stand before an international tribunal for war crimes."

While over one hundred journalists and media professionals had been killed to date in the besieged enclave, a prominent Israeli journalist was oblivious to the decimation of members of his profession.[11] Zvi Yehezkeli, Channel 13's Arab affairs correspondent, was speaking on the channel when he made this suggestion: "In my opinion the IDF should have launched a more fatal attack with 100,000 killed in the beginning," arguing that "such a fatal attack" would have led to a ceasefire and the release of hostages earlier on.

Moreover, while countless unspeakable atrocities continue to be committed day and night by the IDF in Gaza—in large measure enabled by the international community's appalling inaction and apathy—the fate of the Palestinians in what remains of the West Bank looks grim, and the Israeli grip on the al-Aqsa mosque is dangerously tightening. The racist Israeli settlers continued rampaging throughout the West Bank, hell-bent as they are on driving farmers and shepherds off their lands. And neither the far-right government nor the army did anything to stop them. As reported by David Shulman,[12] President Joe Biden and Secretary of State Antony Blinken both warned that this settler violence must be curbed. On November 8, Prime Minister Benjamin Netanyahu made an empty public gesture: "There is a tiny handful of people" he said, "who take the law into their own hands . . . We are not prepared to tolerate this." The same day, he reassured his supporters, including the hundreds of thousands of settlers in the territories: "I told President Biden that the accusations against the settlement movement are baseless."

On December 29, Francesca Albanese, the United Nations Special Rapporteur on Human Rights in the Occupied Palestinian Territories

---

10 Sam Sokol, "Far-right ministers call to 'resettle' Gaza's Palestinians, build settlements in Strip," *The Times of Israel,* January 1, 2023.

11 Middle East Eye Staff, "War on Gaza: Israeli journalist says army should have killed 100,000 Palestinians," December 20, 2023.

12 David Shulman, "A Bitter Season in the West Bank," *The New York Review,* December 21, 2023.

(OPT), described Israel's actions against the Palestinians in Gaza as "the monstrosity of our century" in a post on her official X (formerly Twitter) account. Israel, she wrote, "is bombing areas of Gaza it had designated as 'safe.' It is wiping out entire families, making countless children orphans and forcing countless men and women to survive their offspring. Each story is excruciating."[13] Albanese was commenting on a post by another X user which carried a video depicting a Palestinian father placing a pack of biscuits into the hands of his dead son. "I went to get you these biscuits, son. Keep them! Take them with you!" the grief-stricken father tells his dead boy in the video. The initial post explained: "His little son asked him for something sweet. He risked the dangers, leaving his home to cross Gaza to find something sweet for his little boy. He came home to find an Israeli missile had taken his son and wife." This is just one among over 18,000 children killed to that date by the Israeli air strikes and bombardment. The youngest of these children was one day old. He was killed and his death certificate was issued before his birth certificate was![14] In a later post, Albanese repeated: "Yes: what Israel is doing to the Palestinians, especially in Gaza, is the monstrosity of our century," adding: "Western complacency is turning into complicity." Expressing its displeasure at the United Nations, which has criticized Israel's targeting of civilians, Israel decided to refuse visas to UN staff members. "We will stop working with those who cooperate with the Hamas terrorist organization's propaganda," Eli Cohen, Israel's minister of foreign affairs, posted on X.[15]

Stunned by the speed with which incitement to genocide and other extreme speech had been normalized in Israel, a group of prominent Israelis accused the country's judicial authorities of ignoring "extensive and blatant" incitement to genocide and ethnic cleansing in Gaza by influential public figures. In a letter[16] to the attorney general and state

---

13 "South Africa files application at ICJ charging Israel with genocidal acts against Palestinians in Gaza—as it happened," *Ahram online,* Dec. 29, 2023.

14 As informed by Mustafa Barghouti, Secretary general and co-founder of Palestinian national initiative in an interview with Sky news, "Israel-Hamas war: Israel keeps driving you with lies, lies, lies, says Mustafa Barghouti," November 7, 2023. To watch the interview: https://www.youtube.com/watch?v=Gvw2kQ6IaKw

15 *Al-Jazeera,* "Israel denies visas to UN staff as it hits back against Gaza war criticism," December 25, 2023.

16 Emma Graham-Harrison and Quique Kierszenbaum "Israeli public figures accuse judiciary of ignoring incitement to genocide in Gaza," *The Guardian,* January 3, 2024.

prosecutors, they demand action to stop the normalization of language that breaks both Israeli and international law: "For the first time that we can remember, the explicit calls to commit atrocious crimes, as stated, against millions of civilians have turned into a legitimate and regular part of Israeli discourse," they wrote. "Today, calls of these types are an everyday matter in Israel." Signatories of such an unprecedented letter include one of Israel's top scientists, Royal Society member Prof. David Harel, alongside other academics, former diplomats, former members of the Knesset, journalists and activists. The letter ends with a resounding depiction of an overwhelming sentiment among the Israelis: "The Israeli is embroiled in trauma which will take years to heal. This is precisely the substrate on which immoral monsters are liable to grow, and are growing."

For his part, *Haaretz* columnist Gideon Levy pointed out that the evil can no longer be hidden by any propaganda. "Even the winning Israeli combo of victimhood, Yiddishkeit, chosen people and Holocaust can no longer blur the picture. The horrifying October 7 events have not been forgotten by anyone, but they cannot justify the spectacles in Gaza. The propagandist who could explain killing 162 infants in one day—a figure reported by social media this week—is yet to be born, not to mention killing some 10,000 children in two months," he writes in an editorial.[17] The suffering in the Gaza Strip, he added, is enormous in scope and causes despair. "It has no explanation, nor does it need one. Suffice it for the reports coming out of Gaza and being broadcast all over the world except in one tiny state, whose eyes are shut and whose heart is sealed."

Finally, in an outstanding piece[18] that went viral on the internet, renowned international relations theorist John Mearsheimer wrote:

---

17 Gideon Levy, "There's No Way to 'Explain' the Degree of Death and Destruction in Gaza," *ZNetwork*, December 28, 2023.

18 John J. Mearsheimer, "Death and Destruction in Gaza," John's Substack, December 12, 2023. Mearsheimer has attracted attention for co-authoring, with Stephen M. Walt, and publishing the article "The Israel Lobby and U.S. Foreign Policy," which was subsequently published as a book by Farrar, Straus and Giroux in September 2008. This seminal work provoked both howls of outrage and cheers of gratitude for challenging what had been a taboo issue in America, that is the impact of the Israel lobby on U.S. foreign policy. It remains as relevant today as it was when published in the aftermath of the Israel-Lebanon war of 2006.

I do not believe that anything I say about what is happening in Gaza will affect Israeli or American policy in that conflict. But I want to be on record so that when historians look back on this moral calamity, they will see that some Americans were on the right side of history. What Israel is doing in Gaza to the Palestinian civilian population—with the support of the Biden administration—is a crime against humanity that serves no meaningful military purpose.

He outlined seven main instances showcasing the criminal conduct of Israel both in Gaza and the West Bank before concluding: "As I watch this catastrophe for the Palestinians unfold, I am left with one simple question for Israel's leaders, their American defenders, and the Biden administration: have you no decency?"

The United States Doubles Down

In an eye-opening analysis,[19] Harvard University professor of international relations Stephen M. Walt delves into the highly contentious question of the root causes of the ongoing war on Gaza. Inevitably, the tendency to look for someone to blame is impossible for many to resist. For Israelis and their supporters, he says, pinning all the blame on Hamas is like stating the obvious. On the contrary, for those more sympathetic to the Palestinian cause, they see the tragedy as the inevitable result of decades of Israeli occupation and harsh and prolonged treatment of the Palestinians. Yet for others, there is plenty of blame to go around, and thus seeing one side as wholly innocent and the other as solely responsible is a sure recipe for unwise judgment.

Where, then, to start the quest to find the culprit? While rightly recognizing that the point of departure is inherently arbitrary—Theodor Herzl's 1896 book, *The Jewish State*? The 1917 Balfour Declaration? The Arab revolt of 1936? The 1947 U.N. partition plan? The 1948 Arab-Israeli war, or the 1967 Six-Day War?—the professor's inner compass points him in the direction of the year 1991, when the United States emerged as the unchallenged external power in Middle East affairs and began trying to construct a regional order that served its interests. Walt

---

19 Stephen M. Walt, "America Is a Root Cause of Israel and Palestine's Latest War," *Foreign Policy*, October 18, 2023.

singles out the key episodes thereafter whose adverse consequences brought us to the events of October 7 and their tragic aftermath: the 1991 Gulf War; the September 11, 2001 attacks and the subsequent U.S. invasion of Iraq in 2003; the abandonment by President Donald Trump of the 2015 Joint Comprehensive Plan of Action with Iran and adoption of a policy of "maximum pressure" toward this important country; the ill-conceived Abraham Accords; and the enduring failure to bring the so-called peace process between Israel and the Palestinians to a successful end. Prof. Walt believes that the 30-years-long U.S. management of the region ended in disaster. He concluded his article by saying: "If the end result of Biden and Secretary of State Antony Blinken's current minis-trations is merely a return to the pre–October 7 status quo, I fear that the rest of the world will look on, shake its head in dismay and disapproval, and conclude that it's time for a different approach."

Stephen Walt is far from being alone in drawing such a conclu-sion. In his recent book,[20] former National Security Council member and veteran Middle East expert Steven Simon attempted to explain how U.S. foreign policy in the Middle East collapsed. Tracing forty years of U.S.'s efforts to shape the region from the Iranian revolution in 1979 to Benyamin Netanyahu's return to power in Israel in December 2022, Simon drew stark lessons: Washington's Middle East strategy has been, as his book's title suggests, "delusional," fabricated in the continual "superimposition of grand ideas" by policymakers convinced of their own virtuous intentions toward a region about which they knew little and cared less. As he writes, "It is a tale of gross misunderstandings, appalling errors, and death and destruction on an epochal scale."

To give just one example of this policy, for the second time in December the Biden administration bypassed Congress to greenlight an emergency weapons sale to Israel, which only intensified and broadened its attacks on the Gaza Strip despite growing international outrage. U.S. Secretary of State Antony Blinken told Congress that he had made a second emergency determination to immediately approve a $147.5m sale of equipment to Israel, including fuses, charges, and primers that make 155mm shells functional.[21] According to a State Department spokesperson, "Given the urgency of Israel's defensive needs, the

---

20 Steven Simon, *Grand Delusion: The Rise and Fall of American Ambition in the Middle East* (Penguin Random House, 2023).

21 Jennifer Hansler and Oren Liebermann, "Biden admin again bypasses Congress to sell military equipment to Israel," *CNN*, December 29, 2023.

Secretary notified Congress that he had exercised his delegated authority to determine an emergency existed necessitating the immediate approval of the transfer." The same source explained that "The United States is committed to the security of Israel, and it is vital to U.S. national interests to ensure Israel is able to defend itself against the threats it faces." Earlier that same month, the administration rushed forward a sale of thousands of munitions to Israel, bypassing the standard 20-day period that congressional committees are typically afforded to review such a sale. The State Department sent an emergency declaration to the oversight committees that more than 13,000 tank shells would be delivered to Israel without any *further information, details or assurances."* The *Wall Street Journal* reported that the war "is generating destruction comparable in scale to the most devastating warfare in modern record … By mid-December, Israel has dropped 29,000 bombs, munitions and shells on Gaza, destroying or damaging nearly 70 percent of homes."[22]

Neither the exponential rise of Palestinian deaths, now surpassing 40,000 with thousands more still missing or under the rubble, nor the universal outrage led to any fundamental change in the staunchly pro-Israel position the Biden administration took from the start of the war. And still, anyone expecting a major rupture between President Biden and the Israeli prime minister "ought to lie down and wait quietly until the feeling passes. If needed, they should keep Biden's *Washington Post* op-ed from the weekend handy … Indeed, the president's persona, politics and policy choices have virtually pre-empted such an outcome."[23] In that op-ed President Biden wrote that the U.S. won't back down from the challenge of Russian President Vladimir Putin and Hamas: "Both Putin and Hamas are fighting to wipe a neighboring democracy off the map. And both Putin and Hamas hope to collapse broader regional stability and integration and take advantage of the ensuing disorder. America cannot, and will not, let that happen. For our own national security interests—and for the good of the entire world."

---

22 Jared Malsin and Saeed Shah, "The Ruined Landscape of Gaza After Nearly Three Months of Bombing," December 30, 2023.

23 Aaron David Miller, "Why Biden won't do more to restrain Netanyahu," *CNN,* November 23, 2023. To read the op-ed, see: "Joe Biden: The U.S. won't back down from the challenge of Putin and Hamas," The White House, November 19, 2023: https://www.whitehouse.gov/briefing-room/statements-releases/2023/11/19/icymi-joe-biden-the-u-s-wont-back-down-from-the-challenge-of-putin-and-hamas/

Despite the internal and external pressure, there was no indication that the president might support a ceasefire and has intimated to Israel—let alone pressed—that it set a timeline for ending its military operation in Gaza. His words in the *Washington Post* seemed to rule that out, even while knowing full well that this position damages America's standing and image abroad, further isolates it around the world—leaving it to find itself in a defensive crouch and at odds even vis-à-vis its closest Western allies—as it becomes a lonely protector of a country engaged in genocide.

Why is it so? The answer lies in unexpected developments of overriding importance that will likely prove to be a game-changer in the not-distant future.

In effect, historically, U.S. President Harry Truman was the first world leader to officially recognize Israel as a legitimate Jewish state on May 14, 1948, only eleven minutes after its creation. His decision came after much discussion and advice from the White House staff who had differing viewpoints. Some advisors felt that creating a Jewish state was the only proper response to the Holocaust and would benefit American interests. Others took the opposite view, concerned that the creation of a Jewish state would cause more conflict in an already tumultuous region.[24] While acknowledging this recognition of Israel as one of his proudest moments, Truman also admitted that no issue was "more controversial or more complex than the problem of Israel." As the President told his closest advisers, these attempts to resolve the issue of a Jewish homeland left him in a condition of "political battle fatigue."[25]

Truman's announcement, making the United States the first nation to recognize Israel, stunned everyone. Most surprised were Warren R. Austin, the U.S. representative at the United Nations, and his delegation. It is said that Austin was phoned from Washington, D.C. to be informed of the President's decision while he was attending the United Nations General Assembly's session. He "had to leave the floor of the General Assembly to take his call, and, after hearing the shocking news without informing anyone in the U.S. delegation, he went home, leaving the acting ambassador of the United States, Francis Sayre, to take to the podium to tell the delegates the news and that he had known nothing about Truman's recognition. The entire General Assembly was in a state

---

24 See Harry S. Truman Presidential Library and Museum.

25 Allis Radosh and Ronald Radosh, *A Safe Haven, Harry S. Truman and the Founding of Israel* (New York: HarperCollins Publishers, 2009).

of pandemonium."[26] As expressed by David K. Niles, a Jewish staff member of the Truman's team, if President Franklin Delano Roosevelt had lived and Truman not been president, there probably would not have been an Israel. Certainly, "if Franklin D. Roosevelt had been in office, support at critical moments would most likely have not been offered. Without Truman, the new state of Israel might not have survived its first difficult years, and succeeded thereafter."[27]

A secret Central Intelligence Agency (CIA) document entitled "The Consequences of the Partition of Palestine,"[28] dated November 28, 1947, confirms the latter assessment:

> Armed hostilities between Jews and Arabs will break out if the UN General Assembly accepts the plan to partition Palestine into Jewish and Arab States as recommended by the UN Special Committee on Palestine (UNSCOP). Inflamed by nationalism and religious fervor, Arabs in Syria, Lebanon, Iraq, Transjordan, Egypt, and Saudi Arabia as well as Palestine are determined to fight against any force, or combination of forces, which attempts to set up a Jewish state in Palestine. While the governments of the Arab States are not expected to make official declarations of war, they will not attempt to keep their people (especially fanatical tribesmen) from joining the battle; they may even encourage such action and furnish clandestine assistance as well ... The Zionists, for their part, are determined to have a state in Palestine or, in the view of extreme elements, all of Palestine and Transjordan as well. Whatever the UN recommends, they will attempt to establish a Jewish state after the British withdrawal (now set by the British for August 1948). The Jews are expected to be able to mobilize some 200,000 fighters in Palestine, supplemented to a limited extent by volunteers and recruits from abroad ... Initially, they will achieve marked success over the

---

26 Allis Radosh and Ronald Radosh, "A Safe Haven."

27 Allis Radosh and Ronald Radosh, idem.

28 This document was declassified in part in 2013. To read the sanitized copy approved for release: https://www.cia.gov/readingroom/docs/CIA-RDP78-01617A003000180001-8.pdf

Arabs because of superior organization and equipment. As the war of attrition develops, however, the
Jewish economy (severely strained by mobilization)
will break down ... Without substantial outside aid in
terms of manpower and material, they will be able to
hold out no longer than two years ... The U.S., by supporting partition, has already lost much of its prestige
in the Near East. In the event that partition is imposed
on Palestine, the resulting conflict will seriously dis-
turb the social, economic, and political stability of
the Arab world, and U.S. commercial and strategic
interests will be dangerously jeopardized ... With the
U.S. committed to partition, such developments will
be shelved indefinitely. The poverty, unrest, and hopelessness upon which Communist propaganda thrives
will increase throughout the Arab world, and Soviet
agents (some of whom have already been smuggled
into Palestine as Jewish DP's [Displaced Persons] will
scatter into the other Arab states and there attempt to
organize so-called "democratic movements" such as
the one existing today in Greece. If the UN recommends partition, it will be morally bound to take steps
to enforce partition, with major powers acting as the
instruments of enforcement. The dangerous potentialities of such a development to U.S.-USSR relations
need no emphasis.

Nevertheless, it was not until the 1960s, under President John F.
Kennedy, that Washington began to provide military hardware to Israel,
and the first explicit U.S. pledge to maintain Israel's qualitative military
edge—an assurance of Israel's military superiority over its rivals—came
in a 1982 letter from President Ronald Reagan to Israeli prime minister
Menahem Begin.[29] As recalled by Adnan Abu Amer,[30] many analysts in
Israel remember that in 1948 America did not help the Zionist terror
gangs to occupy Palestine, and in 1956 it forced Israel to withdraw from

29 Shalom Lipner, "How Israel Could Lose America," *Foreign Affairs,*
December 29, 2023.
30 Adnan Abu Amer, "Israeli doubts are growing about relying on the
United States," *Middle East Monitor,* March 31, 2022.

Egyptian territory, which led eventually to the 1967 war. They also believe that although the U.S. intervened in the 1973 war, Israel could have achieved more on its own.

In truth, although the bilateral cooperation has been turbulent at times, "it has maintained a steady upward trajectory. U.S. security, diplomatic, and economic assistance has bolstered Israel's position in a volatile region. Having a 'big brother' over its shoulder has enabled Israel to punch above its demographic weight and geographic size, projecting strength well beyond its borders. And the United States' commitment to Israel has endured through both Democratic and Republican Presidents, including the most recent holders of that office," says Shalom Lipner. Chuck Freilich concurred with this analysis: "For the most part, as a small actor facing numerous and often severe threats, but with limited influence of its own, reliance on the U.S. has become the panacea for virtually all of Israel's national-security challenges. Israel can and does appeal to other countries, but this is usually of marginal utility, and what the U.S. cannot achieve, Israel almost certainly cannot, so there has often been limited interest in even trying."[31]

Conversely, not long ago, Max Fisher pointed out[32] that that was the conventional wisdom, and it had been true for decades. Israeli leaders and voters alike, he said, treated Washington as essential to their country's survival. However, while Israel still benefits greatly from American assistance, security experts and political analysts noted that the country had quietly cultivated, and may have achieved, effective autonomy from the United States. The issue of overreliance by Israelis on the United States for their security and the survival of their "Jewish state," particularly in the event of their country being embroiled in a major war, suddenly rose to prominence when the Russian-Ukrainian war started. Viewing Ukraine as seemingly left alone to deal with Vladimir Putin caused alarm bells to ring in Tel Aviv. Therefore, a new "self-reliant" Israel, it was thought, must be pursued, one in which it "does not need U.S. troops in any capacity to defend it. Ultimately, such self-reliance will grant Israel greater freedom of action and remove a significant lever of pressure used against it in the past."[33]

---

31 Chuck Freilich, "How Long Could Israel Survive Without America?," *Newsweek,* July 14, 2017.

32 Max Fisher, "As Israel's Dependence on U.S. Shrinks, So Does U.S. Leverage," *The New York Times,* May 24, 2021.

33 Ramzy Baroud, "Can Israel exist without America? The facts suggest a changing reality," *Middle East Monitor,* April 5, 2022.

Max Fisher went as far as to think that Israel no longer needed American security guarantees to protect it from neighboring states, with which it had mostly made peace. Nor did Israel see itself as needing American mediation in the Palestinian conflict, which Israelis largely found bearable and supported maintaining as is. "Once reliant on American arms transfers, Israel now produces many of its most essential weapons domestically. It has become more self-sufficient diplomatically as well, cultivating allies independent of Washington. Even culturally, Israelis are less sensitive to American approval—and put less pressure on their leaders to maintain good standing in Washington," he said. And while American aid to Israel remained high in absolute terms, he added, Israel's decades-long economic boom has left the country less and less reliant: in 1981, American aid was equivalent to almost 10 percent of Israel's economy; in 2020, at nearly $4 billion, it was closer to 1 percent. He concluded his article with a preposterous assertion by Mizrahi-Arnaud: "Now, after nearly 50 years of not quite wielding that leverage to bring an end to the Israeli-Palestinian conflict, it may soon be gone for good, if it isn't already. Israel feels that they can get away with more." Mizrahi-Arnaud added, to underscore her point, "When exactly is the last time that the United States pressured Israel?"

This hubris and image of invincibility fostered and entertained for half a century were shattered on October 7. As the war on Gaza was then entering its eleventh-month mark, the Palestinian resistance alone—with no air force, no navy, no tanks, not even a regular army—was still holding and inflicting increasing damage to the IDF, leaving Israel as yet to achieve any of its three stated goals: eliminating Hamas, freeing the kidnapped Israeli citizens, and ensuring that no element in Gaza can threaten Israel again.

In the meantime, both Israel and the United States needed to defend themselves against criminal charges: the former for committing genocide, the latter for failing to prevent it. As the UN Secretary-General said: the eyes of the world—and the eyes of history—were watching!

CHAPTER FIVE

THE INEVITABILITY OF PALESTINE'S INDEPENDENCE IN THE LONG TERM

"Victorious warriors win first and then go to war, while defeated warriors go to war first and then seek to win."
—SUN TZU[1]

Right from the outset of this analysis of the war on Gaza, I posited that this war is different to the others in many crucial respects and will have lasting and far-reaching consequences. It even has the potential to fundamentally remake the entire Middle East region even as, indeed, it is opening the eyes of the American and world's peoples in so many ways. So far, the emphasis has been put on the highly important and necessary historicization and geopolitical contextualization of the century-old Israeli-Palestinian conflict that is today reaching its pinnacle. Going forward, we'll shift our attention to what's next for the Palestinians, for Israel, for the Middle East region and its impact on the global order. More specifically, and to start with, we'll address Khaled Elgindy's insightful observation according to which all parties concerned concur that there's no going back to the October 6 untenable status quo, and try to answer his challenging question "Where do we go from here?"[2]

On the Meaning of Victory in Ancient and Modern Warfare

More than two thousand years ago, in his timeless treatise *The Art of War* (also known as *The Thirteen Chapters*), the great Chinese military strategist and general Sun Tzu asserted that war was an extension

---

1 Sun Tzu, *The Art of War* (Shambhala Publications, 2005), p. 57.
2 See Amir Nour's article, "The War on Gaza: How We got to the 'Monstrosity of our Century'," *GlobalResearch,* January 8, 2024. https://www.globalresearch.ca/war-gaza-how-we-got-monstrosity-our-century/5845445

of politics and should be pursued in the interests of the greater good for all, the conqueror and the conquered. He believed that for warfare to be defined as anything other than a waste of life and resources, one needed to win. And for victory to be achieved, it is imperative to know yourself and your enemy: "If you know the enemy and know yourself, you need not fear the result of a hundred battles. If you know yourself but not the enemy, for every victory gained you will also suffer a defeat. If you know neither the enemy nor yourself, you will succumb in every battle." The conventional view is that Sun Tzu lived, fought, and composed his master work during the Spring and Autumn Period which preceded the Warring States Period (c. 481–221 BCE) during which the Zhou Dynasty (1046–256 BCE) was declining, and the states once bound to it fought each other for supremacy and control of China.[3]

In same vein, the no less famous 19th century Prussian general Carl von Clausewitz claimed, in his magnum opus military strategy book *On War,*[4] that "War is simply a continuation of political intercourse, with the addition of other means. We deliberately use the phrase 'addition of other means' because we also want to make it clear that war in itself does not suspend political intercourse or change it into something entirely different. That intercourse continues, irrespective of the means it employs. The main lines along which military events progress, and to which they are restricted, are political lines that continue throughout the war into the subsequent peace." It follows that "The political object—the original motive for war—will thus determine the military objective to be reached and the amount of effort it requires."[5]

Clausewitz described military victory as a condition where the enemy's ability to enter battle, resist or resume hostilities is destroyed. He stated that "The key to victory lies in the ability to deny the enemy their objective," thus emphasizing the importance of not only achieving one's own objectives but also preventing the adversary from attaining

---

3 Joshua J. Mark, "Sun-Tzu," *World History Encyclopedia,* July 9, 2020.

4 Carl von Clausewitz, *On War,* translated by Michael Howard and Peter Paret (Princeton University Press, 1976). In fact, the book is an unfinished work: Clausewitz had set about revising his accumulated manuscripts in 1827 but did not live to finish the task. His wife Marie von Brühl posthumously published the book in 1832, and subsequently collected his works and published them between 1832 and 1835 (Source: Wikipedia).

5 Bill Bently, "Clausewitz: War, Strategy and Victory—A Reflection on Brigadier-General Carignan's Article," *Canadian Military Journal* 17, no. 2 (Summer 2017).

theirs. By depriving the enemy of their goals, a military force can strategically weaken and ultimately defeat them. It is interesting to note that Clausewitz's manuscripts were inspired by the stunning military successes during the Napoleonic Wars between 1803 and 1815, which nevertheless, as history has recorded, proved ephemeral. Conversely, Clausewitz's Prussia was convincingly beaten in 1806 in the Jena campaign but came back militarily in the 1813 and 1814 campaigns and again at Waterloo in 1815.[6]

This paradigm encompassing both the linkages between war and politics and the notion of victory has traditionally constituted the norm and the yardstick for assessment and judgement through much of history and up to the 21st century. However, in modern wars—wars which have occurred since the end of the Cold War—while the linkage component is still largely valid, contemporary strategists and military affairs analysts tend to diverge on the notion, or more precisely the meaning, of victory. This is particularly the case regarding asymmetric warfare—a form of war between belligerents whose relative military power, strategy, or tactics are significantly different, and often involving a wide variety of non-state actors, insurgents or resistance movement militias. Henry Kissinger was undoubtedly right when he observed that "A conventional army loses if it doesn't win. A guerilla army wins if it doesn't lose."[7]

I dealt with this subject in an article[8] I wrote in 2018 in which I explained that numerous careful studies have shown that the United States and its allies are blindly following those insurgents' worldview and game plan, which is to "perpetually engage and enervate the United states and the West in a series of prolonged overseas ventures" in which they will undermine their own societies, expend their resources, and increase the level of violence, thereby setting off a dynamic that William Roe Polk has reviewed in length in one of his books.[9] Indeed, Polk reveals a pattern that has been replicated over and over throughout recent history.

---

6 Peter Layton, "Using a Clausewitzian Dictum to Rethink Achieving Victory," *The Bridge,* May 15, 2018.

7 Henry Kissinger, "The Vietnam Negotiations," *Foreign Affairs* 48, no. 2 (January 1969).

8 Amir Nour, "The Twilight of the Empire Age: Whose World Will It Be?," *GlobalResearch,* March 30, 2018: https://www.globalresearch.ca/the-twilight-of-the-empire-age-whose-world-will-it-be-why-america-isnt-great-anymore/5634060

9 William R. Polk, *Violent Politics: A History of Insurgency, Terrorism, and Guerilla War, From the American Revolution to Iraq* (Harper Perennial, 2008).

That is, invaders are naturally disliked by the invaded population, who disobey them, at the start in small ways, eliciting a forceful response on the part of the invader, which in turn increases opposition and popular support for resistance. The ensuing cycle of violence then escalates until the invading forces are obliged either to withdraw, or to resort to methods and means that amount to genocide to gain their ends.

Recent examples of battlefield victors eventually losing the war, or the defeated coming out as winners have been provided by many prominent scholars. In 2006, in an article titled "What Is Victory," Stanford University professor Barrie D. Zimmerman rightly pointed out that "Many wars do not result in unambiguous victory for one side or the other. Fatigue, a recognition that the cost of total victory is too high, or the prospect of endless conflict, leads the players to agree on a cease-fire." The article cited as examples the invasions of Iraq and Lebanon by the U.S. and Israel, respectively, saying:

> Israel realized that the cost of its invasion of Lebanon was more than it had bargained for and agreed to a cessation of hostilities. Initially the Jewish state had announced its aim as freeing the two soldiers captured by Hezbollah, disarming that organization, and removing it from a position in which it could threaten Israel. It achieved none of these aims but still declared victory. Following that lead, President George Bush could declare victory in Iraq. Whether one wishes to view Israel or the United States as a victor depends on whether the glass is half full or half empty.[10]

In these examples as well as in the case of Afghanistan, the strategic success could not be achieved, notwithstanding a superior military force and an immense mismatch between the opponents in terms of firepower and technology at their respective command. The main reason for that is that victory required not only the defeat of the opponents' military capabilities but also the successful resolution of the deeper problems at the root of the conflict.[11]

10 Barrie D. Zimmerman, "What is Victory?," Stanford University, 2006. https://web.stanford.edu/~moore/Victory.htm [URL no longer accessible, retrieved by Grok.]

11 Colonel E.A. de Landmeter, "What constitutes victory in modern war?," *Militaire Spectator,* March 20, 2018.

In understanding victory, says William Martel,[12] a clear distinction between the political aim (the end) and the military aim (one of the means to achieve the end) is essential. Victory can be looked at as an outcome (result), a descriptive statement of the post-war situation, or as an aspiration (ambition or goal) being the driver to accomplish specific objectives through use of force. That's why most scholars and analysts seem to agree that military victories alone do not determine the outcome of modern wars. They consider victory to be the achievement of a predetermined end state.

The notion of a desired end state implies that victory occurs if the outcome of the war corresponds with previously articulated aims, that is, a relation between war aims and war outcomes.[13] It is then critical to define the end before the war begins, and to clearly follow it. War, says Michael Anderson, "is a fluid, complicated thing, and it isn't beyond reason for war aims to morph during a conflict, but at each of those points there must be a clear and understood process for the changed goals to be achieved as there was leading into the war in the first place. A change in war aims can seem like a new war in itself."[14] Indeed, if it's unknown how a war is supposed to end, then how can it be known if, or when, the endgame has been achieved?

Nowadays, as stated by de Landmeter, it is almost inconceivable to wage war without considering the post-war period. Ideally, the object of policy extends into the period after hostilities, and victory is closely linked to concepts of conflict termination and conflict resolution that seek to find lasting solutions.

In answering the big question of what constitutes victory in modern war, Gabriella Blum contends that

> With wars becoming about long-term change, requiring a mix of benevolence and aggression that is carefully tailored to individual targets, the political and civilian dimensions of victory have outgrown the military one. As the attempts to define what success looks like in Afghanistan or Iraq show, the formulation

---

12 William C. Martel, *Victory in War: Foundations of Modern Strategy* (Cambridge University Press, 2011).
13 Robert Mandel, "Reassessing Victory in Warfare," *Armed Forces & Society* 33 no. 4 (2007).
14 Michael Anderson, *On the Meaning of Victory,* The Association of the United States Army, July 26, 2018.

of victory now requires more long-term, abstract, and complex, less tangible and immediate terms. War, in other words, can no longer be reduced into a military campaign.[15]

To put it another way, victory in the "true sense implies that the state of peace and of one's people, is better after the war than before."[16] Such a victory, however, requires considerable patience, because "while the military contest may have a finite ending, the political, social, and psychological issues may not be resolved even years after the formal end of hostilities."[17]

So, how does this paradigm translate in the case of the Israeli-Palestinian conflict? More precisely, has violence meted out on the Palestinians, forcing them to do under duress what Israel wanted in the short term, brought a settled, durable peace? It has obviously not. For Peter Layton, the Israelis are a perfect contemporary example of the validity of said paradigm:

> . . . they [the Israelis] have won many seemingly decisive battles but are still searching for victory. The Palestinians may be scattered and partly live in occupied lands, but Israel is unable to compel them to come to a peaceful resolution of their territorial dis-agreement. The two sides' political differences remain unresolved, so their political interaction—their human intercourse—continues, sometimes violently and oc-casionally at times through war.[18]

Since October 7, this situation has worsened in an unprecedented manner, as it has set in motion a succession of tragic events of Dantesque proportions. What is unfolding right before our very eyes is no less than a fight for survival from the point of view of all the belligerents, namely Israel and the Palestinians, as well as the latter's allies in the potent "axis of resistance" composed of Lebanese Hezbollah, Yemeni Houthis, Iraqi

---

15 Gabriella Blum, "The Fog of Victory," *The European Journal of International Law* 24, no. 1 (2013).

16 B.H. Liddell Hart, *Strategy* (Penguin Group, New York, 1991).

17 Robert Mandel, op cit.

18 Peter Layton, "Using a Clausewitzian Dictum to Rethink Achieving Victory," op cit.

resistance factions, Syria and the Islamic Republic of Iran. Quite understandably, Wesley Clark's shocking utterance "we're going to take out
seven countries in five years"[19] has never ceased to loom over the region.

Collectively trapped in an existential War to End All Gaza Wars

Based on the above-mentioned paradigm, how can we, thus far, assess the ongoing war aims and outcomes as per the belligerents? In other
words, who's winning this war and who's losing it from the military,
legal, moral, and, more importantly, political standpoints? And what's
next, therefore?

Like many other strategists and military analysts, Gershon Hacohen
points out that Israel has continued to confront the threat of war according to the pattern of conflicts from the last century, from the "War of
Independence" in 1948 to the Yom Kippur War in 1973. Thereafter, it has
been struggling to grasp the implications of a new conception of warfare
adopted by its enemies. This conception, he says, "has thrust Israel into a
state of continuous warfare, like a chronic disease without a cure."

When he initially crafted his country's national security doctrine
in the mid-twentieth century, the first Israeli prime minister David Ben-
Gurion acknowledged the fundamental weakness of the State of Israel in
terms of its ability to withstand a prolonged war. Accordingly, he expected
the IDF to decisively win wars fast and developed an offensive striking
force with the directive to transfer any conflict to the enemy's territory
as quickly as possible. General Israel Tal—who designed the Merkava
tank and reached the position of deputy Chief of staff—explained this
perspective at length in his book describing the history of the Israel-
Arab wars from 1948 onward and presents a security theory specific to
Israel from which the fighting doctrines of the Israeli military derive.
Tal concludes that the previous security theory proved valid because
it was based upon a decision to allocate the great portion of available
resources, both intellectual and material, to secure national defense. He
considered that this theory was no longer valid due to political changes
in the Middle East and the development of modern military technologies.

---

19 Watch Wesley Clark's interview with Amy Goodman on Democracy
Now!, March 2, 2007: https://www.democracynow.org/2007/3/2/gen_wesley_
clark_weighs_presidential_bid

Over the decades, Israel's security doctrine has been updated to encompass four fundamental pillars, namely deterrence, early warning, strong defensive capabilities, and decisive and quick victories.

Nevertheless, the Israeli need to end wars quickly was clearly understood and effectively integrated into the perception of warfare developed by Hezbollah and Hamas, with the backing of Iran. They formulated a concept of warfare that is aimed at swiftly negating Israel's decisive capabilities. Over the last 40 years, Islamic organizations have formulated the idea of an ideological-religious war guided by the concept of *Al-Muqawama*—the Arabic word for "resistance."

This idea has been convincingly explained by Ramzy Baroud.[20] Muqawama for Palestinians, he wrote,

> is not an intellectual conversation, or an academic theory. It is not an outcome of a political strategy, either. In the words of Frantz Fanon, referencing wars of liberation, "we revolt simply because (...) we can no longer breathe." Indeed, Palestinian revolts and resistance are a direct outcome of the Palestinian people's refusal to accept the injustices of settler-colonialism, military occupation, protracted sieges and the denial of basic political rights.
>
> For *Muqawama* to be fully appreciated as a unique Palestinian phenomenon, it cannot be delinked from history; neither can it be explored separate from the "popular embrace"—*Al-Hadina al-Sha'biyah lil-Muqawamah al-Filistiniyah*—of the Palestinian people themselves, who have always served as the original source and the main protector of Palestinian resistance in all of its forms.

It can thus be viewed as the inverse of Clausewitz's description of war as "the continuation of politics by other means." Politics therefore is seen as the continuation of war by other means, and negotiation is viewed not as a means to bring about the end of a war but simply as a pause that serves its continuation at a more opportune time under more favorable conditions.

---

20 Ramzy Baroud, "Armed vs Peaceful Resistance—What You Need to Know About Muqawama in Gaza," *Savage Minds,* June 25, 2024.

This concept of resistance has both a physical-military dimension and a cultural-spiritual dimension. The military dimension was described by the commander of the Iranian Revolutionary Guards, Hossein Salami, in 2022: "The Palestinians are ready for ground combat. This is Israel's vulnerability. Missiles are excellent for deterrence ... but they don't liberate land. Ground forces must be deployed, step by step, to liberate it ... Hezbollah and Palestinian forces will move on the ground in a unified military structure."[21]

In truth, the new resistance strategy was essentially the brainchild of Qassem Suleimani, the head of Iran's Islamic Revolutionary Guard Corps Al-Qods Force, who was assassinated in an American missile strike on January 3, 2020. Suleimani was keen on and fully invested in strengthening the coordination work between the different Resistance groups around Israel; a strategy known as "Tightening the noose," which links religious, political, civic and military ideology.

Also, less than two months prior to October 7, Saleh Al-Arouri, Deputy Head of the Political Bureau of Hamas, said in an exclusive interview with Lebanese *Al-Mayadeen* TV that: "the Resistance alliance is prepared and motivated by reason, will, and common interests to partake in a regional war, and the active parties are ready and prepared for it," adding: "The all-out war will be a defeat for Israel, and we see that classical wars have changed, and this is evidenced by the conflict in Ukraine."[22] Later on, the very day of the October 7 attack, Al-Arouri[23] declared in an interview with *Al-Jazeera* that the group is engaged in a battle for freedom: "This is not a [hit-and-run] operation; we started an all-out battle. We expect fighting to continue and the fighting front to expand. We have one prime target: our freedom and the freedom of our holy sites."[24]

Regarding the spiritual-cultural dimension, retired general Hacohen says that Hamas's leadership has taught us that its conduct is

---

21 MEMRI, "IRGC Commander Salami In Interview For Supreme Leader Khamenei's Website: The Palestinians Are Ready Today For Ground Warfare," August 31, 2022.

22 *Al-Mayadeen* English, "Exclusive—Al Arouri: Resistance Axis preparing for all-out war," August 25, 2023. To watch the interview in Arabic: https://www.youtube.com/watch?v=_aoONr4zpdQ

23 He was assassinated by an Israeli drone strike in Beirut's southern suburbs of Dahiyeh, a Hezbollah stronghold, on January 2, 2024.

24 *Al-Jazeera,* "Hamas says it has enough Israeli captives to free all Palestinian prisoners," October 7, 2023.

guided by a deep religious rationale, and "Western cultural observers, who for centuries have separated religious motives from the political, diplomatic, and military considerations of state leaders, have no tools with which to understand the leadership of Iran, Hezbollah, and Hamas, which are driven by religious conviction and carry out their daily work guided by faith." He added that

> It is from this perspective that we can understand the logic employed by Yahya Al-Sinwar in his decision to go to war on October 7. From his point of view, after Hamas fulfilled its duty to take the initiative and act, trends would develop later that would advance the divine intention. If, for example, the war results in a situation in which Israel is forced to submit to American demands for the establishment of a Palestinian state and withdrawal from the West Bank, Al-Sinwar will be perceived as victorious. Despite the massive destruction he has brought down upon Gaza, he will achieve a historical status no less than that of Saladin.

In Hacohen's words, "this insight must be integrated into the foundations of the Israeli security perception because in terms of comprehensive existential considerations, this perception extends beyond the concept of deterrence, which has repeatedly revealed itself to be fragile." What he was referring to is the failure of the ill-named "mowing the lawn" strategy, consisting of Israel reestablishing deterrence through a limited use of force each time a flare-up occurred in Gaza. As a matter of fact, this strategy allowed Hamas and the other Palestinian Resistance groups to carry out a long-term build-up of arms and military infrastructure and to improve their operational capabilities, in particular through the building of an amazingly extensive and highly sophisticated network of tunnels, even infiltrating Israeli territory.

In essence, Hacohen concludes, the war of 1967 was the last military clash to unfold along the lines of World War II, and since then, the world of warfare has changed completely. As a result, he believes that "to seek a victory along the lines of outdated patterns is like asking for the Red Sea to be split again."

Undoubtedly, the era of intermittent cycles of fighting and cease-fires in Gaza is over. There will be no going back to the previous state of affairs. For both the Palestinian resistance and Israel the only order of the day is the vital need to achieve a decisive military outcome. This idea has "sparked extensive debate among experts and senior IDF leaders for many years about how to define 'decisive outcome' and 'victory' and how to apply them to conflicts with non-state actors and terrorist groups. Israel now understands that although the jihadi ideology of Hamas may persist (as have those of the Islamic State, or ISIS, and al-Qaeda), the IDF must dismantle the organization's military capabilities."[25]

It's a truism to say that because of its incomparable conventional military superiority to its adversaries, Israel knows full well that Hamas and the other Palestinian Resistance groups cannot go toe to toe with the IDF. How could a group of armed irregulars numbering in the low tens of thousands, besieged in a tiny territory, and with little access to advanced weaponry, reasonably be a match to a nuclear state, ranked 17th most powerful military in the world,[26] armed and backed by the world's number one, that is the U.S.? Yet, as we said earlier when referring to insurgents' worldview and game plan within the framework of modern asymmetric warfare, Israel in its turn will go down in the history books as another example of a mighty military power losing to a weaker opponent.

As Audrey Kurth Cronin says, "For Israel, perhaps the most galling outcome of this asymmetry is that its armed forces may have played squarely into Hamas's hands by striking Gaza with tremendous force"[27] in response to the Al-Aqsa Flood military operation on October 7. This operation, she claims, "was intended to provoke the Israeli military into an overreaction that would undermine international sympathy for Israel, stoke an uprising in the West Bank and Jerusalem, and rally support for Hamas ... In many ways, the group has succeeded."

Indeed, driven by a blind fury and desire for vengeance, the IDF has called up over 350,000 reservists and launched ferocious attacks by air, land and sea in a collective punishment of the Palestinian civilians that has so far killed and injured close to 6% of the Gazan population— put into perspective, that proportion would be equivalent to killing 20 million Americans—created a humanitarian catastrophe of biblical

---

25 Ramzy Baroud, "Armed Vs. Peaceful Resistance—What You Need to Know about Muqawama in Gaza," *Brave New Europe,* June 26, 2024.

26 Global Firepower, "2024 Military Strength Ranking."

27 Audrey Kurth Cronin, "Hamas's Asymmetric Advantage," *Foreign Affairs,* January/February 2024.

proportions, and is increasingly raising the risk of a wider regional, if not global, war.

With its savage military expedition entering its eleventh month—making it the longest and deadliest it has ever experienced—Israel had yet to achieve any of its three stated strategic goals, which Netanyahu has just once more reiterated: "We will not compromise on anything less than total victory ... That means eliminating Hamas, returning all of our hostages and ensuring that Gaza will no longer pose a threat to Israel."[28] Worse still, Netanyahu is facing a deeply divided war cabinet and knows his right-wing governmental coalition is in great danger of being brought down at any time. Further evidence of this was given when Defense Minister Yoav Gallant, who promised to "wipe Hamas off the face of the earth," replaced the previously equally sacrosanct third objective with a revealing new one, that is "maintaining unity among the people of Israel."[29]

After only two months of fierce fighting, and despite the cataclysmic violence unleashed on Palestinians, an increasing number of establishment strategic analysts started warning that Israel was failing to achieve its political goals and could lose this war. By shattering a status quo that Palestinians find intolerable, Tony Karon and Daniel Levy say, "Hamas has put politics back on the agenda. Israel has significant military power, but it is politically weak."[30] They remind that "History also suggests a pattern in which representatives of movements dismissed as 'terrorist' by their adversaries—in South Africa, say, or Ireland—nonetheless appear at the negotiating table when the time comes to seek political solutions. It would be ahistorical to bet against Hamas, or at least some version of the political-ideological current it represents, doing the same if and when a political solution between Israel and the Palestinians is revisited with seriousness." The authors conclude that "What comes after the horrific violence is far from clear, but Hamas's October 7 attack has forced a reset of a political contest to which Israel appears unwilling to respond beyond devastating military force against Palestinian civilians. And as things stand eight weeks into the vengeance, Israel can't be said to be winning."

---

28 Patrick Wintour, "Netanyahu rules out ceasefire deal that would mean Gaza withdrawal," *The Guardian,* January 30, 2024.

29 Akiva Van Koningsveld, "Gallant: IDF to retain security control in Gaza after Hamas defeated," *The Jewish Chronicle,* January 30, 2024.

30 Tony Karon and Daniel Levy, "Israel is Losing This War," December 8, 2023.

For former prime minister Ehud Olmert, the odds of achieving the complete elimination of Hamas were nil from the moment that Prime minister Benjamin Netanyahu declared it the chief goal of the war. Hamas, he wrote in an opinion,[31]

> is not easily defeated. Of course, Netanyahu knew from the get-go that his rhetoric was baseless and would ultimately collapse in the face of a military and humanitarian reality that would force Israel to reach an end point in the current campaign. That time has now arrived. The defeat of Hamas is a long way away. We haven't even reached the point at which we are in control of the timetable of the war that began on October 7.

As for what is to be done, he believes that "the time has come for Israel to express its readiness to end the fighting. Yes, end the fighting. Not a pause and not a temporary cessation of two, three or four days. An end of hostility—period." This should be conditioned on the release of all the hostages and in exchange, Israel "will have no choice but to release all the Hamas prisoners it holds."

Similarly, for Eyal Hulata, who was Israel's national security adviser from 2021 to 2023, "There is no way this will end when Israel can say we are victorious. Israel lost this war [on] the 7th of October. The only question now is if we are able to remove from Hamas the ability to do this again. And we might succeed, and we might not."[32]

Leading Israeli columnist Nahum Barnea doesn't think otherwise. In an op-ed he wrote in *Yediot Ahronoth,* he called on Israel to adjust its objective of dismantling Hamas in Gaza and affirmed that: "In the last three weeks, the war has not changed reality. It has cost the lives of soldiers, has increased the risk of a humanitarian disaster that Israel will be responsible for, has hurt Israel in the world and hasn't brought us any closer to a victory which does not exist."[33]

---

31 Ehud Olmert, "Israel Must Cease Hostilities and Bring the Hostages Home," *Haaretz,* December 28, 2023.

32 Daniel Estrin, "Israelis are increasingly questioning what war in Gaza can achieve," *NPR,* January 11, 2024.

33 Nahum Barnea, איך יוצאים מהבור שאליו נפלנו (How to get out of the hole into which we fell), *Ynet,* 9 January 2024.

Also, former leader of the Shin Bet domestic security force, Ami Ayalon, said Israel will not have security until Palestinians have their own state, and Israeli authorities should release Marwan Barghouti, jailed leader of the second intifada, to direct negotiations to create one. He also shared the view that the nature of Hamas meant that its destruction was an impossible goal for a military. Hamas is not just a militia, he said, but

> an ideology with an organization, and the organization has a military wing. You cannot destroy ideology by the use of military power. Sometimes it will be rooted deeper if you try. This is exactly what we see today. Today, 75% of Palestinians support Hamas. Before the war, it was less than 50%.[34]

The same opinion was expressed by war cabinet Gadi Eisenkot, thus contradicting his own prime minister. He said that "A strategic achievement was not reached ... We did not demolish the Hamas organization."[35]

Last but not least, former prime minister Ehud Barak stated in an opinion in *Haaretz* that "Hamas has not been defeated, and the chances of recovering the hostages are declining."[36] He added that those who believe that Palestinians in Gaza can be encouraged to migrate voluntarily are delving into dreams that have no basis in reality.

The textbook case of genocide that Israel is carrying out against the Palestinian people has inflamed public opinion across the whole world as shown by the millions of pro-Palestinian protesters marching almost daily in rallies on the streets of major world cities. These multitudes are united in one overarching demand: ending the IDF bombardment of Gaza and Israeli occupation of Palestinian territories. Even in the United States, the staunchest supporter of Israel no matter how gravely damaging this blind support has been to its national and global interests, growing numbers of protesters have taken to the streets of New York City, Washington D.C., Los Angeles and Dallas, among others.

---

34 Emma Graham-Harrison and Quique, "Ex-Shin Bet head says Israel should negotiate with jailed intifada leader," *The Guardian,* January 14, 2024.

35 Nadeen Ebrahim and Vasco Cotovio, "Israeli government divisions deepen as cabinet minister says defeating Hamas is unrealistic," *CNN,* January 20, 2024.

36 Ehud Barak, "Israel Needs an Early Election-Before It's Too Late," *Haaretz,* January 18, 2024.

More significantly, after losing the war of worldwide public opinion, Israel suffered another blow when, on January 26, 2024, the International Court of Justice (ICJ) rejected its petition to throw out a landmark legal case filed by South Africa concerning "alleged violations by Israel of its obligations under the Convention on the Prevention and Punishment of the Crime of Genocide in relation to Palestinians in the Gaza Strip." The ICJ's panel of 17 judges issued, by an overwhelming majority of 15 votes to two, an order,[37] which has binding effect, indicating six provisional instructions to Israel to refrain from acts under the Genocide convention, prevent and punish the direct and public incitement to genocide, and take immediate and effective measures to ensure the provision of humanitarian assistance to civilians in Gaza. Crucially, the Court also ordered Israel to preserve evidence of genocide and to submit a report to the Court within one month of all measures taken in line with its order. Critically, this ruling raises the possibility that Israel's backers in Washington, London, Berlin and other European capitals could face the prospect of being implicated in having aided and abetted genocide at some future date.[38]

As a result of all these momentous events, Washington is now openly and regularly calling for the implementation of the two-states solution. In the words of Maria Fantappie and Wali Nasr,[39] Washington "can no longer neglect the Palestinian issue. In fact, it will have to make resolving that conflict the centerpiece of its endeavor. It will simply be impossible for the United States to tackle other questions in the region, including the future of Arab-Israeli ties, until there is credible path to a viable future Palestinian state."

Just before leaving office, Secretary of State Tony Blinken asked the State Department to conduct a review and present policy options on possible U.S. and international recognition of a Palestinian state after the war in Gaza.[40] The simple fact that the State Department is even considering such options signaled a major policy shift within the Biden

---

37 See official press release of the Court: https://www.icj-cij.org/sites/default/files/case-related/192/192-20240126-pre-01-00-en.pdf

38 Simon Speakman Cordall, "Israel's supporters have been put on notice, say experts on ICJ verdict," *Al-Jazeera,* January 27, 2024.

39 Maria Fantappie and Wali Nasr, "The War That Remade the Middle East: How Washington Can Stabilize a Transformed Region," *Foreign Affairs,* January/February 2024.

40 Barak Ravid, "Scoop: State Department reviewing options for possible recognition of Palestinian state," January 31, 2024.

administration. This is notable as for decades, U.S. policy has been to oppose the recognition of Palestine as a state both bilaterally and in UN institutions, and to stress that Palestinian statehood should only be achieved through direct negotiations between Israel and the Palestinian Authority.

Thanks to their steadfast resistance, boundless bravery, indescribable sacrifices, and the fateful blows they are inflicting on the Israeli occupation forces, the Palestinians have at last, and against all odds, succeeded in having their just cause take front and center at the global stage. Thus, they have decidedly paved the way for a long-awaited independence and a dignified life on their stolen ancestral land.

CHAPTER SIX

WHITHER THE "JEWISH STATE"?

*"We are a people, one people (...) When we sink, we become
a revolutionary proletariat, the subordinate officers of a
revolutionary party; when we rise, there rises also our
terrible power of the purse."*
—THEODOR HERZL[1]

Zionism's Quest for a Substitute Jewish Identity

One of the most qualified specialists in the study of Zionism—its antecedents, motivation, powerbase, claim to the land of Palestine, and the far-reaching repercussions of the creation of the state of Israel on both Jews and Arabs—is undoubtedly the late Egyptian scholar, Dr Abdelwahab Elmessiri. His scholarly interest in and extensive research on Zionism as a political movement led to the publication in 1975 of *The Encyclopedia of Zionist Concepts and Terminology,* acknowledged to be, to this day, the only work of its kind in the Arabic language.

Among many other works he published *The Land of Promise: A Critique of Political Zionism,*[2] which, upon its release in 1977, appealed not only to scholarly readers but also to large elements of the public, for it discusses aspects that, at that time, were not apparent to the public and policymakers alike in the Western countries, or the United States in particular, who at the time failed—and still do today—to recognize the true nature of political Zionism and had accepted the ambiguities and mythicism that blur the differences between Zionism and Judaism. Such an accommodation continues to facilitate the rationalization of and

---

1 Theodor Herzl, *The Jewish State* (New York: Dover Publications, Inc., 1946). The first English-language edition, translated by Sylvie d'Avigdor, was published by Nutt, London, England, 1896. As for the Herzl text, it was originally published under the German title *Der Judenstaat* in Vienna, 1896.

2 Abdelwahab Elmessiri, *The Land of Promise: A Critique of Political Zionism* (New Brunswick, New Jersey: North American, 1977).

support for a Zionist-dominated Israel, while also helping to conceal the mistreatment of the native Palestinian population and the denial of their legitimate and inalienable rights.

In this outstanding book, Elmessiri also expressed his conviction that the situation was not without hope, and suggested which aspects of Zionist policy and practice could be changed or eliminated so that peace and justice could be realized in the "Promised Land." The suggestions he put forward were all the more worthy of interest as none of them would do violence either to the basic tenets of Judaism or to the individual human rights of both the Palestinians and the Jews.

With regard to the subject of Zionism and religious belief, Elmessiri observes that it is difficult to think of a political phenomenon that generates more controversy and elicits more violent reaction than Zionism. Many political movements and institutions, he says, have been described over the years as progressive or counterrevolutionary, nationalist, or settler-colonialist. But unlike Zionism, "very few movements in the twentieth century have been described as being 'much more than a political entity'[3] [and] it is doubtful whether any political outlook has ever been classified as a 'sacred word and concept'[4] and as a 'legitimate religious belief,'[5] not to mention the fact that some Zionists and their sympathizers even view the establishment of a state in the land of Palestine as being the fulfillment of biblical prophecy and an event of apocalyptic significance."

It is precisely this aspect of the controversy surrounding Zionism that made it necessary for the Egyptian scholar to begin his study of this ideology by asserting what he believed is self-evident, namely that Zionism is a political movement, and is not a religious doctrine. He added that the hue and cry in the West, following the adoption of the 1975 United Nations resolution equating Zionism with racism, was a timely reminder of the need to emphasize once more the difference between the religious belief and the political program.

Far from being sacred, Elmessiri affirms, Zionism is a political ideology of complex European origins, rooted primarily in the

---

3 Bishop W. Ralph Ward, President of the United Methodist Church's Council of Bishops, *The New York Times,* November 9, 1975.

4 The first phrase is from a letter sent by the second annual Christian-Jewish Workshop, sponsored by the United States Conference of Catholic Bishops cited in op. cit. The second phrase is used in the same report with no citation of source.

5 "Notes on Zionism by Max Nordau," selected by Chaim Bloch, *Herzl Year Book,* Vol. VII, p. 34.

socioeconomic realities of the Eastern European Jewish ghettoes and in European society of the late nineteenth century; the common denominator among their wide variety of schools of thought being the conviction that the Jews, without waiting for divine intervention, should achieve "autoemancipation" by taking matters into their own hands and terminating their state of perpetual alienation and deep longing, and create a Jewish state of their own or, to use the more precise phrase of Theodor Herzl, "the Jews' state" (*der Judenstaat*).[6] It also was being understood that the Jewishness of this state lay neither in its religious orientation nor in its commitment to Judaism and its values, but instead in its presumed national (ethnic) Jewish character.

That is why, like scores of other authors, Elmessiri highlights the well-established historical fact that many of the founders of Zionism had little concern with Judaism, and even evinced a marked hostility toward its precepts and practices. Indeed, Herzl himself, during a visit to Jerusalem, consciously violated a great number of Jewish religious practices in order to emphasize his new non-religious outlook as distinct from a traditional religious stance.[7] Likewise, his close friend, the Hungarian-born and Germanophile writer and Zionist leader, Max Nordau[8] was a self-avowed atheist who believed that the Torah was "inferior as literature" compared "to Homer and the European classics," and that it was "childish as philosophy and revolting as morality."[9] He even suggested that the day would come when Herzl's *Der Judenstaat* would be given equal status with the Bible, even by its author's religious opponents.[10] In an autobiographical sketch, he wrote: "When I reached the age of fifteen, I left the Jewish way of life and the study of the Torah … Judaism remained a mere memory and since then, I have always felt as a German and as a German only."[11] Similarly, Chaim Weizmann took

6 To be read alongside his complete diaries: https://archive. org/details/TheCompleteDiariesOfTheodorHerzl_201606/ TheCompleteDiariesOfTheodorHerzlEngVolume1_OCR/

7 "Statement by the Lubbavitcher Rebbe, Rabbi Shulem ben Schneersohn, on Zionism" (1903), in Michael Selzer (Ed.), *Zionism Reconsidered.*

8 Max Simon Nordau co-founded the Zionist Organization and coined the term *Muskeljudentum* (muscular Judaism) at the second Zionist Congress held in Basel, Switzerland, on August 28, 1898.

9 Desmond Stewart, *Theodor Herzl: Artist and Politician* (Garden City, New York: Doubleday, 1974).

10 Richard Crossman, *A Nation Reborn: The Israel of Weizmann, Bevin, and Ben-Gurion* (Hamish Hamilton, 1960).

11 *New World Encyclopedia*, "Max Nordau," November 9, 2022.

pleasure at times in "baiting the Rabbis about kosher food,"[12] and a typical group of Zionist *halutzim* (pioneers), deliberately irreligious, and militantly atheistic, marched in defiance of Jewish dietary laws in the early 1920s to "the Wailing Wall on the Day of Atonement munching ham sandwiches."[13]

Elmessiri also informs that the Zionist settlers in Palestine, the first to implement this new philosophy of political Zionism, were unusually careful to stress the non-religious and untraditional nature of their endeavor so that there would be no misunderstanding of their philosophy. That's most probably the reason why they dropped the name "Jews," calling themselves "Hebrews" instead. They used this more modern term in their campaigns in the 1930s and early 1940s, calling for a "Hebrew" rather than "Jewish" state. The current term, "Jewish state," Elmessiri said, originally coined as a non-religious concept, was revived in the 1940s, again with no intended religious connotation.

So, most of the early Zionists have viewed and presented themselves in non-religious terms, and their ideology, patterned after nineteenth-century European nationalism, was intended to replace traditional religious beliefs. Such an amoral projection, replacing deep religious commitment while making full use of it, has always proved to be a more or less sure way for recruiting the masses, and the "fusion of nationalistic outlook with religious fervor was achieved by turning authentic religious doctrine into a national myth."[14]

In light of the foregoing, it comes as no surprise that the Jewish orthodox sect, Neturei Karta (Guardians of the City), for example, characterizes the Zionist rabbis as "the clericals of the false Israel" who "teach a false doctrine."[15] Rabbi Chaim Soloveitchik (1853–1918), who was Rabbi of Brisk, Poland, and the founder of the "Yeshiva approach to Talmudic study," had this to say about Zionism: "The Jewish people have suffered many (spiritual) plagues—the Sadducees, Karaites,

---

12 Amos Elon, *The Israelis: Founders and Sons* (Holt, Rinehart and Winston, New York, 1971).

13 Melford E. Spiro, *Kibbutz: Venture in Utopia* (Harvard University Press, Cambridge, 1956).

14 Arthur Hertzberg (Ed.), *The Zionist Idea: A Historical Analysis and Reader* (New York: Harper & Row, 1956).

15 Cited in Meir Ben-Horin, "Max Nordau: Philosopher of Human Solidarity," Conference on Jewish Social Studies, 1956.

Hellenisers, Shabbatai Zvi, Enlightenment, Reform and many others. But the strongest of them all is Zionism."[16]

In effect, in a 1381-page landmark book, *The Empty Wagon: Zionism's Journey from Identity Crisis to Identity Theft*,[17] considered by many as a definitive treatise on the differences between Judaism and Zionism, Rabbi Yaakov Shapiro explains how and why Zionism represents a hijacking of Jewish identity, or as he puts it, a theft of that identity that is not in line with his religion. Zionism, he says, was conceived to erase classic Jewish identity as a people with a divinely ordained mission and replace it with an identity based on a national polity. This attempt to reengineer Jewish identity resulted in the creation of a "self-deprecating, logically inconsistent, traumatic ideology called Zionism."

It also engendered a belief that no other country in the world adheres to, that is, that Israel is the homeland (heimat) and nationality of the Jewish people scattered all over the Earth, including people who never visited Israel, never were citizens of this country, nor were their family members, nor do they ever plan to be. No Muslim country makes such an absurd claim vis-à-vis the world's Muslims, nor has the Vatican ever professed that it is the country of all Catholics.

Rabbi Shapiro avers that if someone wants to extricate themselves from Zionism's influence, they must maneuver through a mess of false ideology, false Judaism, false history, false politics, and a false worldview. In his comprehensive account and critical examination of the various Zionist schools of thought and their ideologies, the orthodox Jewish scholar points out that the original Zionists were Jews who were influenced by, impressed with, and envied the lifestyle of the Gentiles over that of the Jews. More than anything else, they wanted to be secular, or in the words of Vladimir Ze'ev Jabotinsky, the "diametrical opposite of a Jew"; because they attributed anti-Semitism to the priestly lifestyle of the religious Jews, to people looking at them as "ugly, immoral, and debased." They, therefore, were convinced that if the Jews could become "normal," that is to say, to change their lifestyle, and become indistinguishable from non-Jews, anti-Semitism would end.

As a matter of fact, pioneer Zionists did secularize themselves, but anti-Semitism didn't end. They were rudely awakened to their Jewishness by anti-Semitic violence, especially the string of pogroms

---

16 See Neturei Karta International website: https://www.nkusa.org/
17 Rabbi Yaakov Shapiro, *The Empty Wagon: Zionism's Journey from Identity Crisis to Identity Theft* (Primedia eLaunch LLC, 2018).

that began in Russia in 1881 and thus were stuck between a rock and a hard place: they refused to be Jews, and the Gentiles refused to let them be Gentiles. This is how they resolved that Zionism must be their "Plan B." They basically figured if they can't join the Gentile nations, they'll make a nation of their own by turning all the Jews into a nationality.

In doing so, they created an entirely new society, pretending they were scions of the "ancient people of the Book"—partly to garner support from the Evangelicals and to recruit Jews to populate their future state. Despite Zionism having nothing to do with Judaism but rather being a political movement, many early atheist or agnostic Zionists still claimed God gave the Jews the "Holy Land."

Making the "Good Jews" White and European

On that same subject of the perversion of the Jewish identity, Professor Steven Friedman, one of South Africa's foremost political theorists of mainstream understandings of Jewishness, wrote a thoroughly-researched book, *Good Jew, Bad Jew: Racism, Anti-Semitism and the Assault on Meaning.*[18] In it, he offers a searing analysis of the weaponization of anti-Semitism in service of political objectives that support the Israeli state and global white supremacy. Friedman argues that the changes wrought to Jewish identity form an important element in the ideology which underpins the Israeli state and that they deserve more attention than they have received.

He appropriately reminds us that until the French revolution and the Enlightenment, all Jews were effectively forced to adhere to their religion by their reigning authorities. And when Jews were allowed to choose whether to practice their religion, those who chose not to were still regarded as ethnically Jewish. This made Jewish identity more complicated than that of most other religious or ethnic groups.

The concept of religious tolerance promoted by thinkers of the Enlightenment era led to an unprecedented transformation in the legal and economic status of the Jews. Once enjoying civil rights and being allowed a freedom of movement denied to them for centuries, Western

---

18 Steven Friedman, *Good Jew, Bad Jew: Racism, Anti-Semitism and the Assault on Meaning* (Wits University Press, Johannesburg, 2023). The title of the book is most probably inspired by Mahmood Mamdani's book, *Good Muslim, Bad Muslim: America, the Cold War, and the Roots of Terror* (New York: Pantheon Books, 2004).

European Jews in the nineteenth century rose to high levels in the professions, the arts, business and even government.

Yet, as explained by Stanford University Professor Maxine Schur in a presentation at Oregon-based Reed College,[19]

> beneath the new external acceptance of the Jews, there existed in European society a virulent undercurrent of anti-Semitism which was different than the one that had plagued the Jews in the Middle-Ages or during the Inquisition for it was based not on theological, but secular grounds. It was racial, rooted in bogus biology. Paradoxically, the racial anti-Semitism was given authority and first popularized by a self-confessed proponent of religious tolerance, the celebrated philosopher of the Enlightenment, Voltaire.

Indeed, François-Marie Arouet (1694–1778), known by his nom de plume Voltaire, was famous for his wit and his criticism of Christianity, especially of the Roman Catholic Church, and a staunch advocate of freedom of speech, freedom of religion, and separation of church and state. Furthermore, what matters for our purpose is that he was outspoken in his hostility towards the Jews, and recent scholars such as Arthur Hertzberg[20] have seen him as one of the founders of modern secular anti-Semitism.

In effect, in his 1756 "Essai sur les mœurs et l'esprit des nations" (translated to English as "Essay on the customs and spirit of nations and key facts of history from Charlemagne to Louis XIII"), Voltaire writes:

> The Jews are an ignorant and barbarous people, who have long united the most sordid avarice with the most detestable superstition and the most invincible hatred for every people by whom they are tolerated and enriched ... In all the annals of the Hebrew people, one does not see any generous action. They know neither hospitality, nor liberality, nor clemency. Their sovereign happiness is to practice usury with foreigners

---

19 Maxine Schur, *Voltaire and the Jews* (Reed College, June 20, 2015).

20 Arthur Hertzberg, *The French Enlightenment and the Jews* (New York and London: Columbia University Press, 1968).

> ... Their glory is to set fire to and bloody the small
> villages that they can seize. They slaughter the old and
> the children ... They never know how to forgive when
> they are victorious; they are the enemies of the human
> race. No politeness, no science, no art perfected at any
> time among this atrocious nation.

In a section devoted to Voltaire, the Jewish Virtual Library considers that historically speaking, Voltaire's outlook was a powerful contribution to the creation of the mental climate which made possible the emancipation of the Jews, but at the same time prepared the ground for the future racial antisemitism. Just after Voltaire's death, Zalkind Hourwitz, librarian to the king of France, wrote: "The Jews forgive him all the evil he did to them because of all the good he brought them, perhaps unwittingly; for they have enjoyed a little respite for a few years now and this they owe to the progress of the Enlightenment, to which Voltaire surely contributed more than any other writer through his numerous works against fanaticism."

For Nabila Ramdani, an Algerian-French journalist and columnist, however,

> the celebrated philosopher was an unapologetic racist
> and anti-Semite who inspired Hitler, and the removal
> of his statue in Paris was long overdue ... The problem
> is not simply that Voltaire failed to incorporate perse-
> cuted groups such as Black people and Jews into his
> so-called progressive thinking; it is that his advocacy
> of biological racism and white supremacy still offer
> justification to all kinds of extremists. These include
> Nazi sympathizers traditionally linked to France's
> far-right National Rally (formerly the National Front)
> as well as terrorists who target synagogues and
> mosques.[21]

When restrictions on Jews in Europe began to ease, religious hostility to them as a group became less tenable. In theory at least, Jews could choose not to be Jewish by converting to Christianity, as more than

---

21 Nabila Ramdani, "Voltaire Spread Darkness, Not Enlightenment. France Should Stop Worshipping Him," *Foreign Policy,* August 31, 2020.

a few did. But bigotry is not that easily ended. Those who were preju-
diced against Jews, presumably alarmed that they could now integrate
into society, focused not on the religion of the targets of their bigotry but
on accidents of birth; they began to insist that Jews constituted a separate
and dangerous race. It was the ideologues of this new racism that first
coined the term, "anti-Semitism." The term appeared in Germany in
the 19th century and is commonly associated with the German activist
Wilhelm Marr, who, in 1879, founded the "Antisemiten Liga" (League
of Anti-Semites) following the publication of a pamphlet whose German
title translates as "The Victory of Jewishness over Germanness."[22] It has
remained in usage even though it is inaccurate since Arabs are Semites
too.[23] While anti-Jewish racists often despise Arabs as well, the term was
used to describe a prejudice against Jews only.

After 1948, and more conspicuously in the years following the
June 1967 Israeli-Arab War, the Israeli state and its Western supporters
have endeavored to convert "anti-Semitism" from a description of anti-Jewish racism to a weapon against critics of Zionism, many of whom
happen to be Jews who believe that the state's attitudes and practices
are racist. As it stands, the allegation of racism has now been turned
into a weapon against anti-racists. This is accompanied by another turn-
around: the Israeli state and its supporters seek to turn the campaign
against anti-Semitism from a rebellion against white supremacy into an
endorsement of white Europeanness.

In effect, the use and misuse of anti-Semitism to browbeat Israeli
state opponents is part of a larger reality in which those who do this seek
to change the nature of Jewish identity by distinguishing between "real"
Jews and the rest. They also seek to "flatten out" Jewish identity. Jews
are no longer, like every other group, a complicated mix of differing
opinions and perspectives. Instead, there are only "good" Jews who
attach their identity to the Israeli state and "bad" ones who do not. The
historian Avi Shlaim, responding to claims that all "real" Jews support
the Israeli state, observes:

> Ironically, to treat Jews as a homogeneous group is
> in fact an antisemitic trope. It is antisemites who fail

22 Robert Bernasconi, "Racism" in Sol Goldberg, Scott Ury and Kalman
Weiser (Eds.), Key Concepts in the Study of Anti-Semitism (Pelgrave Macmillan,
2021).

23 Avi Shlaim, "On British Colonialism, Antisemitism, and Palestinian
Rights," *Middle East Eye,* March 1, 2021.

to differentiate between different kinds of Jews, and want to see them all clustered in one place. It is on this basis that Theodor Herzl, the visionary of a Jewish state, predicted that the antisemites will become our most dependable friends.[24]

To be sure, as we have noted earlier, an important source of anti-Jewish hostility is the Christian right, which has held Jews in contempt for centuries.[25] But its religious beliefs also ensure uncritical support for the Israeli state.[26] The fact that these allies of the Israeli state see it as an essential means to achieve the death of the Jewish religion, and that hostility to Jews is deeply embedded in their view of the world, does not repulse Israel and its supporters. Thus, during a state visit to Brazil in 2019, then Prime Minister of Israel Benjamin Netanyahu declared: "We have no better friends in the world than the Evangelical community."[27]

To make sense of this contradictory thinking, Friedman explains, it is crucial to understand that, for those in positions of Jewish authority who peddle this attempt to manufacture a reality that seems entirely unreal, anti-Semitism no longer means prejudice against Jewish people. In the English-speaking world, this development can be dated to the 1970s when Arnold Foster and Benjamin Epstein, who held leadership roles in the American Anti-Defamation League, published *The New Anti-Semitism,*[28] which started something of a cottage industry. It is noteworthy that the Anti-Defamation League was founded to combat anti-Semitism in the United States, but it has since become chiefly a propaganda vehicle for the Israeli state.

For the South African professor, the term "anti-Semitism" has become detached from its moorings. It no longer means racism directed at Jews; it means holding left-wing or egalitarian opinions, which often seems to include being opposed to the white supremacy of which

24 Avi Shlaim, idem.

25 James Carroll, *Constantine's Sword: The Church and the Jews* (Boston and New York: Houghton Mifflin, 2002); and Malcolm Hay, *The Roots of Christian Anti-Semitism* (New York: Freedom Library Press, 1981).

26 Robert Leonhard, *Visions of Apocalypse: What Jews, Christians and Muslims Believe About the End Times, and How Those Beliefs Affect Our World* (The John Hopkins University, 2010).

27 Julian Sayarer, "The Antisemitic Face of Israel's Evangelical Allies," *Jacobin,* February 20, 2022.

28 Arnold Foster and Benjamin R. Epstein, "The New Anti-Semitism" (New York: McGraw Hill, 1974).

anti-Semitism was once a part. The new Jew—or victim of anti-Semitism—is no longer a member of a particular ethnic group; it is a right-wing person, Jewish or non-Jewish, who supports the economic status quo and the racial hierarchies that have reigned in the West for centuries. The new anti-Semite is not a person who hates Jews; it is a person, Jewish or non-Jewish, who embraces egalitarian values. Jewish people are no longer victims of prejudice as a group; they are now divided into two groups—one "good," the other "bad"—and "bad Jews" are one of the groups most likely to be accused of anti-Semitism. This is so because of, and not despite, the fact that the "bad Jews" who are stigmatized as "anti-Semites" tend to be anti-racists.

The American "new anti-Semitism" was a product of the Israeli state and has now become not only a core position among the state's defenders but "one that characterizes the mainstream of most of Western politics."[29]

The claim that hostility to the Israeli state was born of anti-Jewish hatred emerged in that state years before the Americans claimed to have found a new and dangerous anti-Semitism:

> A significant intellectual milestone was in the late 1960s when Israeli researchers began to develop the concept of "new antisemitism." Their view was that the old anti-Jewish sentiment that had taken shape and changed form over the centuries was now directed first and foremost against the Jewish political enterprise of Zionism and Israel.[30]

A recently published study shows that it was the Israeli state itself which started the ball running; the term had been used at a series of seminars organized by the office of the Israeli president in the late 1980s.[31] This view soon became deeply embedded in the Israeli state's ideological battle with its critics.

Opposition to the Israeli state and its actions did not target the Jews; it was aimed at the Israeli state. But central to Zionism's understanding of itself was the claim that it was the vehicle of all Jews, not

---

29 Amos Goldberg, "Anti-Zionism and Antisemitism: How Right and Left Conflate Issues to Deny Palestinian Rights," *Middle East Eye,* April 28, 2022.

30 Amos Goldberg, op. cit.

31 Anthony Lerman, *Whatever Happened to Anti-Semitism? Redefinition and the Myth of the "Collective Jew"* (London: Pluto Press, 2022).

merely those Jews who supported the idea of a Jewish state. As a result, to reject the Israeli state—or even to criticize what it did—was to show hostility to the Jews, even if you happened to be Jewish. Friedman views this logic as false, "just as to oppose apartheid in South Africa was not an expression of prejudice against white people. But it served the purpose of Zionism and its allies."

And so, for the ideologues of Zionism, the "Jewish state" quickly turned from a cure for anti-Semitism to its cause when it was faced by the reality of Palestinian resistance. The Palestinians who wanted their land back were labelled the "new Nazis," hence Netanyahu's false claim that it was the Mufti al-Husseini, not Hitler, who devised the mass murder of European Jews. In truth, Netanyahu was following the lead of Malcolm Hoenlein, an American Jewish leadership figure and vocal supporter of the Israeli state, who told a meeting in Toronto, Canada, that Hitler had reluctantly "followed the wishes of the Mufti when he had decided to kill all Jews."[32]

This invention served an important purpose: it conveniently portrayed Palestinians not as victims of the power of the Israeli state but as powerful Jew-haters whose enmity was even greater than that of the Nazis. It follows, of course, that if Palestinians are Nazis, those who support their cause are, too, the primary effect of which seeks to "delegitimize the Palestinian cause and to practically remove once and for all the Palestine issue from the international agenda."[33]

Furthermore, Friedman rightly calls attention to the fact that "comparing anti-Jewish racism to any other form of racial bigotry is now branded anti-Semitic because it is said to reduce the significance of Jewish suffering—which is the justification for the state." Indeed, President Biden's "special envoy to combat anti-Semitism," Deborah Lipstadt, for instance, has insisted that hatred of Jews is both eternal and unlike any other historical fact; "beginning with her earliest work, which argues that the Holocaust was a unique, incomparable event, Lipstadt has tended to exceptionalize antisemitism as the most ancient, enduring form of prejudice—a constant transhistorical force, resurfacing across eras and continents."[34] Responding to this peculiar claim, American

---

32 Norman G. Finkelstein, "Beyond Chutzpah: On the Misuse of Anti-Semitism and the Abuse of History (Berkeley and Los Angeles: University of California Press, 2005).

33 Amos Goldberg, ibidem.

34 Nathan and Ruth Ann Perlmutter, *The Real Anti-Semitism in America* (New York: Arbor House, 19820.

Jewish Studies scholar Barry Trachtenberg remarks: "If one accepts antisemitism to be eternal, and not a consequence of social or historical factors, then it is a fact of life that will forever push Jewish people into defensive postures. It will make us more nationalist, more reactionary, more militaristic, and more closed off the rest of the world."[35]

Worst still, the claim that opposition to the Israeli state and to its actions is equated with "antisemitism" has become the official position of Western governments, and in some U.S. states, such opposition has even been criminalized.

This outstanding development in the West was spearheaded by the International Holocaust Remembrance Alliance (IHRA), an intergovernmental organization comprising 35 member states and 9 observer countries founded in 1998 by former Swedish Prime Minister Göran Persson, with the declared mission of combating "growing Holocaust denial and antisemitism."[36] Its most potent and damaging instrument is, by far, its definition of anti-Semitism, which has become an article of Zionist faith and is relentlessly portrayed by Zionists as "what the Jewish community wants." Steven Friedman believes that

> The IHRA and its participating governments do not consider this attempt to force all Jews to associate with the state's actions as anti-Semitic. Nor do they acknowledge that, by labelling opposition to the state as hostility to Jews, their definition violates this clause. Thus, the IHRA definition itself becomes anti-Semitic and, consequently, the Western states that endorse and apply it are keeping alive a shameful history of anti-Jewish racism.[37]

By defining hostility to Jews in a way that substitutes a state for an ethnic group, British Jewish author Robert Cohen points out, the IHRA definition also defines what it is to be Jewish:

> By that reckoning, to be Jewish is to deny the possibility that Zionism has played out in racist ways, despite

---

35 Mari Cohen, "Deborah Lipstadt vs. 'The Oldest Hatred'," *Jewish Currents,* February 8, 2022.

36 See International Holocaust Remembrance Alliance, "About Us": http://www.holocaustremembrance.com/about-us

37 Steven Friedman, "Good Jew, Bad Jew," op cit.

the overwhelming evidence to the contrary. And
to be Jewish is to believe that the state of Israel is a
democratic nation like any other, despite Israel's own
constitutional laws defining it as the nation state of the
Jewish people rather than the state of all its citizens ...
To be Jewish, according to the IHRA, is to deny the
truth, ignore reality, and defend the indefensible.[38]

The IHRA definition has since been used relentlessly to stigmatize
political expression and shut down free speech in the Western world,
whether it be by governments or many universities. It has been "wielded
against academics who campaigned for Palestine to deprive them of jobs
and to suppress campaigns against the Israeli state, in particular the BDS
movement."[39]

Nowadays, the Israeli state is seen not only as ally of the West but
also as its representative in the Middle East. Like South Africa before
1994, Friedman observes: "the Israeli state is in, but not of, the region
it finds itself." This further explains why the "Collective West" regards
Israel as "the only democracy in the Middle East," democracy being
often used by Western governments, elites and academics as a code for
"Western," and why former Israeli Prime Minister Ehud Barak dared to
utter the racist claim that Israel is a "villa in the jungle"! Instead of this
misnomer, the more correct definition that should be applied to the Israeli
state would be, in the words of Steven Friedman: "the only Western state
in the Middle East."

All of this perfectly sums up the tenacious prejudice that this
Western-created state is an island of "first world" Western civilization in
a barbaric neighborhood.[40]

Such a prejudice is hardly a novel phenomenon, nor does the
Western racist and supremacist mindset seem to become a fading memory during our times. Indeed, back in 1914, Winston Churchill was not
ashamed to declare:

---

38 Robert Cohen, "We Need to Decolonize Our Understanding of
Antisemitism," *Patheos,* March 6, 2021.
39 Ramona Wadi, "Defeating the IHRA Witch Hunt: An Interview with
Palestinian Activist and Scholar Shahd Abusalama," *Mondoweiss,* February 7,
2022.
40 Lazar Berman, "After Walling Itself in, Israel Learns to Hazard the
Jungle Beyond," *The Times of Israel,* March 8, 2021.

> We are not a young people with an innocent record and
> a scanty inheritance... We have engrossed to ourselves
> an altogether disproportionate share of the wealth
> and traffic of the world. We have got all we want in
> territory, and our claim to be left in the unmolested
> enjoyment of vast and splendid possessions, mainly
> acquired by violence, largely maintained by force,
> often seems less reasonable to others than to us.

Churchill was telling the plain truth to his pairs in the closed meeting of the British Cabinet. As a new academic study shows,[41] uncovering the staggering death tolls and immense wealth extraction that was carried out by the empire during the late 19th and early 20th centuries, the impact of British colonialism on India was devastating. The report estimates that India suffered 165 million excess deaths due to British colonialism between 1880 and 1920, "a figure that is larger than the combined number of deaths from both World Wars and the Nazi holocaust"! It also estimates that during nearly 200 years of colonialism, the British Empire stole at least $45 trillion in wealth from India. Interestingly enough, this new research further highlights how British colonialism in India was not only devastating for the Indian people but also had "a profound impact on the global capitalist system" and "inspired fascist leaders like Adolf Hitler and Benito Mussolini," who then carried out similar genocidal crimes within and outside their own borders.

Much more recently, a further example of this deeply rooted Europhilia was proferred by none other than the High Representative of the European Union for Foreign Affairs and Security Policy, Josep Borrell Fontelles, who, addressing young European diplomats at Bruges, Belgium, said:

> Here, Bruges is a good example of the European
> garden. Yes, Europe is a garden. We have built a
> garden. Everything works. It is the best combination
> of political freedom, economic prosperity and social

---

41 The study, conducted by economic anthropologist Jason Hickel and his colleague Dylan Sullivan, is published in the respected journal *World Development,* under the title "Capitalism and Extreme Poverty: A Global Analysis of Real Wages, Human Height, and Mortality since the Long 16th century." Read its summary here, including a link to the whole paper in pdf form: https://www. sciencedirect.com/journal/world-development/vol/161/suppl/C

cohesion that the humankind has been able to build the three things together ... The rest of the world—and you know this very well, Federica—is not exactly a garden. Most of the rest of the world is a jungle, and the jungle could invade the garden ... Europeans have to be much more engaged with the rest of the world. Otherwise, the rest of the world will invade us, by different ways and means ... Keep the garden, be good gardeners. But your duty will not be to take care of the garden itself but [of] the jungle outside.[42]

Can the "Jewish" and the "Zionist" Questions Be Discussed?

One of the unintended and crucial consequences of the genocidal Israeli War on Gaza is that it has put the "Jewish" and "Zionist" questions once again at the center of international geopolitics.

Today, more than ever before, this state of affairs begs an urgent update of the overheated debate around the future of Zionism, and by extension, the fate of the "Jewish State" it succeeded in creating, by means of brutal force, in the midst of the infamous Western colonial enterprise in the Arab world during the 20th century.

Assuredly, the "Jewish Problem" is anything but new throughout history. Indeed, as Brian Klug[43] observed "The first person who saw the Jews as a problem was Moses, who, time and again, complained to God about them; or maybe it was God who first saw the Jews as problematic." As, indeed, did a succession of Jewish prophets in what the Christians Bible calls the Old Testament, not the least of whom was Jesus among the several that they then killed.

A similar complaint is made in a treatise written in 1543 by the German Reformation leader and pioneer of Protestantism, Martin Luther, titled *The Jews and Their Lies*. This work was among the last of his writings, shortly before he died in 1546 at the age of 63.

When they issued its first English translation in the United States in May 1948, the Christian-American publishers emphasized that they did

---

42 To read the full statement, see "European Diplomatic Academy: Opening remarks by High Representative Josep Borrell at the inauguration of the pilot programme," Official EU website, October 13, 2022.

43 Brian Klug, "Reflections on the Jewish Question, Postcolonial Critique, and Zionism," University of Notre Dame, August 29, 2023.

not do so for sectarian purposes, arguing that they were also publishing the edicts of more than 20 popes who dealt with the Jewish problem. Their edicts, they noted, are as strong—if not stronger—as anything contained in Martin Luther's book, since "the ghettos were established by Papal edict, and the segregation of Christian communities from Jewish communities originated in edicts coming out of Rome."

And because some of the language in the book was quite evidently expected to shock many readers, said publishers further stated to the attention of individuals doubting that these writings originated with the German priest that "the original language may be found in Martin Luther's works in the Congressional Library, Washington, D.C., and in one of several accredited Lutheran seminaries. Numerous clergymen of all denominations are aware of the existence of this work."

In its presentation of the treatise, the Virtual Jewish Library indicates that at the beginning of his career, Martin Luther was apparently sympathetic to Jewish resistance to the Catholic Church. Nevertheless, he expected the Jews to convert to his purified Christianity; when they did not, he turned violently against them.

The following excerpts from both the beginning and the end of the book say it all:

> I had decided not to write anymore, neither of the Jews, nor against the Jews. Because I have learned, however, that those miserable, wicked people do not cease trying to win over to themselves us, that is, the Christians also, I have permitted this booklet to go forth that I might be found among those who have resisted such poisonous undertaking of the Jews, and have warned the Christians to be on their guard against them. I would not have thought that a Christian would permit himself to be fooled by the Jews to share their exile and misery. But the Devil is the God of the world, and where God's word is not, he has easy sailing, not only among the weak, but also among the strong. God help us. Amen.

And:

In my opinion it will have to come to this: if we are to stay clean of the Jew's blaspheming and not become partakers of it, we must separate, and they must leave our country. Thus, they could no more cry and lie to God that we are holding them captive; and we could no more complain that they plague us with their blaspheming and usury. This is the nearest and best advice that makes it safe for both parties.

In modern times, however, the "Jewish Question"—in the sense of being a problem that needs to be solved—was set out by Europe in the 19th century. It was "a question Europe asked itself about the Jews," says Klug. European leaders thought the same about such questions as they thought about the "Oriental," "Armenian," and "Kurdish," among others.

Likewise, in his 1896 pamphlet titled *The Jewish State,* the Budapest-born journalist and founder of political Zionism, Theodor Herzl, confirmed that historical fact and further acknowledged that

The Jewish Question still exists. It would be useless to deny it ... The Jewish Question exists wherever Jews live in perceptible numbers. Where it does not exist, it is carried by Jews in the course of their migrations. We naturally move to those places where we are not persecuted, and there our presence produces persecution ... The unfortunate Jews are now carrying anti-Semitism into England; they have already introduced it into America.[44]

As it happens, the "Jewish Question" in the United States of America was first thoroughly dealt with primarily in a series of articles appearing in The *Dearborn Independent* newspaper from May 22 to October 2, 1920. These were subsequently incorporated in Henry Ford's book published in the same year under the title *The International Jew: The World's Foremost Problem.*[45] It is no wonder that this book was—and still is to this day—considered by many as anti-Judaic and anti-Semitic.

---

44 Theodor Herzl, *The Jewish State.*
45 Henry Ford, *The International Jew: The World's Foremost Problem* (The Dearborn Publishing Co., 1920). Download from: https://www.gutenberg.

And similar to today, Ford reported that the chief difficulty in writing about the Jewish Question during his time was the super sensitivity of Jews and non-Jews concerning the whole matter. There is a vague feeling, he said, that even to openly use the word "Jew" or to expose it nakedly to print, is somehow improper. Hence, "polite evasions like 'Hebrew' and 'Semite' both of which are subject to the criticism of inaccuracy, are timidly essayed, and people pick their way gingerly as if the whole subject were forbidden, until some courageous Jewish thinker comes straight out with the good old word 'Jew' and then the constraint is relieved and the air cleared." The word "Jew," Ford rightly observed, is not an epithet, "it is a name, ancient and honorable, with significance for every period of human history, past, present and to come."

According to the American industrialist, owing to this extreme sensitivity surrounding public discussion of the Jewish Question on the part of Gentiles,

> nothing is changed thereby. The Jew is not changed. The Gentile is not changed. The Jew still remains the enigma of the world ... Poor in his masses, he yet controls the world's finances. Scattered abroad without country or government, he yet presents a unity of race continuity which no other people has achieved. Living under legal disabilities in almost every land, he has become the power behind many a throne.

The business magnate remarked that the emergence of Jews in the financial, political and social spheres has been so complete and spectacular since the war (World War I), that their place, power and purpose in the world are being given a critical attention and a new scrutiny, much of it unfriendly. Such a scrutiny of the nature and super-nationality of "the Jew," he added, is essential to better define and understand the reasons for their power, separateness, and suffering.

To that effect, he was of the view that the "Jewish Question" in America cannot be concealed or silenced by the propagandist publication of matter extremely and invariably favorable to everything Jewish, nor by threats against publications presenting a different view. The Jews of the United States, he said,

can best serve themselves and their fellow-Jews all
over the world by letting drop their far too ready cry
of "anti-Semitism," by adopting a franker tone than
that which befits a helpless victim, and by seeing what
the Jewish Question is and how it behooves every Jew
who loves his people to help solve it.

The reality on the ground, nonetheless, proved to be altogether different. And the series of articles in the *Dearborn Independent* newspaper were met by an organized barrage by mail, wire and voice, with every single item carrying the wail of persecution. In reaction, Ford commented by saying:

One would think that a heartless and horrible attack
were being made on a most pitiable and helpless people—until one looks at the letterheads of the magnates
who write, and at the financial ratings of those who
protest, and at the membership of the organizations
whose responsible heads hysterically demand retraction. And always in the background there is the threat
of boycott, a threat which has practically sealed up the
columns of every publication in America against even
the mildest discussion of the Jewish Question.

Malek Bennabi, the Algerian thinker who also wrote about the "Global Jew" in his 1951 book,[46] had this to say about Henry Ford's imbroglio due to his outstanding albeit most unwelcome publication:

. . . In fact, the Jewish "boss" has behind him all the
banks that his ancestors created, and everywhere
he has cousins established, some in Paris, some in
London, some in Berlin and others in New York.
Anyone who is unaware of the crucial importance of
this international cousinship, of these economic kingdoms, is learning this the hard way. When, about 1920,
Ford thought himself strong enough to denounce the
occult power that was spreading over all of America,

---

46 Malek Bennabi, "Vocation de l'Islam, Deuxième partie" (translated from Arabic), December 5, 1951.

> he proved both his ignorance of the real force he want-
> ed to fight and his boastfulness. But the great Kahal,
> who had been disturbed by the insubordination of the
> Gentile, had made his arrangements. And six months
> later, the great, the powerful, the extremely wealthy
> Ford had to publicly apologize to the Jewish commu-
> nity. He had understood.

With regard to the question of political Zionism, as wished for by Henry Ford, there are today not one "courageous Jewish thinker [who] comes straight out with the good old word Jew" but many, who do not shy away either from addressing challenging issues regarding their fellow-Jews nor from calling a spade a spade.

In October 2003, the late New York University professor and internationally renowned historian Tony Judt wrote an essay in the *New York Review of Books (NYRB)* entitled "Israel: The Alternative."[47] The reaction to this outstanding article was swift and vicious and, in the case of the American response, verged on hysteria. In effect, within a week of its publication, the editor of *NYRB* had received several thousand letters on Judt's essay—more than on any in its history—and the Jewish Professor, who, up to then, had been widely respected for his core commitment to justice and intellectual honesty and loudly acclaimed for his lucid studies of 19th and 20th century social history, in particular his panoramic study[48] of Europe after World War II, became, almost overnight, the object of great furor, defamation and ostracism.

Readers, among whom were numerous renowned scholars and heads of Jewish organizations, accused him of belonging to the "Nazi Left," of hating Jews, of denying Israel's right to exist; distinguished professors at American universities canceled their *NYRB* subscriptions; Andrea Levin, executive director of the "Committee for Accuracy in Middle East Reporting in America" accused him of "pandering to genocide" and being "party to preparations for a final solution"; Alan Dershowitz of Harvard made the analogy with Adolf Hitler's "one-state

---

47 To read the full essay: https://archive.globalpolicy.org/security/issues/israel-palestine/2003/1025alternative.htm

48 Tony Judt, *Postwar: A History of Europe Since 1945* (Penguin Press, London, 2005).

solution for all of Europe," and David Jeffrey Frum, a former speech-writer for President George W. Bush, charged him with advocating "genocidal liberalism."

Judt's essay opened with the sentence: "The Middle East peace process is finished. It did not die: it was killed," followed by the notion that "The president of the United States of America has been reduced to a ventriloquist's dummy, pitifully reciting the Israeli cabinet line." He went on to contend that Israel

> has imported a characteristically late-nineteenth-century separatist project into a world that has moved on, a world of individual rights, open frontiers, and international law. The very idea of a "Jewish state," a state in which Jews and the Jewish religion have exclusive privileges from which non-Jewish citizens are forever excluded is rooted in another time and place. Israel, in short, is an anachronism;

that it

> remains distinctive among democratic states in its resort to ethnoreligious criteria with which to denominate and rank its citizens. It is an oddity among modern nations, not as its more paranoid supporters assert because it is a Jewish state and no one wants the Jews to have a state; but because it is a Jewish state in which one community, Jews, is set above others, in an age when that sort of state has no place;

and that

> in a world where nations and peoples increasingly intermingle and intermarry at will; where cultural and national impediments to communication have all but collapsed; where more and more of us have multiple elective identities and would feel falsely constrained if we had to answer to just one of them; in such a world Israel is truly an anachronism. And not just an anachronism but a dysfunctional one.

Judt also cited the prominent Labor politician Avraham Burg, who wrote: "After two thousand years of struggle for survival, the reality of Israel is a colonial state, run by a corrupt clique which scorns and mocks law and civic morality."[49] Unless something changes, Judt declared, "Israel in half a decade will be neither Jewish nor democratic." He then uttered the "anathema" that "the time has come to think the unthinkable," that is "the bringing to an end of Israel as a Jewish state, and the establishment in its place of a binational state of Israelis and Palestinians."

In his essay, Prof. Judt explained that, in one vital attribute, Israel is quite different from previous insecure, defensive microstates born of imperial collapse in so far as it is a democracy; hence, as such, its present dilemma due to its occupation of the lands conquered in 1967. Israel, he said, faces the following three "unattractive choices":

- It can dismantle the Jewish settlements in the Occupied Territories, return to the 1967 state borders within which Jews constitute a clear majority, and thus remain both a Jewish state and a democracy, albeit one with a constitutionally anomalous community of second-class Arab citizens;

- It can continue to occupy "Samaria," "Judea" and Gaza, whose Arab population, when added to that of present-day Israel, will become the demographic majority, in which case Israel will be either a Jewish state (with an ever-larger majority of unenfranchised non-Jews) or it will be a democracy. But logically it cannot be both;

- It can keep control of the Occupied Territories but get rid of the overwhelming majority of the Arab

---

49 Avraham Burg is a former head of the Jewish Agency and Speaker of the Knesset, Israel's Parliament, between 1999 and 2003. His essay first appeared in the Israeli daily Yediot Aharonot; it has been widely republished, notably in *Forward* (August 29, 2003) – "A Failed Israeli Society Collapses While Its Leaders Remain Silent" (https://forward.com/news/7994/a-failed-israeli-society-collapses-while-its-leade/); the *London Guardian* (September 15, 2003) – "The end of Zionism" (https://www.theguardian.com/world/2003/sep/15/comment); and in the French newspaper *Le Monde* (September 11, 2003 – "La révolution sioniste est morte" (https://www.mafhoum.com/press5/159C73.htm).

population, either by forcible expulsion or by depriving them of land and livelihood, leaving them
no option but to go into exile. In this way Israel
could indeed remain both Jewish and at least formally democratic, but at the cost of becoming the
first modern democracy to conduct full-scale ethnic
cleansing as a state project, something which would
condemn Israel forever to the status of an outlaw
state, an international pariah.

As Judt put it, the historian's task is precisely "to tell what is almost
always an uncomfortable story and explain why the discomfort is part of
the truth we need to live well and live properly. A well-organized society
is one in which we know the truth about ourselves collectively, not one
in which we tell pleasant lies about ourselves."

Another of those thinkers is Maj. Gen. (ret.) Gershon Hacohen
whose very incisive critique we have previously referred to. In part three
of his above-mentioned contribution,[50] he asked: "What has Zionism
achieved?" And answered: "The imposition of doubt." The sudden strike
by Hamas, he explained, thrust the Zionist idea back to the dilemma
of its earliest days. It prompted an echoing of the doubt cast during
Herzl's visit: "You might solve the Jews' problem, but you won't solve
the problem of Judaism." On October 7, he added, "we were forcefully
confronted with the fundamental Zionist question: What do the Jews
want in the Land of Israel?"

He was actually paraphrasing another "courageous Jew thinker" in
the person of Dan Miron, a professor of 20th century Hebrew literature
who, in a book[51] published in 2005, touched upon the Zionist dilemma
and disputed its ultimate goal. To that effect, he said:

> ... [T]he expectation of Zionism that the distancing of
> Jews from European societies and their concentration

---

50 Maj. Gen. (ret.) Gershon Hacohen, "A New Existential War—Part III:
Forming a Clear Post-War National Vision Means Returning to the Roots of
Zionism," BESA Center Perspectives Paper no. 2,251, January 8, 2023.

51 Dan Meron, "Healing for Touching" (translated from Hebrew),
2005. See my related contribution, "The war on Gaza: Towards Palestine's
Independence Despite the Doom and Gloom": https://www.globalresearch.ca/
war-gaza-towards-palestine-independence-despite-doom-gloom/5848373

in their own country would lead to the disappearance
of antisemitism did not materialize. Even the security
of Zionism, which was supposed to be able to extricate
the Jewish people from existential threats, leading to a
new Jewish existential activism, did not come to frui-
tion and may not reach the goal it set for itself.

Miron argues that in the two main dimensions of the Zionist vision
outlined in Theodor Herzl's magnum opus—that is to say, finding a solution to the problems of antisemitism and the need to physically protect
Jews from persecution around the world—expectations have yet to pan
out, notwithstanding over a hundred years since the beginning of the
Jewish emigration to Palestine and over fifty years of the state of Israel's
existence. Thus, in the first dimension, Miron believes that the Zionist
vision has become caught in a deadlock, given that antisemitism has
emerged in a new form that is more sophisticated: now it is ostensibly
not hatred of Jews as Jews, but merely criticism of the state of Israel, and
fierce antipathy is directed against Jews worldwide whenever they voice
complaints about actions that threaten the state of Israel, actions they
feel endanger them as well. As for the second dimension, Miron is of
the opinion that there exists a fear that despite Israel's independence and
military strength, the historical development of Zionism and its success
in achieving Jewish statehood have only led to the replacement of one
type of existential threat with another.

Hacohen shares this perspective. In essence, he says, Zionism has
merely swapped ailment A, like past pogroms—a Russian word meaning
devastation—in Kishinev for ailment B, like the Iranian nuclear threat or
the Simchat Torah massacre, the assault on the kibbutz of Nahal Oz and
the adjacent military base near the northern Gaza Strip on the morning
of October 7, 2023. In other words, the movement that was supposed
to solve antisemitism has instead generated, over the past two decades,
a new and equally dangerous form of it, in the guise of anti-Zionism.
Reflecting on the October 7th Operation "Al-Aqsa Flood" conducted
by several Palestinian Resistance groups and the earlier entrance on the
scene of the Iranian-led "Axis of Resistance"—which wiped out layers
upon layers of Israelis' conventional wisdom in terms of how they think
about themselves and their path forward—the retired military officer
considers that the state of Israel is now "in one of the most difficult crises

130 THE MONSTROSITY OF OUR CENTURY

it has ever known. It suffered an unprecedented blow and it is required to receive an unprecedented punishment."

Such a punishment took a turn for the worse when—in retaliation for an April 1, 2024 Israeli attack on the Iranian consulate building in Damascus, Syria, that killed several Iranian military commanders and other local personnel, Iranian Revolutionary Guards launched "Operation True Promise" through a massive air attack—which was indeed unprecedented—on designated targets inside Israel, including two air bases in the Negev desert from which Israeli aircraft were used to strike said consulate. Over 300 drones and missiles navigated more than 1,700 kilometers above Iran's neighbors, including Iraq and Jordan—both of which are home to U.S. military bases—before penetrating Israel's airspace. Even though Israel employed all of its extensive integrated anti-missile defense system comprised of the Iron Dome, the Arrow and David's Sling missile interceptors and U.S.-made Patriot missile batteries in addition to the layers of U.S., British, and Israeli aircraft, and U.S. and French shipborne anti-missile defenses, several Iranian missiles succeeded in striking Israel's heavily-protected airfields and air defense installations.

In the aftermath of this Iranian attack, the leader of Israel's opposition, Yair Lapid, as well as many analysts and former Israeli officers believe that Israel's key defensive policy of deterrence—which has long been an obsession of the country's political and military circles and regarded as a vital pillar of its security—has been severely damaged once again after the Al Aqsa Flood on October 7, 2023. From now on, writes commentator Ben Caspit in *Ma'ariv* newspaper, "The Iranians have lost their sense of fear. No more proxies, undercover agents and covert terror attacks. From now on, it is Iran against Israel, out in the open. Israeli deterrence, which got Iran to swallow its pride every time anew and not to attack Israel directly, has now been shattered."[52]

---

52 Peter Beaumont, "Iran attack shows Israeli deterrence policy 'shattered,' Netanyahu critics say," *The Guardian*, April 15, 2024.

For his part, Scott Ritter[53] recounted in a recent article[54] that back in 2007, during an address to the American Jewish Committee, he told the crowd that the last thing he wanted to see was a scenario where Iranian missiles were raining down on the soil of Israel. He therefore warned that "unless Israel changes course, this is the inevitable outcome of a policy driven more by arrogance than common sense." On the night of April 13–14, 2024, his concerns were effectively played out live before an anxious international audience. Commenting on that event, Ritter said: "The 'Missiles of April' represent a sea-change moment in Middle Eastern geopolitics—the establishment of Iranian deterrence that impacts both Israel and the United States ... Moreover, Iran has been able to accomplish this without either disrupting its strategic pivot to the east or undermining the cause of Palestinian statehood." He therefore concluded that "Operation True Promise" will go down in history as "one of the most important military victories in the history of modern Iran, keeping in mind that war is but an extension of politics by other means."

In the final analysis, more than ever before in its short history, the "Jewish state" is now in deep and multifaceted trouble. In the past, writes Jacques Baud in his illuminating recent book,[55] "the term antisemitism meant a sickly hatred of the Jew. Today, it means protesting against the bombing of women and children! . . . Israel has always sought to impose itself by force, and this strategy is not a winning one. Today, the Palestinian David is defeating the Israeli Goliath."

Yet neither Theodor Herzl's vision of a soft solution to the "Jewish Question" through a successful creation of a Jewish homeland in Palestine, nor Vladimir Ze'ev Jabotinsky's security approach based

---

53 Scott Ritter spent the better part of a decade trying to protect Israel from Iraqi missiles, both during his service in Desert Storm, where he played a role in the counter-SCUD missile campaign, and as a United Nations weapons inspector, where he worked with Israeli intelligence to make sure Iraq's SCUD missiles were eliminated. He has been writing about Iran for more than two decades and published two books on related subjects: *Target Iran: The Truth about the White House's Plans for Regime Change* and *Dealbreaker: Donald Trump and the Unmaking of the Iran Nuclear Deal.* Since the October 7 attacks, he has been a staunch supporter of the Palestinian cause. He wrote a long article titled "Why I no longer stand with Israel, and never will again," in which he explained his position: https://www.scottritterextra.com/p/why-i-no-longer-stand-with-israel

54 Scott Ritter, "The Missiles of April," *Scott Ritter Extra,* April 14, 2024.

55 Jacques Baud, *Operation Al-Aqsa Flood: The Defeat of the Vanquisher* (Max Milo editions, March 2024).

on his hard *Iron Wall*[56] policy—which was equally advocated by David Ben-Gurion—have so far helped the Jews fulfil their dream of living in peace, away from an age-old, entrenched and pervasive antisemitism, in "their own normal state, where they could be accepted as a nation among nations, a state among nation-states."

Furthermore, 76 years after its founding, Israel has yet to overcome the basic contradiction that has defined it from the very beginning: Can it be Jewish *and* democratic?[57]

Snapshots of the Abrahamic Religions in the West

In 2008, Professor of Political Science and History at the University of California, Los Angeles, Anthony Pagden published one of the best books, *Worlds at War: The 2,500 Year Struggle Between East & West,*[58] concerning the history of the long and Manichean struggle between East and West, from classical times to the conflicts of the twenty-first century, including the protracted and seemingly insoluble Israeli-Arab and Israel-Palestine conflicts.

In this illuminating masterpiece of stunning scope and relevance, Pagden argues that the differences that divide West from East go deeper than politics, deeper than religion; and to understand this volatile relationship, and how it has played out over the centuries, it is necessary to go back before the Crusades, before the birth of Islam, and even before the birth of Christianity. For him, the starting point should be set in the fifth century BCE. Europe, he goes on to say, was born out of Asia and for centuries the two shared a single history. But when the Persian emperor Xerxes, commonly known as Xerxes the Great, son of Darius the Great, tried to conquer Greece in 480 BCE—with initial victories securing control of mainland Greece but ending in defeat in Platatea the following year—a struggle began which has never ceased.

---

56 Jabotinsky stated that "Zionist colonization must either stop, or else proceed regardless of the native population. Which means that it can proceed and develop only under the protection of a power that is independent of the native population—behind an iron wall, which the native population cannot breach." To read the full document, click on the following link: https://en.jabotinsky.org/media/9747/the-iron-wall.pdf

57 See Eran Kaplan, "On its 75th birthday, Israel still can't agree on what it means to be a Jewish state and a democracy," *The Conversation,* May 10, 2023.

58 Anthony Pagden, *Worlds at War: The 2,500-Year Struggle between East & West* (Oxford University Press, 2008).

Later on, the conflict resumed when Alexander the Great and then the Romans tried to unite Europe and Asia into a single civilization—as symbolized by the historically famous "Susa weddings."[59] Even more bitter battles continued unabated after the conversion of the West to Christianity and much of the East to Islam, two universal religions, each claiming world dominance. These battles culminated with the destructive episode of the Crusades during the Middle Ages and were followed by Western colonization of almost all of the Islamic territories starting in the nineteenth century. They continue to our times under the pretext of the so-called American-led "War on terrorism" after the events of September 11, 2001.[60]

Arnold J. Toynbee addressed the issue of Islam's place in history and its relations with the West in his 1948 monumental *A Study of History,* which has been acknowledged as one of the greatest achievements of modern scholarship. He wrote:

> In the past, Islam and our Western society have acted
> and reacted upon one another several times in suc-
> cession, in different situations and alternating roles.
> The first encounter between them occurred when the
> Western society was at its infancy and when Islam
> was the distinctive religion of the Arabs in their heroic
> age ... Thereafter, when the Western civilization has
> surmounted the premature extinction and had entered
> upon a vigorous growth, while the would-be Islamic

---

59 As recounted by Ian Worthington in his book titled *Alexander the Great: A Reader* (Routledge, 2011), the Susa weddings were arranged by Alexander the Great in 324 BCE, shortly after he conquered the Achaemenid Empire. In an attempt to wed Greek culture with Persian culture, he and his officers held a large gathering at Susa and took Persian noblewomen in matrimony. The collective weddings involved 80 couples and blended various Greek and Persian traditions. Celebrating his own Persian wife, Alexander intended for these new unions to help him begin identifying himself as a son of Persia and thereby legitimize his claim as the heir of the Persian kings of the Achaemenid dynasty. It was also expected that any children produced from these marriages would, as the progeny of both Greece and Persia, serve as a symbol of the two civilizations coming together under Alexander's Macedonian Empire.

60 See my related articles titled: "Islam and the West: What Went Wrong and Why," March 6, 2018 (https://www.islamicity.org/14457/islam-and-the-west-what-went-wrong-and-why/) and "9/11 and the Green Scare: It's High Time for a Paradigm Shift," March 13, 2018 (https://www.globalresearch.ca/911-and-the-green-scare-its-high-time-for-a-paradigm-shift/5631878).

state was declining towards its fall, the tables were turned.[61]

The British historian further noted that in that life-and-death struggle, Islam, like Christendom before it, had triumphantly survived. Yet, this was not the last act in the play, for "the attempt made by the medieval West to exterminate Islam failed as signally as the Arab empire-builders' attempt to capture the cradle of a nascent Western civilization has failed before; once more, a counterattack was provoked by the unsuccessful offensive. This time, Islam was represented by the Ottoman descendants of the converted Central Asian nomads." After the final failure of the Crusades, Western Christendom stood on the defensive against this Ottoman attack during the late medieval and early modern ages of Western history. The Westerners managed to bring the Ottoman offensive to a halt in the wake of the battle of Vienna that lasted from 1683 until 1699 when a peace treaty between the Sublime Porte and the Holy League was signed at Karlowitz. Thereafter, having encircled the Islamic world and cast their net about it, they proceeded to attack their old adversary in its native lair.

The concentric attack of the modern West upon the Islamic world, according to Toynbee, has inaugurated the present encounter between the two civilizations, which he saw as "part of a still larger and more ambitious movement, in which the Western civilization is aiming at nothing less than the incorporation of all mankind in a single great society, and the control of everything in the earth, air and sea which mankind can turn to account by means of modern Western technique." Thus, the contemporary encounter between Islam and the West "is not only more active and intimate than any phase of their contact in the past, it is also distinctive in being an incident in the attempt by the Western man to 'westernize' the world—an enterprise which will possibly rank as the most momentous, and almost certainly as the most interesting feature in history, even for a generation that has lived through two world wars."

Toynbee drew the conclusion that Islam is once more facing the West with its back to the wall; but this time the odds are more heavily against it than they were "even at the most critical moments of the Crusades, for the modern West is superior to it not only in arms, but also in technique of economic life, on which military science ultimately

---

61 Arnold J. Toynbee, "Islam and the West, and the Future," in *Civilization on Trial* (Oxford University Press, 1948).

depends, and above all in spiritual culture—the inward force which alone creates and sustains the outward manifestations of what is called civilization"—although, with this work being first published in 1947 then 1957, that latter contention of the West's superiority in "spiritual culture" might well be questioned.

On this particular topic, Anthony Pagden points out that by the seventeenth century, with the decline of the Church, the contest has shifted from religion to philosophy: the West's scientific rationality in contrast to those who sought ultimate guidance in the words of God. Thus, the eighteenth and nineteenth centuries witnessed the disintegration of the great Muslim empires—the Ottoman, the Mughal, and the Safavid in Iran—and the increasing Western domination of the whole of Asia. The resultant attempt to mix Islam and Western modernism sparked off a struggle in the Islamic world between reformers and traditionalists which persists to this day. The wars between East and West, Pagden concludes, "have not only been the longest and most costly in human history, they have also formed the West's vision of itself as independent, free, secular, and now democratic. They have shaped, and continue to shape, the nature of the modern world."

In this long sequence of interaction between East and West, or Orient and Occident, Western powers—and Jewish Zionists following in their footsteps—have profusely used the Bible (in both its Old and New Testament) for close to 2000 years, to justify the conquest of land in the Islamic world and everywhere else.

All along, the biblical claim of a so-called "divine promise" of land was integrally linked with the claim of a "divine mandate" to exterminate the indigenous populations of the conquered territorial possessions. This, unavoidably, resulted in the suffering of millions of people and the loss of respect for a religious scripture—despite its incorporation by Christianity in the New Testament bearing the contradictory teachings of Jesus—still depicting God as a merciless and ferocious warrior Yahweh, making covenants with "His chosen people," granting them other people's lands, and commanding them to slaughter and pillage with His blessing and assistance! Expressed in particularly gruesome language, Exodus 20 to 33, for example, dealt with what Yahweh told prophet Moses:

> If you listen carefully to what [My angel] says and
> do all that I say, I will be an enemy to your enemies

and will oppose those who oppose you. My angel will go ahead of you and bring you into the land of the Amorites, Hittites, Perizzites, Canaanites, Hivites and Jebusites, and I will wipe them out. Do not bow down before their gods or worship them or follow their practices. You must demolish them and break their sacred stones to pieces. Worship the Lord your God, and his blessing will be on your food and water. I will take away sickness from among you, and none will miscarry or be barren in your land. I will give you a full life span. I will send my terror ahead of you and throw into confusion every nation you encounter. I will make all your enemies turn their backs and run. I will send the hornet ahead of you to drive the Hivites, Canaanites and Hittites out of your way. But I will not drive them out in a single year, because the land would become desolate and the wild animals too numerous for you. Little by little I will drive them out before you, until you have increased enough to take possession of the land. I will establish your borders from the Red Sea to the sea of the Philistines, and from the wilderness to the Euphrates River. I will give into your hands the people who live in the land, and you will drive them out before you. Do not make a covenant with them or with their gods. Do not let them live in your land or they will cause you to sin against me, because the worship of their gods will certainly be a snare to you.

The Yahweh depicted in the books of the Old Testament between Judges and Deuteronomy is a god whose actions are taught in religious and secular schools in Israel, says Australian senior lecturer in history in the school of social and international studies at Deakin University in Geelong, David Wetherell. A modern secular Israeli, he presumes, may not subscribe to such a god who commands the maltreatment/extermination of the original Canaanites and Hittites but still support Israel's expansion into the lands of the indigenous Palestinians. Still, a citizen of Israel does not need to be a religious Jew to endorse the national mythology, and "the deeds of Israel's national heroes in the Bible have come to non-religious Jews as a means of organizing biblical history to provide moral legitimacy for the walling in of indigenous Palestinians."[62]

In his fascinating and compelling book, *The Bible and Colonialism: A Moral Critique*,[63] Michael Prior issued a profound challenge to theologians, biblical specialists, and everyone interested in reading and understanding the Bible, in particular regarding the moral dimension of the interpretation of those biblical claims. In this book Prior protests at the neglect of the moral question in conventional biblical studies and attempts to rescue the Bible from being a blunt instrument in the oppression of people. He affirms that the land traditions whose legitimization had the authority of "sacred scripture" and have been deployed in support of barbaric behavior in a wide variety of contexts, pose fundamental moral questions relating to one's understanding of the nature of God, of His dealings with humankind and of human behavior. Prior believes that the communities which have preserved and promulgated those biblical traditions must shoulder some of the responsibility for what has been done in alleged conformity with the values contained within them; because, he rightly notes, "according to modern secular standards of human and political rights, what the biblical narrative calls for are war crimes and crimes against humanity," whether it be for the enduring consequences of the bloody colonization of Latin America, of the fabricated Afrikaner nationalism erected as an ideological structure justifying the abhorrent apartheid regime in South Africa and Rhodesia, or, even more so, of the nightmarish and genocidal settler-colonialism in Palestine instigated by political Zionism with the decisive support of the Christian governments of the Western world.

For all the above-mentioned reasons, the settler-colonialism established in the Arab land of Palestine has proved to be infinitely more inextricable than all the other—already resolved—similar cases. Indeed, while the Bible is not the only justification, "it certainly is the most powerful one, without which Zionism is only a conquering ideology. Read at face value and without recourse to doctrines of human rights, the Old Testament appears to propose that the taking possession of the Promised Land and the forcible expulsion of the indigenous population is the fulfilment of a biblical mandate."[64] It logically follows then, as

---

62 David Wetherell, "Israel and the God of War," *Financial Review*, December 23, 2004.

63 Michael Prior, CM, *The Bible and Colonialism: A Moral Critique* (England: Sheffield Academic Press, 1997).

64 David Wetherell, idem.

remarked by Caitlin Johnstone, that "Everything about Israel is fake. It's a completely synthetic nation created without any regard for the organic socio-political movements of the land and its people, slapped rootless atop an ancient pre-existing civilization with deep roots. That's why it cannot exist without being artificially propped up by nonstop propaganda, lobbying, online influence operations, and mass military violence."[65]

How Jewish Zionism was created by Christian Evangelicals

Many readers of the following lines will surely be surprised to learn that many well-established facts regarding much of the core beliefs of the Zionist ideology that Zionists try to erase from history do not actually come from Judaism, but from Evangelical Christianity. In effect, as the already existing literature and some newly disclosed Western archives show beyond any doubt, Christian Zionism was in existence centuries before any Jew ever thought of Zionism.

American orthodox Rabbi Yaakov Shapiro, who has attained an enviable place among both rabbinic scholars in orthodoxy and anti-Zionist public intellectuals, did an outstanding job in going over the history and the ideology of Western Christian Zionism and its influence on the Jews across the world. In tackling such a daunting task, he starts with defining what it means to be a Jew. A Jew, he explains, is not a nationality or a race or an ethnicity or a culture. Rather, a Jew is anyone who accepts and keeps the 613 commandments (mitzvot) of the Torah, including the Ten Commandments given by God to Prophet Moses at Mount Sinai, not one less. Shapiro calls it a "job description"—and it's a tough one indeed. It is therefore an anti-nationalist and anti-racist definition of Judaism: anti-Zionist in short.

Rabbi Shapiro then informs that it was the European Christian Evangelicals that first tied the existence of Israel to the Jewish Bible—the Old Testament as the Christians call it—because in Judaism no Jewish authority ever has done such a thing. Indeed, the Evangelicals believe that the Jews must be assembled in their Holy Land, having a state in Palestine, before the Messiah comes either to kill or convert all the Jews to Christianity. On the contrary, the Jews never wanted to return to the Holy Land en masse until the Jewish Messiah (Ha-mashiach), often referred to as King Messiah arrives, and peace would come to reign the

65 Caitlin Johnstone, "Everything About Israel Is Fake," *GlobalResearch*, June 11, 2024.

world, and the universe would be ruled by a spirit of God. The ideology of modern Zionism is thus much more Christian Evangelical than it is traditional Jewish. In fact, a 2013 Pew Research Center survey[66] even concluded that

> twice as many white evangelical Protestants as Jews say that Israel was given to the Jewish people by God (82% vs. 40%). Some of the discrepancy is attributable to Jews' lower levels of belief in God overall; virtually all Evangelicals say they believe in God, compared with 72% of Jews (23% say they do not believe in God and 5% say they don't know or decline to answer the question). But even Jews who do believe in God are less likely than Evangelicals to believe that God gave the land that is now Israel to the Jewish people (55% vs. 82%).

It emerges from the historical compilation made by Shapiro and from other sources that:

- As early as 1585, a man by the name of Reverend Francis Kett—who was burned for heresy—published a book called *The Glorious and Beautiful Garland of Man's Glorification*, in which he discusses the Jewish national return to Palestine.

- In 1611, English clergyman and biblical commentator Thomas Brightman's pamphlet called "Apocalipsis Apocalypseos" was published. It described the process of the Jews' so-called return to the Holy Land and their subsequent conversion to Christianity, saying "Only if this happens would England be blessed by their God."

- In 1621, lawyer and member of the Parliament of England for Canterbury, Sir Henry Finch, published a book whose title was *The World's Great Restauration, or Calling of the Jews, and with them of all Nations and Kingdoms of the Earth to the Faith of Christ*, in which he called for the Jews to invoke their rightful claims to the Promised Land, reestablish themselves there, and convert to Christianity.

---

66 Michael Lipka, "More white Evangelicals than American Jews say God gave Israel to the Jewish people," Pew Research Center, October 3, 2013.

- In 1649, English puritan Christians who lived in Holland, Johanna Cartwright and her son Ebenezer, presented a petition to the English parliament of Oliver Cromwell to allow the Jews into England, so that England, with the help of Holland, could then transport the Jews to Palestine where they needed to be, according to the Christian Evangelical belief.

- In 1771, Joseph Eyre, a minister of the Church of England, published a book titled *Observations Upon the Prophecies Relating to the Restoration of the Jews,* in which he reiterated that according to Christianity, the Jews are going to return to Palestine from the lands of their dispersion.

- During the years 1793–1795, Baptist minister James Bicheno published a book called *The Signs of the Times* predicting the imminent overthrow of the Pope and the ingathering of the Jews from their exile, in preparation for their conversion to Christianity.

- At the end of the 1700s, after the traumatic changes engendered by the American and French revolutions, the British, like many other Europeans, believed that the world was in the middle of a great upheaval. And as is usually the case at the turn of each and every millennium, people would turn to their religions to seek stability and psychological comfort. In particular, the invasion and occupation of the Ottoman territories of Egypt and Syria (1798–1801) by the Napoléon Bonaparte-led forces of the French First Republic were viewed as a sign that the Jews were coming back to the Holy Land. All the more so as Napoléon appealed to the Jews of Africa and Asia to join him in marching against Syria and restoring the Kingdom of Jerusalem. The Jews, however, showed no interest in Napoléon's offer: the religious among them believed that they belonged in exile all over the world and that their return to the Promised Land bore no resemblance to what Napoléon offered them; and the non-religious Jews, or the assimilated Jews of Germany and Western Europe, had no interest in abandoning their plans to be assimilated into European society.

- The early and mid-1800s saw increasingly more Christian Zionist activity in the attempt to both liberate the Jews from their exile and reestablish them in Palestine as well as to convert them to Christianity. And so, on February 15, 1809, the "London Society for Promoting Christianity Amongst the Jews" was founded with the main aim to convert the Jews to Christianity. The Society changed its name several times since its inception. It still exists today and is known as "The Church's Ministry Among Jewish people" (CMJ). It is one of the 10 official mission agencies of the Church of England. Besides the UK, it has branches in Israel, the U.S., Ireland, France, Canada, South Africa, Hong Kong and Australia. The Society is not only a precursor of Zionism, but also the initiator of what is now the "messianic Jewish movement." Messianic Jews consider themselves Jews and not Christians; they don't believe in most of the Torah and consider Jesus as the Messiah. Their declared mandate, as published on their website, reads as follows: "We believe the mandate God has given to us is to be a witness to the Jewish People about the Messiah, and to educate the Church on the Jewish roots of her faith and understanding that God has not finished with Israel. We also believe that God is doing a restorative work between His people, as through Yeshua the dividing walls between us are being broken down."

- In 1830, the British-born John Thomas, who was then living in New York, founded yet another Christian sect called the "Christadelphians," a restorationist and nontrinitarian denomination. Thomas wrote a book titled *Hope of Israel,* in which he suggested that the Jewish nation could successfully be reconstituted in its so-called ancestral homeland through the political assistance of England.

- In 1839, the Church of Scotland itself published a memorandum to the Protestant monarchs of Europe for the restoration of the Jews to Palestine.

- In 1848, British Tory politician and pre-millennial Evangelical Anglican Anthony Ashley-Cooper, 7th Earl of Shaftesbury, became president of the London Society for Promoting Christianity Amongst the Jews. He, more than anybody else, is responsible not only for pushing the idea of the creation of the state of Israel, but also for successfully getting Christian Zionism to become the official political policy of England. In 1853, he wrote to the prime minister, Lord Aberdeen, that Greater Syria was "a country without a nation" in need of "a nation without a country... Is there such a thing? To be sure there is, the ancient and rightful lords of the soil, the Jews!" In his diary that year he wrote: "these vast and fertile regions will soon be without a ruler, without a known and acknowledged power to claim dominion. The territory must be assigned to someone or other... There is a country without a nation;

and God now in his wisdom and mercy, directs us to a nation without a country." This is commonly cited as a precursor of the phrase "A land without a people for a people without a land," by which Shaftesbury was echoing another British proponent of the restoration of the Jews to Palestine, Dr Alexander Keith. The phrase would be promulgated to the world over a century later by Israeli Prime Minister, Golda Meir.

- In 1851, the Italian politician Benedetto Musolino wrote a book[67] in which he called for a Jewish municipality in the Holy Land, under the sovereignty of the Ottoman empire, where the national religion would be Judaism and the national language would be Hebrew.

- In 1884, William Henry Hechler, who was a Restorationist Anglican clergyman and promoter of Zionism, published a book called *The Restoration of the Jews to Palestine According to Prophecy*. In it, he called for the Jews to return to Palestine as a prerequisite for the coming of the Christian Messiah, and based on complex calculations of scriptural interpretation, held that in 1897 or 1898 the Jews would be returned to Palestine. It is important to note that this Protestant pastor, who undertook missionary work in Germany, was also the personal tutor of Prince Ludwig, the son of the Grand Duke of Baden and the uncle of the future Kaiser of Germany, William II.

- In 1887, shortly after the outbreak of the Russian pogroms, American Christian Zionist William E. Blackstone authored a book called *Jesus is Coming,* in which he insisted Jews have a biblical right to Palestine. He sent a petition to President Benjamin Harrison with over 400 signatures, lobbying for the U.S. to work together with the European countries to return Palestine to the Jews. In this petition, Blackstone used the argument that the Jewish refugees from persecution, which comprised about 2 million Russian Jews, had nowhere to go and that the only solution to their plight was a Jewish state in Palestine.

- In 1895, British Prime Minister Benjamin Disraeli bought controlling interests in the Suez Canal, and two years later the British gained control of Cyprus, thereby establishing themselves as a key player in areas in and around the Holy Land and boosting significantly the expectation of the achievement of the long-sought creation of a Jewish state in Palestine.

---

67 Benedetto Musolino, *Gerusalemme ed il Popolo Ebreo* (Jerusalem and the Jewish People) (Roma: La Rassegna Mensile d'Israel, 1951).

- It is against such a backdrop that Theodor Herzl published his pamphlet "Der Judenstaat"[68] in 1896, which, according to William Hechler, was a clear fulfilment of the Christian prophecy. Hechler thereupon sought out to inform Herzl of this "miracle"! Herzl recorded in his diary his first meeting with the Reverend: "The Rev. William H. Hechler, chaplain to the British Embassy in Vienna, called on me. A likeable, sensitive man with the long grey beard of a prophet. He waxed enthusiastic over my solution. He, too, regards my movement as a 'prophetic crisis'— one he foretold two years ago. For he had calculated in accordance with a prophecy dating from Omar's reign (637–638) that after 42 prophetical months, that is, 1,260 years, Palestine would be restored to the Jews. This would make it 1897–1898. When he read my book, he immediately hurried to Ambassador Monson (British Ambassador in Vienna) and told him: the fore-ordained movement is here! Hechler declares my movement to be a "Biblical" one, even though I proceed rationally in all points. He wants to place my tract in the hands of some German princes. He used to be a tutor in the household of the Grand Duke of Baden, he knows the German Kaiser and thinks he can get me an audience." So, besides granting Herzl access to powerful leaders, Hechler did his own lobbying among the high-ranking state leaders he knew, in particular among the Protestants of Germany, England and the U.S. The U.S., by and large, has always supported Zionism. President John Quincy Adams said that he would like it if the Jews were again an independent government and no longer persecuted. For his part, Abraham Lincoln said to the Canadian Christian Zionist Henry Wentworth Monk: "Restoring the Jews to their homeland is a noble dream shared by many Americans."

- Last but certainly not least, 1909 saw the publication by Oxford University Press of the *Scofield Reference Bible,* edited and annotated by the American Bible student Cyrus Ingerson Scofield. It is a widely circulated Bible containing the entire text of the traditional, Protestant King James version published in 1611, and is known for

---

68 It's worth indicating here that the first Zionist books that were printed before Herzl's pamphlet—that's to say centuries after the Evangelical literature we have summarily mentioned—were Moses Hess's "Rome and Jerusalem: The Last National Question" published in Leipzig, Germany, in 1862, in which he argued for the Jews to return to Palestine and proposed a socialist country, and Russian-Polish Leo Pinker's "Auto-Emancipation" published in Berlin, Germany, in 1882 and considered as a founding document of modern Jewish nationalism, especially Zionism.

having popularized dispensationalism[69] at the beginning of the 20th century. It was revised by the author in 1917 and sales of it are said to have exceeded two million copies by the end of World War II. One of its most innovative features is that it comprises what amounts to a commentary on the biblical text alongside the Bible instead of in a separate volume, the first to do so in English since the Geneva Bible of 1560. More significantly, central to Christian Zionist belief is Scofield's commentary (italicized below) on Genesis 12:3: "'I will bless them that bless thee.' *In fulfilment closely related to the next clause, 'And curse him that curseth thee.' Wonderfully fulfilled in the history of the dispersion. It has invariably fared ill with the people who have persecuted the Jew—well with those who have protected him. The future will still more remarkably prove this principle.*"

• Drawing on Scofield's tendentious interpretation, Christian Zionist John Hagee claims that "The man or nation that lifts a voice or hand against Israel invites the wrath of God."[70] But as Stephen Sizer rightly points out in his definitive critique,[71] "The promise, when referring to Abraham's descendants, speaks of God blessing them, not of entire nations 'blessing' the Hebrew nation, still less the contemporary and secular state of Israel." It might be worthwhile to add to Sizer's reflection the important fact that the Arabs—of whom the Palestinians—are also descendants of Abraham through his first son Ishmael.

Britain's (and France's) Promises and Betrayals

So, after centuries of relentless preaching and planning on the part of Western Christian Evangelicals, the early twentieth century finally provided them with the Jewish cooperation they needed—mainly after the formation of the British Zionist Federation in 1899—to fulfil their desire to see the Jews restored in Palestine, which represents the beginning of the "redemption" according to Protestant restorationist Christianity. This is how Britain issued the ominous Balfour Declaration in 1917. Lord

---

69 For a definition of this theological approach to the Bible, read Darrell L. Bock, "Dispensationalism," *St. Andrews Encyclopedia of Theology,* University of St. Andrews, August 24, 2023.

70 Maidhc O Cathail, "The Scofield Bible—The Book That Made Zionists of America's Evangelical Christians," *Washington Report on Middle East Affairs,* October 2015.

71 Stephen Sizer, *Christian Zionism: Road-Map to Armageddon?* (Intervarsity Press Academic, 2004).

Balfour himself, as we mentioned earlier, was a devout Christian,[72] a racist and a Zionist. In 1906, as the then leader of the opposition, Balfour met with Chaim Weizmann[73]—together with Jewish MP and Minister Herbert Samuel and banker Lord Lionel Walter Rothschild—who lobbied him to support the creation of a Jewish homeland in Palestine. Balfour commented: "Their love for their country refused to be satisfied by the Uganda scheme. It was Weizmann's absolute refusal to even look at it which impressed me."

The Declaration was quite simply just a letter from the Foreign Secretary to Lord Rothschild, hence having no legal legitimacy. Later, when it was incorporated into the 1922 Mandate of Palestine, what was initially just a political sentiment was transformed into British policy[74] promising the Jews a land which was at the time an integral part of Syria and belonging to the Ottoman Empire, of which Britain had no legal right to give away.[75]

The exploration of the British archival documents held in the National Archives in Kew Garden—which detail the drafting stages of the Declaration—amply demonstrates the vast oversights, insincerity and a complete lack of consideration for the Palestinian people that has ignited and fueled decades of violence and injustice in the Middle East region. Historian Elizabeth Monroe has described the Declaration as "one of the greatest mistakes in our [British] imperial history."[76]

In the years preceding the publication of the Declaration, the British government had already entered into two very opposing agreements in the Levant. The first was the notorious Sykes-Picot Agreement of 1916,

---

72 He wrote a book on Christian theology in 1894 called *The Foundations of Belief: Being Notes Introductory to the Study of Theology.*

73 Chaim Azriel Weizmann was born in Motol (Russian empire) in 1874. He settled in London upon taking up a science appointment at the University of Manchester. Being a chemist by training, he gave valuable assistance to the British munitions industry during World War I. This achievement signally aided the Zionist political negotiations he was then conducting with the British government. In 1917, he was President of the British Zionist Federation, and he headed the World Zionist Organization in 1920. He later became the first President of the state of Israel (from 1949 to 1952).

74 See Janko Scepanovic, *Sentiments and Geopolitics and the Formulation and Realization of the Balfour Declaration* (CUNY Academic Works, 2014).

75 Kathy Durkin, *The Ambiguity of the Balfour Declaration: Who Caused it and Why?* (CreateSpace Independent Publishing Platform, 2013).

76 Elizabeth Monroe, *Britain's Moment in the Middle East 1914–1956* (London: Chatto & Windus, London, 1963).

in which British statesman Sir Mike Sykes and French politician François Georges-Picot carved up the map of the Middle East between France and Britain with pencils on a napkin, assuming that the Ottoman Empire would fall.[77] The second agreement was named the Hussein-McMahon agreement. It was comprised of a series of correspondences and formal pledges made between Hussein bin Ali, the Sherif of Mecca, and Sir Henry McMahon, the High Commissioner for Egypt.[78] As the Great War commenced, Britain realized that Arab nationalists could be of benefit to them; they therefore solicited their loyalty to fight the Ottomans and in return McMahon promised Arab independence to Hussein on the advent of the Ottoman Empire being defeated. The British had therefore "already double crossed and betrayed two peoples before a third agreement on the destiny of Palestine had even been declared."[79]

Over the last one hundred years historical propaganda and biased colonial discourse have constructed the history of the Israeli-Palestinian conflict and written its dominant narrative. This discourse, both within historiography and academia, has proven to be a powerful tool serving to manipulate public understanding of this conflict and to justify the continued denial of basic rights to the Palestinian people. However, as Noam Chomsky wrote in the book *Gaza in Crisis: Reflections on Israel's War Against the Palestinians*[80] that he co-authored with Ilan Pappé: "Anyone who dares to dive into the ocean of words to be found in the political and diplomatic documents in the various national archives understands how precarious is the story extracted from these heaps of documents left behind by the chattering classes that shaped our lives over the last two centuries."

As a matter of fact, among the above-mentioned British archival documents, especially those included in the War Cabinet files, are various letters written by Lord Edwin Samuel Montagu, who was then the only Jewish member of the Cabinet, in which he opposed the

77 Joe Stork, "Understanding the Balfour Declaration," *Middle East Research and Information Project,* 1972.

78 See *The McMahon-Hussein Correspondence, 14 July 1915–10 March 1916:* http://www1.udel.edu/History-old/figal/Hist104/assets/pdf/readings/13mcmahonhussein.pdf

79 Hannah Bowler, in Sameh Habeeb and Pietro Stefanini (Eds.), *Giving Away Other People's Land: The Making of the Balfour Declaration* (The Palestinian Return Centre, 2017).

80 Noam Chomsky and Ilan Pappé, *Gaza in Crisis: Reflections on Israel's War Against the Palestinians* (Chicago: Haymarket Books, 2010).

Declaration, saying: "I have never heard it suggested even by their most fervent admirers, that either Mr. Balfour or Lord Rothschild would prove to be the Messiah."[81] Alongside his protests—both before and after the Declaration was made public—was a list of forty-five prominent British Jews who vehemently expressed their opposition to the Declaration and abhorrence of Zionism, as well as figures showing that just six percent of the Jewish population of Great Britain supported Zionism. One of those prominent Jewish anti-Zionists was philanthropist, scholar and founding President of the World Union for Progressive Judaism, Claude Montefiore.[82]

A closer look at the different archives reveals the following main arguments:

• Said these 45 Jewish people ardently resented Zionist efforts to convince Jews that they were an ethnic-racial group who constituted a nation. They believed it was an injustice to turn over control of a land to those who then constituted only 7% of the population,[83] and noted that the Holy Land is holy to Jews, Christians and Muslims alike. They further pointed out the practical implications of Zionism and its challenge, both for those who would emigrate to Palestine and those assimilationist Jews who wouldn't leave their countries of residence.

• Zionism was viewed by many Jews, and primarily by rabbis, as an anti-Jewish rebellion comparable to Luther's challenge to the Church of Rome. Looking outside the British Jewish community, Montagu gives the testimony of Italy's second Jewish prime minister, Luigi Luzzatti: "Jews must acquire everywhere full religious liberty as existing in the United States and in Italy. In Palestine, delivered from the Turks, Jews will live, not as sovereigns but as free citizens, to fertilize their fathers' land. Judaism is not a Nationality but a Religion."

---

81 NA CAB 21/58 Pamphlet written by Edwin S. Montagu (1917).

82 In his works "Nation or Religious Community?" and "Race, Nation, Religion and the Jews," published, respectively, in 1917 and 1918, Montefiore stated that "The establishment of a 'National Home for the Jewish Race' in Palestine presupposes that the Jews are a nation, which I deny, and that they are homeless, which implies that in the countries where they enjoy religious liberty and the full rights of citizenship, they are separate entities, unidentified with the interests of the nations of which they form parts, an implication which I repudiate." See CAB21/58 letter from Lenard Cohen (October 1917).

83 Michael Meyer, *Response to Modernity: A History of the Reform Movement in Judaism* (Oxford: Oxford University Press, 1990).

• With regard to Judaism and politics, Chief Rabbi Dr Hermann Adler
was of the opinion that

> When we dwelt in the Holy Land, we had a political
> organization of our own: we had judges and kings to
> rule over us. But ever since the conquest of Palestine
> by the Romans, we have ceased to be a body politic;
> we are citizens of the country in which we dwell ... To
> Mr. Goldwin Smith's question, "What is the political
> bearing of Judaism?," I would reply that Judaism has
> no political bearing whatever. The great bond which
> unites us is not one of race, but the bond of a com-
> mon religion. We regard all mankind as brethren. We
> consider ourselves citizens of the country in which we
> dwell, in the highest and fullest sense of the term, and
> esteem it our dearest privilege and duty to labor for its
> welfare.

• At the time of the drafting of the Declaration all British foreign policy
was created along lines that sought to benefit the Empire, and Palestine
was viewed as a territory of the utmost importance to the future security and wellbeing of the British Empire. This line of argument finds
that it was the British government who invited the Zionists into the
negotiations and opened up the debate, thus contradicting common
claims that it was Zionist leaders who courted and persuaded the
Cabinet to fulfil their desires. Indeed, the archives show that the War
Cabinet gained its first introduction to the idea of a Jewish Palestine
from Herbert Samuel. In a memorandum in 1915 titled "The Future of
Palestine," Samuel wrote:

> From the standpoint of British interests there are sev-
> eral arguments for this policy [annexation of Palestine
> to the British Empire] if wider considerations should
> allow it to be pursued: 1. It would enable England to
> fulfil in yet another sphere her historic part of civilizer
> of the backward countries; 2. ... Palestine, small as it
> is in area, bulks so large in the world's imagination,
> that no Empire is so great but its prestige would
> be raised by its possession ... particularly if it were

avowedly a means of aiding the Jews to reoccupy the country; 3. ... Although Great Britain did not enter the conflict [World War I] with any purpose of territorial expansion, being in it and having made immense sacrifices, there would be profound disappointment in the country if the outcome were to be the securing of great advantages by our allies, and not for ourselves ... Certain of the German colonies must no doubt be retained for strategic reasons. But if Great Britain can obtain the compensations, which public opinion will demand, in Mesopotamia and Palestine, and not in German East Africa and West Africa, there is more likelihood of a lasting peace; 4. The belt of desert to the east of the Suez Canal is an admirable strategic frontier for Egypt. But it would be an inadequate defense if a great European Power [that is, France] were established on the further side; 5. The course which is advocated would win for England the lasting gratitude of the Jews throughout the world. In the United States where they number about 2,000,000, and in all the other land where they are scattered, they would form a body of opinion whose bias, where the interest of the country of which they were citizens was not involved, would be favorable to the British Empire.

The minutes from War Cabinet meeting 245 seemed to concur with Samuel's analysis: "The Secretary of State for Foreign Affairs stated that he gathered that everyone was now agreed that, from a purely diplomatic and political point of view, it was desirable that some declaration favorable to the aspirations of the Jewish nationalists should now be made. The vast majority of Jews in Russia and America, as, indeed, all over the world, now appeared to be favorable to Zionism. If we could make a declaration favorable to such an ideal, we should be able to carry on extremely useful propaganda both in Russia and America." Moreover, the archives show that the Foreign Office sent influential Zionists on a mission to achieve these aims. Aaron Aaronsohn was one such Zionist, who was sent to both the U.S. and Russia by the Foreign Office to spy and infiltrate Jewish communities.

- The discovery of oil in Persia by the British company Anglo-Persian in 1908 may have played a latent role in the formulation of Zionist policy. In a Foreign Office memorandum titled "The Oilfields of Russia and Mesopotamia" it was explained that the "security of this country and the British Empire is dependent on oil."

With regard to the no less perfidious and duplicitous attitude of France vis-à-vis the origins of the Israeli-Palestinian conflict in general and the support given to Zionism in particular, Lord Montagu writes in a document labelled "SECRET" and titled "ZIONISM"[84] he circulated on the 9th of October 1917:

> The Cabinet has been informed that the French Government are in sympathy with Zionist aspirations. It has recently come to my knowledge officially that the French Ambassador has approached our Foreign Office with a proposal to establish a Jewish nation in El Hasa in Arabia [in today's Saudi Arabia], oblivious of the fact that although this is technically Turkish territory, we have concluded so recently as 1915 a treaty which roughly promises to support Bin Saud and his followers in the occupation of the country. I quote this to prove that the French are anxious to establish Jews anywhere if only to have an excuse for getting rid of them, or large numbers of them.

Through this testimony Montagu was actually just confirming the content of a letter at the time addressed on June 4, 1917, by Jules Cambon, then secretary general of the French Quai d'Orsay, to Nahum Sokolow, a leader of the Zionist movement, who publicly supported the establishment of a Jewish national home in Palestine. In this letter which precedes the Balfour declaration by five months, the French diplomat wrote:

> You were good enough to present the project to which you are devoting your efforts, which has for its object the development of Jewish colonization in Palestine. You consider that, circumstances permitting, and the

---

84 British Record Office, CAB24/28

independence of the Holy Places being safeguarded on the other hand, it would be a deed of justice and of reparation to assist, by the protection of the Allied Powers, in the renaissance of the Jewish nationality in that Land from which the people of Israel were exiled so many centuries ago. The French Government, which entered this present war to defend a people wrongfully attacked, and which continues the struggle to assure the victory of right over might, can but feel sympathy for your cause, the triumph of which is bound up with that of the Allies. I am happy to give you herewith such assurance.

At the time, the letter was not released for publication, and it was no sooner sent than regretted as the French Quai d'Orsay returned to its habitual anxiety and duplicity on the subject, as recounted by David Pryce-Jones in *Betrayal: France, the Arabs, and the Jews.*[85] Indeed, on January 15, 1919, Foreign Minister Stephen Pichon instructed Pierre Paul Cambon, the French ambassador in London, to draw to the British government's attention that Zionist propaganda should not be allowed to become cause for trouble in the Middle East, saying: "The allied authorities should abstain from all actions or declarations which might arouse unrealizable expectations in the Jews ... The Zionists must understand once and for all that there could be no question of constituting an independent Jewish state in Palestine, nor even forming some sovereign Jewish body." Three days later Cambon wrote to Pichon that he could hardly believe the conversation he had just had with Lord Balfour, who reportedly said to him: "It would be interesting to be present at the reconstitution of the Kingdom of Jerusalem." Cambon replied that according to the apocalypse such a reconstitution would signal the end of the world, and Balfour came back: "It would be still more interesting to be present at the end of the world"!

In sum, the examination of the British archival documents clearly shows that the Balfour Declaration was a product of four key mindsets: desperation for victory in World War I, imperialism, antisemitism and Orientalism.

---

85 David Pryce-Jones, *Betrayal: France, the Arabs, and the Jews* (New York: Encounter Books, 2006).

In her speech[86] at a dinner organized in London on November 2, 2017 to mark the 100th anniversary of the Balfour Declaration, Prime Minister Theresa May said that the Declaration was "one of the most important letters in history," that "we are proud of our pioneering role in the creation of Israel," that she will "absolutely not" apologize for this landmark document. She also slammed the BDS movement and considered "abhorrent" a "new and pernicious form of anti-Semitism which uses criticism of the actions of Israeli government as a despicable justification for questioning the very right of Israel to exist." No wonder then that Benjamin Netanyahu flew to London to attend the dinner, and that no Palestinian leader was invited.

May's exclusion of Palestinians from her celebration reflects with uncanny accuracy their scornful disregard in the Balfour Declaration one hundred years ago. The British "treated the Palestinians as non-people then, and still treat them as non-people today."[87]

A Naked Settler Colonialism Fast Approaching Its Demise

According to the Cornell Law School Legal Information Institute, settler colonialism has "an additional criterion that is the complete destruction and replacement of indigenous people and their cultures by the Settler's own in order to establish themselves as the rightful inhabitants."

Many scholars apply the term to Israel's founding as well. Late Australian historian Patrick Wolfe, for one, clearly referred to the Zionist settler project in Palestine as an example of settler colonialism in a seminal essay[88] published in 2006. As practiced by Europeans, he wrote,

> Both genocide and settler colonialism have typically employed the organizing grammar of race. European xenophobic traditions such as anti-Semitism, Islamophobia, or Negrophobia are considerably older than race, which, as many have shown, became discursively consolidated fairly late in the eighteenth century ... Settler colonialism destroys to replace.

---

86 To read the full text of the speech: https://www.timesofisrael.com/full-text-of-mays-speech-at-balfour-declaration-centenary-dinner/

87 Peter Oborne, "100 years after Balfour: the reality which still shames Israel," *OpenDemocracy*, November 2, 2017.

88 Patrick Wolfe, "Settler colonialism and the elimination of the native," *Journal of Genocide Research* 8 (December 21, 2006).

As Theodor Herzl, founding father of Zionism, observed in his allegorical manifesto/novel, "If I wish to substitute a new building for an old one, I must demolish before I construct."[89] Settler colonialism is an inclusive, land-centered project that coordinates a comprehensive range of agencies, from the metropolitan center to the frontier encampment, with a view to eliminating the indigenous societies... The colonizers come to stay: invasion is a structure not an event.

In Palestine, however, the native society has not been eliminated. Palestine is not "as Jewish as England is British," as Chaim Weizmann once candidly expressed Zionist goals. Instead, as Rashid Khalidi wrote in 2018,

The population of the entire country from the river to the sea, unified by decades of occupation and colonization since 1967, is today at least half Palestinian, and that proportion is growing. The natives are still there, and they are restless. Those Palestinians who have managed to remain in historic Palestine—in spite of the ceaseless efforts to dispossess them—continue to resist erasure. Outside of Palestine, an equal number remain profoundly attached to their homeland and to the right of return. The Palestinians have not forgotten, they have not gone away, and the memory of Palestine and its dismemberment has not been effaced. Indeed, wider international audiences are increasingly aware of these realities.[90]

When one looks at white settler colonies, Joseph Masaad insightfully observes,[91] the only ones that have survived are the ones who have been successful in absolutely eliminating and annihilating the native population, either completely or basically retaining a small minority of

89 Theodor Herzl, *Old-New Land* [Altneuland, 1902], translated by Lotta Levensohn (New York: M. Wiener, 1941), p. 38.

90 Rashid Khalidi, "Israel: 'A Failed Settler-Colonial Project'," Institute for Palestine Studies, May 10, 2018.

91 Prof. Joseph Masaad, interviewed by Rania Khalek, *BreakThrough News,* June 5, 2024.

them. We see this especially in the United States, Canada, Australia and New Zealand.

The situation is quite different in other settler-colonial places like South Africa, Algeria, Rhodesia, Kenya, Mozambique, Angola and Namibia, where the attempts to establish settler-colonies have failed, and as a result, those countries achieved their independence in the early 1960s and through the mid-1990s. And the reason why those attempts did not succeed is because the native populations have always outnumbered the white settler intruders.

The Western-Zionist settler-colonialism in Palestine clearly belongs to the latter project. As mentioned before, Theodor Herzl had foreseen the absolute need to expel the native Palestinian population and replace it with Jewish immigrants coming mostly from Eastern and Western European countries; a sine qua non condition for the successful establishment of a "Jewish state" in the "Holy Land."

Later on, in the 1920s and 1930s, Zionist ideologues and activists came up with concrete schemes and plans on how to bring this about, and started to implement their designs even before the 30th of November 1947, the day the United Nations General Assembly passed the Partition Plan Resolution. Indeed, by the time Israel was finished with the expulsions by December 1948, the Zionists had successfully evicted more than 90% of the Palestinian population in the territories they illegally occupied by brutal force.

According to Prof. Masaad, the major mistake the Zionists made was to conquer the remaining part of Palestine in 1967, adding to Israel a large number of Palestinians, not only the indigenous populations of the West Bank, the Gaza Strip, and East Jerusalem. As a result of that, the demographic situation changed dramatically in Israel, affecting the survivability of the settler colony, at least on a demographic basis.

As referred to earlier, several Israeli officials, including Benjamin Netanyahu and Ehud Barak, have made predictions over the last few years, saying they were not sure Israel will survive to its 80th or 100th birthday. That kind of worry is based essentially on the internal fissures, the demographic contraction of Israel, and the fact that there's no new major pool from which to draw additional Jewish immigrants. The six million or so American Jews, for instance, have never shown a willingness, or at least have never been a large percentage of American Jewry that showed an interest in moving to Israel. Even though many individual

Jews may be strongly supportive of Israel, that does not mean that they are all Zionists, or they're going to move en masse to Israel.

Accordingly, Joseph Masaad goes on to say, the mass murder and genocidal policies of the Israeli government are not necessarily irrational. The issue is not only to eliminate the Palestinians physically and demographically, but also to forestall the possibility of resistance in the future. However immoral, this kind of behavior is quite rational, and was followed by many of the settler-colonial countries—witness the appalling atrocities and mass killings committed by the British in Kenya in the 1950s and 1960s; the American support for the Portuguese in the South African war on the guerrillas in Angola and Mozambique between 1962 and 2000; the Western support to the French in Algeria where any uprising by the Algerian natives against their cruel and sadistic French settlers would be met with massive murders of tens of thousands of Algerians, so much so that hundreds of thousands of Algerians were killed by the French during the war of independence between 1954 and 1962; and the U.S. troops going to support France after its defeat in Dien Bien Phu in Vietnam in 1954, continuing the war at the behest of the French and then independently until 1975.

In light of the above, there's nothing special about the ongoing Western support for Israel. Israel's President Isaac Herzog has been banging on about how Israel is defending Western civilization, and that were it to fall, Europe would be next. The exact same discourse has recently been repeated by Netanyahu in his latest address to the U.S. Congress, saying:

> We meet today at a crossroads of history. Our world is in upheaval. In the Middle East, Iran's axis of terror confronts America, Israel and our Arab friends. This is not a clash of civilizations. It's a clash between barbarism and civilization. It's a clash between those who glorify death and those who sanctify life. For the forces of civilization to triumph, America and Israel must stand together. Because when we stand together, something very simple happens. We win. They lose ... The ICC is trying to shackle Israel's hands and prevent us from defending ourselves. And if Israel's hands are tied, America is next. I'll tell you what else is next.

> The ability of all democracies to fight terrorism will
> be imperiled. That's what's on the line.[92]

Netanyahu's lies were met with dozens of standing ovations on the part of the overwhelming majority of the audience. The rare but re- sounding dissenting voices came from inside the Capitol with Rashida Tlaib holding a War Criminal sign, and from the outside with thousands of protesters chanting "free Palestine" and also calling Netanyahu a war criminal.

We have also heard from German Head of the European Union Ursula von der Leyen that the Jewish values of Israel are European val- ues. And indeed, perhaps she's right! Such "shared values" include the values of colonialism and genocide. It is worth recalling here that the tone of the EU's support for Israel had already been set when she tweeted a photo of the European Commission building in Brussels lit up in an Israeli flag. She pointedly said: "Israel has the right to defend itself—to- day and in the days to come. The European Union stands with Israel."[93]

Shrewdly explaining the justification for the European Union's solidarity with Israel, including and notably Germany's purported love for European Jews and its regret over the Holocaust, Prof. Masaad says that after World War II, the Europeans "made the discovery that the Jews were actually white European people." Their regret was therefore "not that you should not kill people that are different from you, but instead that you should not kill people that are just like you, meaning white European, since Jews, subsequent to the Holocaust, began to be integrat- ed in Europe at the level of cultural value." As for the belief that non- white people should continue to be killed, it has never been questioned, and we've seen many examples of this in European colonial policies since 1945—from the Algerian and Vietnamese genocides in the case of France, to what the United States has done in Korea, Vietnam, Central and Southern Africa, Central and South America, Afghanistan, Iraq etc.

In his book, *Good Muslim, Bad Muslim,* referred to earlier, Mahmood Mamdani provides a similar explanation, saying that by the beginning of the twentieth century, it was a European habit to distinguish between "civilized wars" and "colonial wars." The former were governed

---

92 "We're protecting you: Full text of Netanyahu's address to Congress," *The Times of Israel,* July 25, 2024. https://www.timesofisrael.com/were-protecting-you-full-text-of-netanyahus-address-to-congress/
93 Niamh Ni Bhriain and Mark Akkerman, "Partners in Crime: EU complicity in Israel's genocide in Gaza," Transnational Institute, June 4, 2024.

by the "laws of war" and the latter by the "laws of nature," meaning that wars between "people like us" were to be fought within rules that were meant to limit their barbarity, but wars against people who were not full members of "Western civilization" were not bound by any rules at all. Mamdani traces the beginnings of the massacres of colonized people to the first years of the 19th century, when the indigenous Australians were slaughtered by colonists in Tasmania. This was imitated by wholesale slaughters, *inter alia* in French Algeria, German Namibia, and Belgian Congo.

Also worthy of mention in this respect is the Nazi establishment of extermination camps in occupied Poland, not in Germany. There were, of course, concentration camps in Germany, but these were used as forced labor camps, not death camps. So, by "siting the camps to the east of Germany, the Nazis were, in effect, removing them from Western Europe where such barbarism was not considered acceptable. The east of Europe became, in a sense, a colony inhabited by people who were not considered Aryan and therefore not fully European. They were thus subject only to the laws of nature." And in the words of Frantz Fanon, "Nazism transformed the whole Europe into a veritable colony."[94]

This Western support is thus "part and parcel of their support for white supremacy in their own countries and elsewhere," and the unstinting support that Israel is obtaining from powerful Western powers—apparently unshaken by any of its crimes and excesses.

This is also why today, we see most of the support for the Palestinians coming precisely from peoples who have suffered under countries who had set up settler colonies previously, like Algeria, South Africa and Namibia.

Seventy-six years ago, says Ghada Karmi,[95]

> an anomalous state was imposed on the Arab Middle East. The new creation was alien in every sense to the region's culture and anti-colonial struggle ... The new state went on to violate international law repeatedly, attack its neighbors, persecute the native Palestinian population, and impose a system of apartheid rule over

---

94 Johanna Jacques, "A 'Most Astonishing' Circumstance: The Survival of Jewish POWs in German War Captivity During the Second World War," *Social and Legal Studies* 30, no. 3, 2021.

95 Ghada Karmi, "Why is Israel so vital to the West?," *Middle East Eye,* May 18, 2023.

them ... If instead, Israel had been left to fend for itself, the Palestinian struggle for freedom would have been short, and the settler community in Palestine would gradually and peaceably have been absorbed into the region.

John Mearsheimer, one of the most distinguished professors of political science in the world, discussed the current predicament of the state of Israel and its uncertain future at the Center for Independent Studies, explaining "why Israel is in deep trouble."[96] Three months later, Mearsheimer's co-author of the celebrated book *The Israel Lobby and U.S. Foreign Policy,* Stephen Walt, wrote an opinion[97] in which, he too, says that Israel—whose Zionist project has been getting worse at defending itself for decades—is "in serious trouble." He concluded his analysis by saying that Israel's vengeful and shortsighted behavior has inflicted enormous harm on innocent Palestinians for decades and continues to do so today, warning that Israel's decline in strategic judgement must be reassessed for the sake of its own survival.

Prof. Richard D. Wolff is even more affirmative in this respect, saying, "History suggests that Benjamin Netanyahu or his successors will eventually be disconnected from the United States. Their last alliance will hasten the end of Israel's settler colonialism."[98]

For his part, Prof. Yuval Noah Harari, concurring with the view that Israel destroyed Gaza materially while Gaza destroyed Israel morally, sees an even greater danger for Israel and Judaism, maybe one of the biggest turning points in Jewish history. What is happening right now in Israel, he said, is a worst-case scenario that could destroy 2,000 years of Jewish thinking, culture, and existence. He warned that "If Israel continues on its present trajectory, what we are facing is the potential of an ethnic cleansing campaign in Gaza and in the West Bank, resulting in the expulsion of two million, maybe more, Palestinians from there, the establishment of a Greater Israel, the disintegration of Israeli democracy,

96 John Mearsheimer, "Why Israel Is in Big Trouble," Centre for Independent Studies, May 17, 2024. To read the transcript of the discussion: https://scrapsfromtheloft.com./opinions/why-israel-is-in-deep-trouble-john-mearsheimer-with-tom-switzer-transcript/

97 Stephen M. Waltz, "The Dangerous Decline in Israeli Strategy," *Foreign Policy,* August 16, 2024.

98 Richard D. Wolff, "Settler Colonialism: 'It Ends with Us' in Palestine and Israel," *Brave New Europe,* January 30, 2025.

and the creation of a new Israel which is based on an ideology of Jewish supremacy and on the worship of what were completely anti-Jewish values for the last two millennia (...) This will be the new Judaism, and maybe the only Judaism."[99]

As its genocidal war on Gaza continues, Israel and its Western backers are getting more desperate than ever in defending their mass murder of tens of thousands of Palestinian civilians. And with Zionism exposed to much of the world for its unprecedented savagery in the 21st century, it's becoming clear that this project is not only unsustainable but may even be approaching its demise.

99 Watch the interview: *Yuval Noah Harari on Israel, AI, and the Future | Unholy Live in London* [35:27], Unholy Podcast YouTube channel, June 8, 2025. https://youtu.be/pB5Ul3GHFxA

CHAPTER SEVEN

THE ROAD AHEAD IN THE "HOLY LAND"

*"Those who cannot remember the past
are condemned to repeat it."*
—GEORGE SANTAYANA[1]

Requiem for the Deeply Held Two-State Delusion

The Settler Colonialist and Ethno-Nationalist Roots of Zionism

An extensive examination of Theodor Herzl's wittings and movement shows clearly that from its very beginnings to the politics and policies of the state of Israel today, Zionist thought has permanently and resolutely embraced the dominant European discourses of the late nineteenth and early twentieth centuries, including anti-Semitism.

In his 1896 *Der Judenstaat*—"state 'for,' or 'of' Jews" would be a literal and more accurate English translation—Theodor Herzl articulated his vision and blueprint for a future "Jewish state" in Palestine by highlighting his scheme as a venture beneficial to both the "current sovereign authority"—then embodied by the Ottoman sultan—and the European colonial powers "under whose protectorate" the new state would come into being and continue to exist: "If His Majesty the Sultan were to give

---

1   Said by George Santayana (b. Jorge Agustín Nicolás Ruiz de Santayana y Borrás) in his book, *Reason in Common Sense*. He was a Spanish-American philosopher, essayist, poet, and novelist born in Spain and raised and educated in the United States from the age of eight. At the age of 48, he left his academic position at Harvard University and permanently returned to Europe. *The Life of Reason,* subtitled *The Phases of Human Progress,* is a book published in five volumes from 1905 to 1906 [Source: Wikipedia]. This oft-quoted aphorism has been incorrectly attributed to Edmund Burke and Winston Churchill, among others.

us Palestine" he wrote, "we could offer to resolve Turkey's finances. For Europe, we would form part of a bulwark against Asia there, we would serve as the advance post of civilization against barbarism."

As recalled by Nora Scholtes in her thoughtful and richly researched study submitted for the Degree of Ph.D. in Postcolonial Studies,[2] French Marxist historian and sociologist Maxime Rodinson is commonly said to be the first contemporary "Western" scholar to have positioned Zionism/ Israel within its colonial, and more specifically settler colonial, context. Rodinson recognized in Herzl's propositions a clear manifestation of Zionism as a "colonialist phenomenon":

> It would have been difficult to place Zionism any more clearly within the framework of European imperialist policies ... The [Zionist] perspective was inevitably placed within the framework of the European assault on the Ottoman Empire, this "sick man" whose complete dismemberment was postponed by the rivalries of the great powers but who, in the meantime, was subjected to all kinds of interference, pressures, and threats. An imperialist setting if there ever was one ... The Europeanism of the Zionists made it possible for them to present their plan as part of the same movement of European expansion that each power was developing on its own behalf.

In effect, throughout his writings and speeches, Herzl never missed an opportunity to present the Zionist idea as a quintessentially colonial project, one that would also serve the interests of the Europeans, and more broadly the whole of the "civilized" world. In his *Der Judenstaat* he wrote: "The world will be liberated by our freedom, enriched by our wealth, magnified by our greatness"; and in a speech he delivered in London in 1891, he declared:

> We want to carry culture to the East. And once again, Europe will in turn profit from this work of ours. We will create new trade routes—and none will be more interested in this than England with its Asiatic

---

2 Nora Scholtes, *Bulwark Against Asia: Zionist Exclusivism and Palestinian Responses* (University of Kent School of English, 2015).

possessions. The shortest route to India lies through
Palestine ... What could I, poor barbarian from the
Continent, tell the inhabitants of England about these
things [progress and industry]. They are our superiors
in all technical achievements, just as their great politicians were the first to see the necessity for colonial expansion. That is why the flag of Greater-Britain waves
over every sea ... And so I should think that here in
England, the Zionist idea, which is a colonial one,
should be easily and quickly understood in England,
and this in its most modern form.[3]

For Desmond Stewart, there is no doubt that "Herzl's stencil for
obtaining a territory and then clearing it for settlement was cut after the
Rhodesian model."[4] Mark Levene equally argues that Herzl "had an
agenda that closely followed and sought to emulate the essential contours
of European empire-building in Africa."[5] It was thus within the context
of Western colonialism in Africa that the idea of acquiring a territorial
basis for the establishment of a "Jewish entity" was most contemplated,
more precisely in the Uasi Ngishu plateau, near Nairobi, Kenya, and not
in Uganda as is commonly reported.

Nevertheless, although Herzl did not exclude the option that "The
Society"[6] would "take what it will be given under a charter" in what
he called a "neutral land" in order to materialize his colonial-Zionist
project—since Argentina was another country envisioned for a possible
mass settlement for the Jews—he was convinced that Palestine would
be the most powerful asset in attracting a Jewish mass following. As

3 Quoted in Nora Scholtes, Op cit.
4 Desmond Stewart, "Herzl: Artist and Politician," Hamish Hamilton,
London, 1974.
5 Mark Levene, "Herzl, the Scramble, and a Meeting That Never Happened:
Revisiting the Notion of an African Zion," in: Bar-Yosef, E., Valman, N. (eds)
"'The Jew' in Late-Victorian and Edwardian Culture: Between the East End and
East Africa," Palgrave Macmillan, London, 2009.
6 In *Der Judenstaat* Herzl writes: "The plan, simple in design, but
complicated in execution, will be carried out by two agencies: The Society of
Jews and the Jewish Company. The Society of Jews will do the preparatory
work in the domains of science and politics, which the Jewish Company will
afterwards apply practically. The Jewish Company will be the liquidating agent
of the business interests of departing Jews, and will organize commerce and
trade in the new country."

the Jews' "ever-memorable historic home," he writes in *Der Judenstaat,* "that name alone would be a tremendously stirring rallying cry for our people." Furthermore, it is reported that when it was known that Herzl was wavering on the option of Palestine as a Jewish homeland in favor of East Africa or South America, he received a Bible from William Blackstone, an American Christian Zionist, in which every reference to "Israel" or "Zion" had been underlined in red, together with a letter urging him to insist Zionists settle only in Palestine.[7]

Ultimately, the East-Africa scheme proposed by the British, which was indeed hotly debated during the 6th Zionist Congress held in Basel on August 23, 1903, was rejected, both because of a lack of support by the critical mass of Russian Jews and because the British government faced a strong local opposition on the part of British settlers in its African territories to the idea of a Jewish colony in the area.

And so, by the time of Herzl's death the following year, the East-Africa and Argentina options had all but vanished from the agenda of the Zionist leadership. In a 1914 article in the German newspaper *Die Welt,* a special issue on the tenth anniversary of Herzl's death, Herzl's East-Africa proposal is described by Bernstein as a "historical derailment," a desperate and well-intentioned, but ultimately misguided attempt at providing emergency help to Eastern Europe's persecuted Jews. Herzl, he indicated, "grasped the Uganda-straw immediately after the pogrom in Kishinev ... He impatiently searched for a quick rescue ... even if only in the form of a 'night shelter.' It was the greatest sacrifice that Herzl has made for his people. He sacrificed, even if only for a moment, his life's ideal."[8]

From that point onwards, the new leadership concentrated all its efforts on the implementation of the most preferred solution, that is the creation of a purely Jewish state in Palestine, mainly by way of ethnic cleansing. The terminology of "ethnic cleansing" only entered the popular vocabulary in recent times. The concept used by Zionist thinkers was "transfer," and Herzl's true plans with regard to Palestine's non-Jewish population are well-documented in his diary, where as early as 1895 he put forward this idea, writing: "We shall try to spirit the penniless

---

7 Donald Wagner, *Dying in the Land of Promise* (London: Melisende, 2000).

8 S. Bernstein, "Theodor Herzl im Lichte des Ostjudentums" (Theodor Herzl in the Light of Eastern Jewry), *Die Welt,* July 3, 1914, cited by Nora Scholtes, op cit. https://sammlungen.ub.uni-frankfurt.de/cm/periodical/pageview/3355506

population across the border by procuring employment for it in the transit countries, while denying it any employment in our own country."

Maxime Rodinson asserts that the root cause of all of Zionism's future failings is consubstantial with its very colonial founding vision:

> Once the premises were laid down, the inexorable logic of history determined the consequences. Wanting to create a purely Jewish, or predominantly Jewish, state in an Arab Palestine in the twentieth century could not help but lead to a colonial-type situation and to the development (completely normal, sociologically speaking) of a racist state of mind, and in the final analysis to a military confrontation between the two ethnic groups.

Gabriel Piterberg agrees with Rodinson's early analysis: "From the moment Zionism's goal became the resettlement of European Jews in a land controlled by a colonial European power, in order to create a sovereign political entity, it could no longer be understood just as a central or east European nationalism; it was also, inevitably, a white-settler colonialism."[9]

The unavoidable consequence of such vision is what Ahad Ha'am already warned against back in 1891: "if the time comes when the life of our people in Eretz Israel develops to the point of encroaching upon the native population, they will not easily yield their place."[10] A decade before Ha'am made his prescient comment, Palestine's population was some 460,000. Of these, around 400,000 were Muslim Arabs; about 40,000 were Christian, mostly Greek Orthodox; and the remainder, Jews. How challenging these figures are to the falsehood of one of Zionism's most cherished founding myths—that of "a land without people for a people without land"– and how shockingly ill-intentioned was Herzl's omission of *any* reference to "Arabs" or "Palestinians" in his 30,000-word pamphlet!

Assuredly, Herzl's dream of a national home for the Jews that would end both their own age-old insecurity within the diaspora and Gentiles'

---

9 Gabriel Piterberg, "Settlers and their States," *New Left Review*, no. 62 (March–April 2010). https://newleftreview.org/issues/ii62/articles/gabriel-piterberg-settlers-and-their-states

10 Ahad Ha'am, "Truth from Eretz Israel," op cit.

anti-Semitism has inexorably transformed into a nightmare both for Jews and Palestinians and for the world, which is still held hostage to their struggle, with no apparent solution in a completely transformed and blood-soaked "Holy Land."

Nightmare is precisely the key word in the title of the brilliant book[11] by Peter Rodgers, a former Australian journalist and ambassador to Israel, devoted to the tragic drama caused by the pursuit of Herzl's dream by his Zionist followers to the present day. Whatever their historical or emotional attachment to the land they came to rule, Rodgers asserts, the Jews of Israel had supplanted another people, a people who would not forget. The making of one nationalist dream has indeed involved the unmaking of another. But for how long and for what price?

The Aussie ambassador's well-researched study tells a story of sorrow and anger in a balanced manner – insofar as this is possible— which, obviously entails the risk of drawing fire from both Jews and Palestinians, but this, he says, is sadly part of the twisted logic of the conflict. The story told shows how little the dynamics of the conflict between Jew and Palestinian have changed; how eerily reminiscent today's antagonisms and falsehoods are of yesteryear's; how "modern" leadership is anything but; and how much today's self-righteous intransigence owes to what went before. Furthermore, it poses the vital question: "have the nationalist dreams of both peoples been doomed by the determined refusal of Jew and Palestinian to contemplate what life must be like for the other?"

To epitomize the opposing views of the protagonists, Rodgers, in his concluding remarks, quotes Yasser Arafat as saying that "the womb of the Arab woman" is one of the Palestinians' most potent weapons, and Shimon Peres, as writing of a deepening chasm between Israelis and Palestinians, commenting typically: "We are sorry but not desperate." Rodgers reacted to these last words by saying: "He might perhaps have added wisely, not yet."

The Origin and Enduring Adverse Consequences of a Bad and Unjust Idea

The idea of establishing two states for two peoples in historic Palestine came together in 1936 when Lord William Robert Wellesley Peel was appointed by the British government to head a commission

---

11 Peter Rodgers, *Herzl's Nightmare: One Land, Two Peoples* (London: Constable, 2005).

of inquiry, formally known as "Palestine Royal Commission," with a view to investigating the causes of unrest among Palestinians and Jews in Palestine following a six-month-long Arab general strike. The unrest intensified after the April 1920 San Remo Conference awarded the United Kingdom a mandate to control Palestine, which had been part of the Ottoman Empire until its dismemberment in the wake of its defeat in the First World War.

In a widely acclaimed book containing a wealth of fascinating untapped archival material and primary sources, Israeli journalist and historian Tom Segev reconstructs in vivid detail the tumultuous three decades of the British mandate in Palestine, when "anything seemed possible and everything went awry." Tom Segev argues that the British, far from being pro-Arabist as commonly thought, consistently favored the Zionist position, thereby ensuring the creation of the "Jewish state"; and that they did so out of the mistaken and anti-Semitic belief—"a uniquely modern blend of classical antisemitic preconceptions and romantic veneration of the Holy Land and its people"—that the "Jews turn the wheels of history." At first, he writes, the British were received as an army of liberation; both Arabs and Jews wished for independence and assumed they would win it under British sponsorship. The Promised Land had, by the stroke of a pen, become "twice-promised," and as a result, "confusion, ambiguity, and disappointment were present at the very beginning." In sum, although the British took possession of "one Palestine, complete" as noted in the receipt signed by the British High Commissioner, "Palestine was riven, even before His Majesty's Government settled in."

Therefore, as it unavoidably turned out, Britain was caught in the middle of a bloody fight between two competing national movements. There were those in the British administration who identified with the Arabs and those who identified with the Jews; and there were also those who found both repugnant: "I dislike them all equally" wrote General Sir Walter Norris "Squib" Congreve, emphasizing that "Arabs and Jews and Christians, in Syria and Palestine, they are all alike, a beastly people. The whole lol of them is not worth a single Englishman." High Commissioner Wauchope compared himself to a circus performer trying to ride two horses at the same time. Of these two horses, he said in a lecture, "one cannot go fast and the other would not go slow." In fact, as Chaim Weizmann rightly observed, the British were fooling the Arabs, fooling the Jews, and fooling themselves. And Segev was equally right to conclude that from the start there were, then, only two possibilities:

that the Arabs defeat the Zionists or that the Zionists defeat the Arabs: "War between the two was inevitable."

With its formal approval by the League of Nations in 1922, the mandate incorporated the Balfour Declaration of 1917, which provided for both the establishment of a Jewish national home in Palestine for a minority Jewish population and the preservation of the civil and religious—but not the political or national—rights of non-Jewish indigenous Palestinian majority. Desiring political autonomy and resenting the continued Jewish immigration into their ancestral land, Palestinian Arabs disapproved of the British mandate, and by 1936 their dissatisfaction had grown into open rebellion.

The Peel Commission published its report in July 1937, admitting that the mandate was unworkable and, therefore, proposing that Palestine be partitioned into three zones: an Arab state, a Jewish state, and a neutral territory containing the holy places. Even though it initially accepted these proposals, by 1938 the British government recognized that such partitioning would not be feasible and ultimately rejected the Commission's report. And by the time the post-World War Two newly-created United Nations Organization voted the infamous Resolution 181 devising the partition of Palestine in 1947—giving 56% of historic Palestine along with 80% of the coast and the most fertile land to the Jewish minority side, and only 43% to the Palestinian majority side—the binational idea, and its array of supporting factions, had dissolved, soon to be followed by a civil war in Mandatory Palestine, the confirmation of the termination of the British mandate on May 14, 1948, the Israeli "Declaration of Independence" on the same day, and the outbreak, the following day, of the first Arab-Israeli war on May 15, 1948—which ended with a final armistice agreement concluded in July 1949, also demarcating the so-called "Green Line" which separated Arab-controlled territory from Israeli-occupied territories until the 1967 Arab-Israeli war.

In the aftermath of the Six-Day (June) War, on November 22, 1967, the UN Security Council adopted Resolution 242 in an effort to secure a "just and lasting peace" in the Middle East. The Israelis willingly supported the resolution because it called on the Arab states to accept Israel's "right to live in peace within secure and recognized borders free from threats or acts of force." Arab states, however, reacted in a very disparate way: Egypt and Jordan accepted it from the outset because it called for Israel to withdraw from "territories occupied in the recent conflict," and the Palestine Liberation Organization (PLO), headed by

Yasser Arafat, rejected it until 1988 for the main reason that it lacked explicit references to Palestinians and their inalienable national rights. As far as the League of Arab States as a whole is concerned, it convened a Summit in Khartoum, Sudan, on September 1, 1967, which adopted the "Khartoum Resolution," famously known for its "Three Noes" contained in its third operative paragraph,[12] namely: no peace, no negotiation, no recognition of Israel. Although Resolution 242—and UNSC's Resolution 338 adopted on October 22, 1973 following the Yom Kippur/ Ramadan War, and calling for a ceasefire and for the implementation of Resolution 242 "in all of its parts"—was never fully implemented, it nevertheless constituted the basis of international diplomatic efforts to end the Arab-Israeli conflict until the 1978 Camp David Accords and remains, to this day, at least theoretically, an important touchstone in any negotiated resolution to this longstanding conflict.

The U.S. Takes Over the Stewardship of the International Peace Efforts

As history teaches us, peace efforts aimed at re-building peace almost always follow destructive wars. The two Iraq wars of 1991 and 2003 paved the way for renewed peace efforts to resolve the Israeli-Palestinian Conflict, first within the framework of the 1991 Madrid Conference and the 1993 Oslo Agreement peace process, and then through such initiatives as "The Roadmap to Peace" of the "Quartet" in April 2003, the "Geneva Accord" published in October 2003, the Bush administration-convened peace conference at Annapolis in November 2007, the "Kerry Initiative" in 2013–2014, and the "Paris Conference" of January 2017, intended to "preserve the two-state solution and create incentives that would move the parties closer to direct negotiations."[13]

---

12 Paragraph 3 reads as follows: "The Arab Heads of State have agreed to unite their political efforts at the international and diplomatic level to eliminate the effects of the aggression and to ensure the withdrawal of the aggressive Israeli forces from the Arab lands which have been occupied since the aggression of 5 June. This will be done within the framework of the main principles by which the Arab States abide, namely, no peace with Israel, no recognition of Israel, no negotiations with it, and insistence on the rights of the Palestinian people in their own country."

13 Greg Shapland and Professor Yossi Mekelberg, "Israeli-Palestinian Peacemaking: What We Can Learn from Previous Efforts?," *Chatham House,* July 24, 2018 (updated December 14, 2020).

The Madrid Conference marked the first time that Israelis had sat down at a conference table with Arabs since the Geneva Conference in December 1973, and the first time in which all four of the frontline Arab states, as well as Palestinian representatives sat down with Israelis since the Lausanne Conference of 1949. With the defeat of Iraq at the hands of an American-led military coalition in the Gulf War of January–March 1991 and the end of the Cold War between the United States and the Soviet Union that same year, the George Bush administration

> felt that it had to "reward" the Arab countries, especially Syria, for their participation in the coalition against the Iraqi regime and that the time was right to use the immense power and prestige of the United States in the Middle East to push for a peaceful solution to the Arab-Israeli conflict. To do so, the United States proposed reconvening the international conference provided for by UN Security Council Resolution 338 of 1973, but which had been held in abeyance ever since.[14]

Against the backdrop of the seismic shift in the global geopolitical landscape brought about by the September 11, 2001 events, and the dismal failure of the Oslo Agreements to achieve the hoped-for "two-state solution" within the intended time frame, the collective Arab stance towards Israel evolved dramatically. Thus, in 2002, during their annual summit in Beirut, Lebanon, the twenty-two members of the Arab League proposed the Arab Peace Initiative (API), which called for normalizing relations with Israel on the condition of the establishment of a viable Palestinian state. The API was initially meant to be a framework to peacefully end the decades-old conflict. While that framework still remains intact today.

> The API has played a different function since the Arab Spring jolted the region into an intense zero-sum game between Saudi Arabia and Iran. From then on, Saudi official discourse treated the API as a focal point in the

---

14 Michael Fischbach, "Madrid and the Oslo Agreement, 1991–1993: Short-Lived Promises of a Negotiated Settlement," *Interactive Encyclopedia of Palestinian Question,* Institute for Palestine Studies, September 13, 2023.

Kingdom's pragmatic policy toward Israel. It gained a simultaneous function that allowed the Saudis to express their willingness for cooperation, yet still distance themselves from such willingness by emphasizing the centrality of Palestinian rights.[15]

Later on, with successive bilateral (Israeli-Palestinian), regional, and international peace efforts failing and falling to the wayside, the API was eventually overshadowed, if not deemed clinically dead, when the United Arab Emirates (UAE), Bahrain, Morocco and Sudan—with regional political mastodon Saudi Arabia programmed to be next—signed normalization agreements with Israel in 2020 and 2021 within the framework of the Abraham Accords, without guarantees for Palestinian rights.

The UAE showed the way in this regard. On the pretext of stopping Israel's plan to annex parts of the West Bank in July 2020, Abu Dhabi engaged in negotiations with Tel Aviv to normalize relations, further encouraged by and "sweetened" with a U.S. offer to sell the wealthy pro-Western Emirate 50 F-35 combat jets—an offer that has not materialized so far, while hundreds of those highly technologically advanced fighter jets have been sold by Washington to its other allies around the world, starting, of course, with Israel.

The tiny and vulnerable kingdom of Bahrain, home to the U.S. Fifth Fleet, quickly followed suit. And in December 2020, in a joint declaration between the U.S., Morocco, and Israel, Rabat and Tel Aviv agreed to normalize relations, and as a "reward" to the Alawite monarchy, President Donald Trump, having lost the re-election one month earlier, and just a few days before he left office, decided unilaterally through a tweet[16] that the U.S. recognizes Morocco's sovereignty over the illegally occupied territory of Western Sahara, thus enacting one of the most shocking U-turns in American foreign policy.[17]

As for the internally tormented and externally fragilized Sudan, it was, in the same month of December, removed from Washington's

---

15 Aziz Alghashian, "A Revived Arab Peace Initiative from Saudi Arabia Could Save the Middle East," *The Cairo Review of Global Affairs,* Winter 2024.

16 https://x.com/realDonaldTrump/status/1337067019385057290?ref_src=twsrc%5Etfw

17 To read the official "Proclamation on Recognizing The Sovereignty Of The Kingdom Of Morocco Over The Western Sahara," The White House, December 10, 2020: https://trumpwhitehouse.archives.gov/presidential-actions/proclamation-recognizing-sovereignty-kingdom-morocco-western-sahara/

sanctions list against "state sponsors of terrorism," and in January 2021, signed the Abraham Accords Declaration, but has yet to formally sign a bilateral agreement with Israel, deeply engulfed as it is in a devastating and unending civil war.

Finally, as is well-known today, the prospect of the signing of a groundbreaking Saudi-Israeli agreement within the same framework was only thwarted by the events of October 7, 2023 led by Palestinian Resistance movements, to the great dismay of the "Arab normalizers" and their Western backers and protectors.

Less than two months before he died, the famous statesman and veteran of American diplomacy, Henry Kissinger, did an interview[18]— the last he would ever do. In it, he said the two-state solution to the Israeli-Palestinian conflict was no longer viable and that it "doesn't guarantee that what we saw in the last weeks [the 7th of October attacks] won't happen again." He added: "I believe the West Bank should be put under Jordanian control rather than aim for a two-state solution which leaves one of the two territories determined to overthrow Israel."

On July 18, 2024, the Knesset put the final nail in the coffin of the two-state solution. Israel's parliament passed a resolution that overwhelmingly and firmly opposed the establishment of a Palestinian state. Such a state in the heart of the Land of Israel, the motion says, "will pose an existential danger to the State of Israel and its citizens, perpetuate the Israeli-Palestinian conflict and destabilize the region," and "Promoting the idea of a Palestinian state at this time will be a reward for terrorism and will only encourage Hamas and its supporters to see this as a victory, thanks to the massacre of October 7, 2023, and a prelude to the takeover of jihadist Islam in the Middle East."

The resolution was co-sponsored by parties in Netanyahu's coalition together with right-wing parties from the opposition. It passed with 68 votes in favor, and only 9 lawmakers, all from the Arab-majority Ra'am and Hadash-Ta'al parties, voted against it.

Slamming the passing of this resolution and summing up what that move really means in practice, Mustafa Barghouti, the Secretary-General of the Palestinian National Initiative, highlighted the fact that "No Zionist party from both the government and the opposition voted against the

---

18 Rolf Dobelli, "Henry Kissinger's (Maybe) Last Interview: Drop the 2-State Solution," *Politico,* February 12, 2023.

resolution,"[19] which "represents a rejection of peace with Palestinians and an official declaration of the death of [the] Oslo agreement."

Similarly, senior Palestinian Authority official Hussein al-Sheikh condemned the resolution, saying the Knesset's rejection "confirms the racism of the occupying state and its disregard for international law and international legitimacy, and its insistence on the approach and policy of perpetuating the occupation forever."

For his part, United Nations Secretary-general António Guterres declared that "Recent developments are driving a stake through the heart of any prospect for a two-state solution ... We must change course. All settlement activity must cease immediately," adding that the settlements were a flagrant violation of international law and an obstacle to peace with Palestinians.

The Case for the Only durable Solution: One Democratic State from the River to the Sea

Bad Students of History

General Vo Nguyen Giap, the great military strategist[20] and political leader who led Vietnamese communist forces to victories in successive wars against Japan, France,[21] South Vietnam and the United States, once famously said:

> The imperialists are bad students. Yes. We taught them
> the right lessons, didn't we? But they learn the lessons
> badly, although they are lessons of historical signifi-
> cance: the debacle in Algeria, in Cuba—the stinging
> debacle in Vietnam. Well, these are events that herald
> and have contributed to the collapse of colonialism

19 Mustafa Barghouti was likely referring to the lawmakers from opposition Leader Yair Lapid's center-left Yesh Atid and the more left-leaning Labor Party, who left the plenum to avoid backing the measure, even though they had previously spoken in favor of a two-state solution.

20 Giap was also the author of *People's War, People's Army: the Viet Cong Insurrection Manual for Underdeveloped Countries,* a manual of guerrilla warfare based on his own experience, published in 1961. To download the book as reproduced by the U.S. Armed Services Technical Information Agency: https://apps.dtic.mil/sti/tr/pdf/AD0292744.pdf

21 Especially the decisive battle of Dien Bien Phu on May 7, 1945, which—together with the Algerian War of Liberation of 1954–1962—brought the French colonialist regime to an end.

and also to the inevitable collapse of neocolonialism. However, these students, bad students, want to repeat grades.[22]

Later on, in the same vein, Gideon Rose argued in a penetrating look at American wars over the last century[23] that time and again American presidents and their advisers have focused more on beating up the enemy than on the need for careful postwar planning. Such a phenomenon, which challenges the Clausewitzian dictum that war is simply a continuation of political intercourse with the addition of other means,[24] led them to blindly stumble into turmoil during the final stages of almost each and every major conflict from World War I to Iraq and Afghanistan.

The latter experiences were the most prominent examples of this phenomenon, not an exception to the rule. As U.S. Central Command (CENTCOM) commander Tommy Franks put it to the deputy Secretary of Defense on the eve of the second Iraq war, "you pay attention to the day after, I'll pay attention to the day of."[25] In reality, though, history will recall that nothing of the sort has come about.

Likewise, after its year-long genocidal war on Gaza—which now threatens to become a full-scale regional conflict, or worse, after Netanyahu's decision to assassinate Hezbollah leader Hassan Nasrallah[26] and wreak havoc on Lebanon, a country Israel hopes to colonize as well, as part of its messianic or irredentist Zionist folly of an "Eretz Yisrael Hoshlema" (Greater Israel)[27]—Israel finds itself in the ex-

---

22 Watch related video: https://x.com/nxt888/status/1691124304300363777

23 Gideon Rose, *How Wars End: Why We Always Fight the Last Battle, A History of American Intervention from World War I to Afghanistan* (New York: Simon & Schuster, 2010).

24 See Amir Nour, "Towards Palestine's Independence Despite the Doom and Gloom." https://www.globalresearch.ca/war-gaza-towards-palestine-independence-despite-doom-gloom/5848373

25 Tommy Frank with Malcolm McConnell, *American Soldier* (New York: HarperCollins, 2004).

26 Ben Norton, "Hezbollah leader Nasralllah defeated ISIS, protected Lebanon's Christians, fought Israeli colonialism," *Geopolitical Economy Report,* September 29, 2024. https://youtu.be/sxYAn-Ci4jE?si=5EXXhLMfwB58egTa&sfnsn=wa

27 The concept of "Greater Israel" has been a cornerstone in the ideological and strategic development of the Zionist movement. This idea envisions a Jewish state extending far beyond its modern borders, rooted in biblical descriptions and historical claims ("On that day the LORD made a covenant with Abram and said 'To your descendants I give this land, from the Wadi [or river] of Egypt to the

act same above-mentioned predicament as America, its closest ally, supplier of deadly arms, and unconditional diplomatic shielder. As Gideon Rose rightly pointed out, "lessons from previous wars can serve as cognitive blinders, narrowing the way officials think about the situations they face, and power can be a trap, underwriting hubris and folly." In 2001, Benjamin Netanyahu said: "We must beat them up, not once but repeatedly, beat them up so it hurts so badly, until it's unbearable."[28]

---

great river, the Euphrates"; and "Every place on which the sole of your foot treads shall be yours. Your territory shall be from the wilderness to the Lebanon and from the River, the river Euphrates, to the western sea." Source: *Bible Gateway,* Genesis 15:18 and Deuteronomy 11:24). It stretches from the "River of Egypt [the Nile] to the Perat River [the Euphrates]," thus including parts of Egypt, modern-day Israel, the West Bank, East Jerusalem, Gaza Strip, Lebanon, Jordan, Syria, and Iraq. Central to this vision are three influential figures: Theodor Herzl, Rabbi Fischmann, and Oded Yinon. Herzl, the father of modern political Zionism, laid the groundwork with his pragmatic and diplomatic efforts. Rabbi Fischmann expanded on Herzl's vision, emphasizing the religious and historical significance of the Promised Land. Oded Yinon introduced a strategic dimension, proposing a plan to secure Israel's dominance through the fragmentation of neighboring states. Together, their visions and strategies have profoundly shaped Israeli policy and regional dynamics. For further information on this subject, read:
- Douglas C. Youvan, "Herzl, Fischmann and Yinon: The Greater Israel." https://www.researchgate.net/publication/382108240_Herzl_Fischmann_and_Yinon_The_Greater_Israel
- Amir Nour, "Quand Oded Yinon s'allie avec Sykes-Picot le résultat c'est le chaos" (When Oded Yinon Allies with Sykes-Picot, the Result Is Chaos). https://algerienetwork.com/blog/quand-oded-yinon-sallie-avec-sykes-picot-le-resultat-cest-le-chaos-when-oded-yinon-allies-with-sykes-picot-the-result-is-chaos/
- Oded Yinon, "A Strategy for Israel in the Nineteen Eighties." https://archive.org/details/astrategyforisraelintheninteeneighties
- Anshel Pfeffer, "'Lebanon, Part of the Promised Land': Israel's Messianic Right Wing Targets New Territory for Settlements," *Haaretz,* June 18, 2024.
- Mark Fish, "Is Lebanon part of Israel's Promised territory?," *The Jerusalem Post,* September 25, 2024. The concluding paragraph of this article reads: "If one looks at a map, they will be astounded by how far north this river [Euphrates] extends and how vast the Land of Israel truly is. While we may not be able to reclaim all of it in our time, Hashem will surely return it to us soon." This article was quickly taken down, but is luckily archived: https://archive.ph/2024.09.29-103032/https://www.jpost.com/judaism/article-821680#selection-753.448-753.481
- Jerusalem Post staff, "Israeli Rabbi calls for Israel to conquer Lebanon and settle it," *The Jerusalem Post,* September 25, 2024.

28 In a video filmed in 2001, in which he makes a series of unguarded admissions about his first period as prime minister, from 1996 to 1999. It follows

Precisely because the notion of "war-as-combat" is deeply ingrained in the thinking of both American and Israeli militaries and peoples at large, and the essential political aspects of the war are often neglected, if not lost in the fog of war, it is more than doubtful that current American and Israeli policymakers think clearly about what they are doing today and how to ward off a looming doom; and notwithstanding the fact that their two countries are the strongest powers in the world and in the Middle East region respectively, they will likely stumble miserably once again, and will therefore have nobody to blame but themselves for failing to understand that there's no military solution to the Israeli-Palestinian conflict. Only a political settlement—one characteristically off the beaten track or once discarded as illusory or too radical—can achieve this desired goal.

Israel/Palestine: One State or Two States?

So, if the two-state solution proposed by the Oslo Accords has failed and seems more remote than ever, if not definitely dead thirty years on, isn't it about time to consider alternatives to the prevailing untenable status quo, or even worse, to endless war? All the more so, since the illusion that the conflict can be ignored or "managed" has been shattered in a resounding manner in October 2023. The current bout of fighting is forcing the U.S., the EU and regional powers to reassess their old approaches and reappraise the wrong and costly assumption that they can safely ignore the conflict.

Nowadays, it appears that the old/new idea of a "one-state" between the Mediterranean Sea and the Jordan River—a democratic state, with full and equal rights for the populations residing in Israel, East Jerusalem, the West Bank, and the Gaza Strip, as citizens—is the best workable option and, most importantly, the only durable solution to an intractable conflict that has lasted too long and cost too much blood and treasure.

---

him during a visit to the West Bank settlement of Ofra to meet with the family of a man killed in a Palestinian shooting, as described in 2010 by the London-based, Middle East-focused outlet *The National:* "The film was shot, apparently without Mr. Netanyahu's knowledge, nine years ago, when the government of Ariel Sharon had started reinvading the main cities of the West Bank to crush Palestinian resistance in the early stages of the second intifada. At the time Mr. Netanyahu had taken a short break from politics but was soon to join Mr. Sharon's government as finance minister." To watch the video: https://www.youtube.com/watch?v=mvqCWvi-nFo&t=63s

After all, if we properly take stock of past experiences, can't we justifiably ask what if self-determination for both Palestinians and Israelis is not necessarily based on territory but on citizen's rights?

This idea of a single state is not new. Back in 1930, rabbi, scholar and political activist Judah Leon Magnes already wrote an essay[29] in which, in contradistinction to the then Zionist leadership, he expressed his strong preference for the establishment of a bi-national, Jewish and Arab state through an agreement with Palestine's Arab population.[30] And when the Peel Commission made its 1937 recommendations about partition and population transfer for Palestine, Magnes sounded the alarm by saying:

> With the permission of the Arabs we will be able to receive hundreds of thousands of persecuted Jews in Arab lands ... Without the permission of the Arabs even the four hundred thousand [Jews] that now are in Palestine will remain in danger, in spite of the temporary protection of British bayonets. With partition a new Balkan is made.[31]

And in an article in *Foreign Affairs* magazine in January 1942, he suggested a joint British-American initiative to prevent the division of mandatory Palestine. This move was followed, pursuant to the Biltmore Conference,[32] by the foundation—with Henrietta Szold[33]—of a small bi-nationalist party called "Ihud" (Unity). In 1946, Magnes again opposed

---

29 Judah Leon Magnes, "Like All the Nations?," *Weiss Press,* 1930.

30 Ben Reiff, "Mandate 100, 'Neither a Jewish State nor an Arab State': How Zionist Bi-Nationalism Tried and Failed to Change the Face of the Middle East," *Fathom Journal,* April 2020.

31 Quoted in the *New York Times,* July 18, 1937.

32 The Biltmore Conference was called by the *Extraordinary Zionist Conference,* and was held from May 6 to May 11, 1942 in New York. Due to the war, no Zionist Congress could be held that year. *The Extraordinary Zionist Conference* was thus called to serve a similar purpose of forming Zionist policy. The joint statement issued at the end of the session was known as the Biltmore Program. It reiterated Zionist demands for unrestricted Jewish immigration to Palestine and that Palestine should serve as a Jewish Commonwealth (Source: *Jewish Virtual Library*).

33 Henrietta Szold was an essayist, editor, social and communal worker, and Zionist organizer. In 1912, she created "Hadassah," the Women's Zionist Organization of America, which later became the largest and most powerful Zionist group of the United States.

the partition plan before the Anglo-American Committee of Inquiry in Jerusalem and submitted 11 objections to partition to the United Nations Special Committee on Palestine.[34] Finally, by mid-1948, when the conflict between the Jews and Arabs of Palestine was in full swing, Magnes expressed the hope that if a Jewish state were declared, the United States would impose economic sanctions; and also supported a 1948 U.S. trusteeship proposal, in which the UN would freeze the partition decision and force both sides into a trusteeship with a temporary government ruling Palestine, until conditions suited another arrangement. During the 1948 War, he lobbied for an armistice and proposed a plan for a federation between Israel and a Palestinian state, which he called the "United States of Palestine," under which the two states would be independent, but operate joint foreign and defense policies, with Jerusalem as the shared capital. Magnes predicted that even if a Jewish state was established and defeated the Arabs, it would experience a never-ending series of wars with the Arabs.[35]

The notion of a one state in all of historic Palestine was espoused by Palestine Liberation Organization (PLO) in its original charter[36] in 1964, which called for the establishment of a single, democratic, and secular state for Jews, Muslims and Christians. The PLO only abandoned the idea in the context of the diplomatic negotiations within the framework of the Oslo Accords, hence fundamentally swinging its ideological compass and reorienting its political struggle and efforts toward the realization of the two-state path to peace.

With the benefit of hindsight, one can say that the PLO's historic embrace of Oslo was a huge sacrifice, incommensurate with the petty initial "rewards" of a peace process which eventually led nowhere but to an equally historic, and furthermore tragic, impasse.

As the peace process started to show signs of fraying at the edges in the late 1990s, an increasing number of analysts started to suggest

---

34 Justus D. Doenecke, "Principle and Expediency: The State Department and Palestine, 1948," *Journal of Libertarian Studies,* 1978.

35 Ofri Ilany, "1948 Diaries: Saving the Jews from Themselves," *Haaretz,* May 5, 2008.

36 The first version of the "Palestinian National Charter" was adopted on May 28, 1964. It was then extensively amended, with the addition of seven articles in 1968. And in April 1996, many of its articles which were deemed inconsistent with the Oslo accords were wholly or partially nullified, as is stated in the following letter from the Palestinian Authority President Yasser Arafat to the Israeli Prime minister Shimon Peres. http://www.pna.gov.ps/Government/gov/The_Amendment_of_the_Palestinian_National_Charter.asp

acknowledging a "one-state reality"[37]—an ambiguous reference to the continued entanglement of Israelis and Palestinians on the ground—as the starting point for negotiating a workable solution.

Thus, Palestinian-American academic Edward Said wrote: "It is time to question whether the entire process begun in Oslo in 1993 is the right instrument for bringing peace between Palestinians and Israelis. It is my view that ... real peace can come only with a binational Israeli-Palestinian state."[38]

In 2003, as referred to earlier,[39] Tony Judt stated that:

> The time has come to think the unthinkable. The two-state solution—the core of the Oslo process and the present "road map"—is probably already doomed. With every passing year we are postponing an inevitable, harder choice that only the far right and the far left have so far acknowledged, each for its own reasons. The true alternative facing the Middle East in coming years will be between an ethnically cleansed Greater Israel and a single, integrated, binational state of Jews and Arabs, Israelis and Palestinians.

In the same year, Ari Shavit wrote an insightful article[40] in which he quoted two popular Israeli figures. Meron Benvenisti was one of them. Deputy mayor of Jerusalem from 1971 to 1978, a columnist and author, Benvenisti said: "We are living in a binational reality, and it is a permanent given. What we have to do is adapt our thinking and our concepts to this reality."

> The conclusion is that the seemingly rational solution of two states for two nations can't work here. The model of a division into two nation-states is inapplicable. It doesn't reflect the depth of the conflict and doesn't sit

---

37 David Remnik, "The One-State Reality," *The New Yorker,* November 10, 2014.

38 Edward Said, "The One-State Solution," *The New York Times Magazine,* January 10, 1999.

39 See Amir Nour, "The Twilight of the Settler Colonialist Project in Palestine," *GlobalResearch,* August 17, 2024.

40 Ari Shavit, "Cry, the beloved two-state solution," *Haaretz,* August 6, 2003.

with the scale of the entanglement that exists in large parts of the country. You can erect all the walls in the world here but you won't be able to overcome the fact that there is only one aquifer here and the same air and that all the streams run into the same sea. You won't be able to overcome the fact that this country will not tolerate a border in its midst.

The other figure was Haim Hanegbi, a journalist for the Israeli daily *Ma'ariv*. He argued that if Israel remains a colonialist state in its character, it will not survive. Maybe, he added, "in the end we have to create a new, binational Israel, just as a new, multiracial South Africa was created."

Prof. Joel Kovel,[41] who approaches the subject from an Israeli perspective, argued that "Israel is an incorrigible human rights offender because, by discriminating against Arabs, it is guilty of state-sponsored racism." Considering that Zionism and democracy are essentially incompatible, Kovel concludes that a two-state solution is fundamentally hopeless as it concedes too much to the regressive forces of nationalism, wherein lie the roots of continued conflict, and believes therefore that the best hope for peace in Israel is to return to the idea of a one-state solution, where Jews and Palestinians can co-exist in a secular democracy.

Speaking presciently about the future of Palestine[42] back in 2010, John Mearsheimer said:

The story I will tell is straightforward. Contrary to the wishes of the Obama administration and most Americans—to include many American Jews—Israel is not going to allow the Palestinians to have a viable state of their own in Gaza and the West Bank. Regrettably, the two-state solution is now a fantasy. Instead, those territories will be incorporated into a "Greater Israel," which will be an apartheid state bearing a marked resemblance to white-ruled South Africa. Nevertheless, a Jewish apartheid state is not politically

41 Joel Kovel, *Overcoming Zionism: Creating a Single Democratic State in Israel/Palestine* (Pluto Press, New York, 2007).

42 John J. Mearsheimer, "The Future of Palestine: Righteous Jews vs. New Afrikaners," at Palestine Center, Washington, D.C., April 29, 2010.

viable over the long term. In the end, it will become a democratic bi-national state, whose politics will be dominated by its Palestinian citizens. In other words, it will cease being a Jewish state, which will mean the end of the Zionist dream.

In sum,

there are great dangers ahead for the Palestinians, who will continue to suffer terribly at the hands of the Israelis for some years to come. But it does look like the Palestinians will eventually get their own state, mainly because Israel seems bent on self-destruction.

Even the Israeli strategic analyst Yossi Alpher, who does not agree with the one-state option, noted that: "By 2017, Israel and Palestine were slowly sliding down a slippery slope towards a single political entity."[43]

Making or Breaking Hope for Peace in the City of Peace

It is against this bleak backdrop that, on March 1, 2018, a new initiative based on the old idea emerged when the "One-State Foundation" was launched.[44] The initiative holds:

first, that the current situation in Palestine and Israel is untenable; second, that the negotiating process that emanated from the Madrid Peace Conference and Oslo Accords on the basis of a two-state solution has reached a dead end as the final status issues degraded to become effectively non-negotiable; third, that this obstructs the realization of the hopes and aspirations of the Palestinian and Israeli peoples; fourth, that the time has come to rethink the question in its entirety; and, fifth, that any new thinking has to reflect realities on the ground and, above all, the reality that more than

43 Yossi Alpher, "Two States or One? Reappraising the Israeli-Palestinian Impasse," The Carnegie Endowment for International Peace, September 18, 2018.

44 To read the Democratic State Manifesto: https://onestatecampaign.org/all/en-manifesto/

fifty years after the Israeli occupation of the whole of
Palestine, a form of unity over political, economic,
and security matters already exists.[45]

In recent years, and particularly since the resurgence of the polem-
ical issue of West Bank annexation, beginning in the fall of 2019, a substantial debate over the One-State reality has raged between proponents
of the two-state "international consensus" and those of the one-state
"alternative," both among and between Palestinians and Israelis, and on
the global stage. In the West, the one-state alternative has been boosted
over the years by quite knowledgeable academics and militants such
as Edward Said, Tony Judt, John Mearsheimer, Ian Lustick, Virginia
Tilley, Ilan Pappé, Avi Shlaim, Shlomo Sand, and Ali Abunimah, the
Palestinian-American co-founder of Electronic Intifada.

A significant milestone in this regard was registered when four
well-known professors published an article in *Foreign Affairs* magazine
entitled "Israel's One-State Reality."[46] In this essay, the authors argue
that the two-state solution is dead because there is already a one-state
reality, no matter what anyone thinks. In other words, between the
Mediterranean Sea and the Jordan River, only one state, namely Israel,
controls the entry and exit of people and goods, oversees security, and
has the capacity to impose its decisions, laws, and policies on millions
of people without their consent. A one-state reality, the academics go on
to say, could, in principle, be based on democratic rule and equal citizenship, but such an arrangement is not on offer at the moment. Forced
to choose between Israel's Jewish identity and liberal democracy, Israel
has chosen the former; it has locked in a system of Jewish supremacy,
wherein non-Jews are structurally discriminated against or excluded in
a tiered scheme: some non-Jews have most of, but not all, the rights that
Jews have, while most non-Jews live under severe segregation, separation, and domination. They, therefore, see no real prospect of negotiating
a Palestinian state, and are of the opinion that the United States should
acknowledge this reality, denounce it, impose sanctions on Israel, while
putting an end to its efforts against the BDS movement and refraining

45 Abdel Monem Said Aly, "The Case for the One-State Solution," *The Cairo Review of Global Affairs,* Winter 2019.
46 Michael Barnett, Nathan Brown, Marc Lynch, and Shibley Telhami, "Israel's One-State Reality: It's Time to Give Up on the Two-State Solution," *Foreign Affairs,* May/June 2023.

from leading those aiming at normalization of relations between Israel and its Arab neighbors.

Reacting furiously to this essay, well-known pro-Zionist Elliot Abrams published an article,[47] which he concluded by saying that by publishing this article, *Foreign Affairs* has "served only one useful purpose: to show us the state of academia. There, the view that one Jewish state is one too many is widely and indeed increasingly popular," and that those who believe otherwise are "well-advised" to learn from this article that "the goal of many of today's academic critics is not to reform the state of Israel. The goal is to eliminate it."

Asked by his *Al-Jazeera* interviewer[48] to give his opinion about this debate, and on his own preferred solution, six months before the outburst of the ongoing war on Gaza, Noam Chomsky indicated that there was something wrong with that debate, because it's omitting a third alternative, namely the one that is being systematically implemented by Israel, ever since 1969 or so: the creation of a "Greater Israel," which will take over. If you want to talk about long-term outcomes, he added,

> you can't just talk about one state and two states. You have to talk about what's happening, "Greater Israel." I understand the reasoning of the one-state advocates, but I think . . . it's almost inconceivable that Israel will ever agree to destroy itself and become a Jewish minority population in a Palestinian-dominated state, which is what the demography indicates. And there's no international support for it. Nothing.

So, his own personal feeling is that the real options are "Greater Israel," or move towards some kind of two-state arrangement. "It's often claimed," he concluded, "that that's now impossible because of the enormous settlement project. Maybe, maybe not. I think if the United States insists, decides to join the rest of the world in supporting some kind of two-state settlement, not just rhetorically, but in practice, Israel will be faced with a very serious decision."

---

47 Elliot Abrams, "As Israel Turns 75, 'Foreign Affairs' Publishes a Call to Eliminate It," Council on Foreign Relations, May 9, 2023.

48 Eliyahu Freedman, "Q&A: Noam Chomsky on Palestine, Israel and the state of the world," *Al-Jazeera Media Network*, April 9, 2023.

As for Israeli historian Ilan Pappé, he sees signs that the ideological hold of Zionism is weakening, and a freer, more democratic Palestine may be possible, telling *Democracy Now!*:

> I think we are seeing processes, important processes, that are leading to the collapse of the Zionist project. Hopefully, the Palestinian national movement and anyone else involved in Israel and Palestine would be able to replace this apartheid state, this oppressive regime, with a democratic one for everyone who lives between the river and the sea and for all the Palestinians who were expelled from there since 1948 until today.

He added: "I am really hopeful that there will be a different kind of life for both Jews and Arabs between the river and the sea under a democratic, free Palestine."[49]

Although polls differ greatly on how Palestinians view the one-state solution, it seems that a half century of crushing Israeli occupation is convincing more and more people in Palestine that the one-state reality is an unbearable fact of everyday life that is not likely to change in the foreseeable future, hence pushing them to support bi-nationalism.

Abdel Monem Said Aly has probably summed up correctly what Palestinians and Israelis alike think about the idea when he said that Palestinians who oppose the idea of a one-state solution argue that a state based on full and equal citizenship between Arabs and Jews could never really exist and that a single state for both would merely be an extension of the current one in which, after seven decades, Israeli Arabs would remain second-class citizens. Indeed, the Palestinians have long resisted the Israeli concept of the single state, which, in the current de facto version, translates into occupation with apartheid on top of it. The Palestinians are also well aware that no Israeli government—let alone the current most far-right and racist one in the whole history of the "Jewish state"—would consider a binational alternative in which the Palestinians were in the majority.

On the other hand, Israeli opponents, who are more numerous, hold that the Zionist project was and remains the establishment of a state with a Jewish majority—something that could not be sustained given current

---

49 Edward Carver, "Israeli Scholar Sees Hope for Democratic Palestine 'To Replace This Apartheid State'," *Common Dreams,* May 21, 2024.

Palestinian population growth rates, which would reduce Jewish Israelis in the future to a minority status.

As a matter of fact, the feeling that another day of conflict will ultimately bring victory continues to prevail on both sides. Still, the many objections do not diminish the fact that the status quo and ongoing occupation create a volatile situation with all the conditions for uprisings, resistance, and at times full-scale war.

On account of the above, if the two-state alternative to the status quo is unreachable, then the one-state alternative could be laid out with solutions for the different objectors on both sides. This would involve a broad restructuring of the existing political system, whether beginning with the Israeli government's conferral of citizenship on Palestinian Arabs in the West Bank and the Gaza Strip or beginning with the creation of a new state altogether. Moreover, mechanisms such as subjecting legislation on vital or constitutional issues to a two-thirds majority vote, or to a minority veto, or some combinations thereof, have been floated to prevent a majoritarian state in which the demographic majority, whether Jewish or Arab, would govern unilaterally.

Some other proponents advocate a binational or consociational arrangement where a federation or confederation would jointly manage economic matters, security, and Jerusalem as a common capital, but maintain separate political structures for Israeli Jews and Palestinian Arabs on some matters of civil law.

While confederation reflects the existing realities of a multifaceted interdependence between the two sides, it also resolves the citizenship crux of the Israeli-Palestinian conflict: the Israelis would always have majority status in their own state and its security, and the Palestinians would have their state with a legitimate place in the Council of Jerusalem, which would be the capital of the confederation. Both the Israeli and Palestinian states would be in a position to interact with their Arab neighbors without animosity for Israel or dependency for the Palestinians. Both would have all symbols of the state from the flag to the seat in the UN, and above all their chosen identities along with the privileges of peace and space throughout historic Palestine.[50]

In the conclusion of her powerfully argued recent book,[51] Palestinian-born academic Ghada Karmi says that the tremendous

---

50 Abdel Monem Said Aly, "The Case for the One-State Solution," op. cit.
51 Ghada Karmi, *One State: The Only Democratic Future for Palestine-Israel* (London and Las Vegas: Pluto Press, 2023).

obstacles facing the "one democratic state solution" may be daunting to some of those who support it in theory, but the fact that something is difficult to realize does not make it any less the right thing to do; nor does the attainment of this solution hinge solely on the wishes of Israel and its supporters. Other factors, she believes, "though now unforeseen or thought improbable," could intervene and alter the situation dramatically. If and when they do, such events "will merely dictate the pace and timing of the one democratic state solution. But the concept itself must have been established long before, not as an immediately attainable goal perhaps, but as a vision, an aspiration and a belief in the ultimate humanity of Palestinians and Jews and all who wish them to prosper."

This "humanity" was precisely the subject of a groundbreaking book[52] in which Richard Forer said:

> The real enemy is not someone or something outside us. The real enemy is the unexamined mind that unconsciously projects its suffering onto the other and then blames or scapegoats the other for its suffering ... If defenders of Israel want to distinguish the source of conflict and find peace as much as they want to be right, they must inquire within. If they do, they will find that just as the real enemy is not someone or something outside us, the real conflict is not Israel versus the Palestinian people or Israel versus a hostile world. The real conflict is the fear of integrating the hard-to-believe but unmistakable reality of Israel's treatment of Palestinians with unquestioned loyalty to the Jewish state. One consideration recognizes Israel's dark side. The other denies it exists.

---

52 Richard Forer, *Wake Up and Reclaim Your Humanity: Essays on the Tragedy of Israel-Palestine* (MindStir Media, 2020). Boulder County, CO—The NYC Big Book Award recognized Forer as the winner in the Cultural and Social Issues category. His book tells the true story of a lifelong supporter of Israel who underwent a remarkable spiritual awakening in which he realized he was as much Muslim or Christian as Jew, and as much Palestinian as Israeli or American. Recognizing that endless conflict only leads to alienation from our true selves, Forer encourages readers to look at the documented history of the Israel-Palestine tragedy and get in touch with how they view and interpret that history. He also offers readers a path that leads to freedom from false beliefs, enemy images, and the illusion of identity to equal rights for all people and a just peace between Palestinians and Israelis.

All in all, if history is any guide—and it is indeed—we must retain its most overarching principle, which is highlighted in the epigraph: "Those who cannot remember the past are condemned to repeat it." And if we do remember history—and we must indeed—then the following key considerations should always be duly taken into account in any reflection or negotiation about peace in the Middle East. They all stand in opposition to partition and division of the Holy Land and point in the direction of one democratic state from the river to the sea as the only genuinely durable solution to the Israel-Palestine conflict.

Primo: There is no military solution to the conflict. Wars, uprisings and permanent political instability have been the distinctive features of the whole Middle East since WWI. And today, for the first time ever, we're witnessing the coming into the picture of a new and mighty regional power in a conflict which has so far involved only Arabs and Jews. Interestingly enough, Iran, a Muslim but non-Arab country, is where the oldest settlement of the Jewish diaspora has been dwelling since King Nebuchadnezzar took the inhabitants of Jerusalem into captivity in 587/6 BCE.

Secundo: In the aftermath of WWII, the world has seen an irresistible wave of decolonization that led to the emancipation of almost all former Western colonies. Israel was thus established against a historical trend of mass decolonization, thence constituting an equally historical anomaly.

Tertio: The only white settler colonies that have not been dismantled are those where the native populations have been effectively eliminated or demographically overwhelmed by foreign settlers (chiefly in the United States, Canada, Australia, and New Zealand). Israel, which is also a settler colony, clearly doesn't belong to this category of settlements. It is more like South Africa, Algeria, Rhodesia, Kenya, Angola, Mozambique, or Namibia, whose native population outnumbered the white settler population, and ended up gaining their independence.

Quarto: The Israel/Palestine problem has been created by Western powers—be it because of the dismemberment of the Ottoman Empire in the wake of WWI, the secret Sykes-Picot Accords of 1916, the failed British mandate for Palestine, the refusal to accept Jewish refugees fleeing Nazi Germany before, during, and after the Holocaust,[53] or the

---

53 Read, among others, David S. Wyman, *The Abandonment of the Jews: America and the Holocaust, 1941–1945* (New York: Pantheon Books, 1984); and Erin Blakemore, "A Ship of Jewish Refugees Was Refused U.S. Landing in

Western-sponsored and ill-advised 1947 UN partition resolution. It's then only fair and imperative that they should resolutely shoulder their moral and political responsibilities in the search and implementation of a fair solution, in the spirit of restorative justice. As for the rest of the "international community," it has consistently supported a two-state solution, as evidenced by the deliberations and positive votes in the United Nations General Assembly and other international fora.

Quinto: Throughout the ages, Arabs—who, like the Jews, are Semites and descendants of Prophet Abraham, hence equally legitimate heirs to the "Holy Land"[54]—have almost always provided protection and refuge to the Jews in Arab/Muslim lands. They have lived peacefully with one another as epitomized by the "Pact of Umar" of 638 AD, the "Golden age of Jewish culture" in Muslim-ruled Al-Andalus, Saladin's "Announcement" of 1187, the settlement of Jews in Arab/Muslim territories after the Reconquista in the 15th century, and their physical protection by Muslim rulers and individuals during WWII. But these Jews had not just tried to genocide them. Zionism ruined everything, as

---

1939. This Was Their Fate," *History.com*, June 4, 2019. For the period during and after the Holocaust:
- Read "The Origin of the Palestine-Israel Conflict Zionism and the Holocaust," *Washington Report on Middle East Affairs*, March 15, 2015;
- Read about the *Évian Conference* convened July 6–15, 1938 at Évian-les-Bains, France, to address the problem of German and Austrian Jewish refugees wishing to flee persecution by Nazi Germany. It was the initiative of U.S. President Franklin D. Roosevelt, and agreed upon by Western European countries. The Roosevelt Plan suggested to take in 100% of Jewish Holocaust survivors. However, the World Zionist Organization refused to participate in the Conference, and other Zionist organizations, including in the U.S., as well as David Ben-Gurion himself, vehemently opposed it, fearing that resettlement of Jews in other states would reduce the number available for Palestine.

54 Read in this regard, Naomi Wolf, "On the meaning of 'God has given us the land'," Facebook, July 25, 2014.

recounted by Orit Bashkin,[55] Michael Warchawski,[56] and Avi Shlaim.[57] It is therefore in Israelis vital and vested interest to understand that if they are to be accepted, once again, in the Arab world, they have to belong to it by integrating in it at all levels. Michael Warchawski was spot on when he said that "I believe that Israel will only be able to be at peace with the Arab world, to create relations of coexistence and neighborliness when it accepts the geopolitical reality that it is situated at the heart of the Arab world...We have made the choice to settle in the Arab world and we must assume this choice and learn to be part of it, even if it takes time."[58]

---

55 Orit Bashkin, *New Babylonians: A History of Jews in Modern Iraq* (Stanford University Press, 2012). In this elegantly written chronicle of the last years of the Jewish presence in Iraq, viewed mostly through the writings of Jewish intellectuals in Iraq at the time and later in Israel, and through interviews with them, Bashkin says that the relatively numerous Iraqi Jewish community was, for the most part, well integrated into Iraqi society, and many of its members consciously identified with Arabic culture, language, and literature as well as with aspects of Arab nationalism and anti-imperialism.

56 Michael Warchawski, "Ils ont oublié ce que c'est qu'être Juif..." (They have forgotten what it is to be Jewish...), *Le Peuple Breton,* December 21, 2017. In this article Warchawski argues that "The Crusades, the Inquisition, the Dreyfus Affair and the Nazi Judeocide were not the work of Muslim culture, and in Arab countries the Jewish minority experienced nothing similar...The genocide of the Jews of Europe is 100% 'made in Europe,' the product of nearly two millennia of Christian civilization. The so-called 'Judeo-Christian civilization' is a racist mystification, and as Jeannette Mandouze, my extraordinary classics teacher and courageous anti-Nazi resistance fighter, used to say, a hyphen often excludes a third party: Judeo-Christian excludes Muslims from the so-called 'civilization.' Now, the link between Judeo and Christian, what has it been made of for nearly two thousand years? Of blood. If we want to talk about a civilization in which the Jews were an essential and legitimate component, let's talk about the four centuries of Andalusia, the summit of medieval Western civilization, or the Iraqi civilization until Zionism came to rot Jewish-Muslim relations in this country.... This has nothing to do with Jewish existence in Europe, where moments of calm and relative harmony are the exception and not the rule, and this continued until the twentieth century."

57 Avi Shlaim, *Three Worlds: Memoirs of an Arab-Jew* (Oneworld Publications, 2023). In this book, Avi Shlaim tells the story of his family's idyllic existence in 1940s Iraq and also claims to possess "undeniable proof of Zionist involvement in terrorist attacks" targeting Jewish sites in Baghdad. He argues that these attacks were orchestrated by the Zionist underground within the country, with the aim of pressuring the hesitant Jewish community to participate in the "Aliyah" (Jewish emigration) to the newly established state of Israel.

58 Dimitri Nicolaidis, Anne Le Strat, and Hugues Jallon, «Dépasser le sionisme? Débat avec Ilan Greilsammer et Michel Warschawski» (Going Beyond Zionism? Debate with Ilan Greilsammer and Michel Warschawski),

Sexto: Jerusalem is considered a "holy city" by all three monotheistic religions and frightening eschatological narratives and announcements about it are also present in all three of them. Fortunately, there is a growing number of religious groups[59] and organizations promoting peace through integration in Israel/Palestine. One of them is "Christians for a Free Palestine."[60]

Perhaps the best and most candid contribution to the debate on the One-State solution is the one made by Shlomo Sand.[61] The Austrian-born (to Polish Jewish survivors of the Holocaust) Israeli Emeritus Professor of History at Tel Aviv University published a book in French in January 2024, translated as *Two Peoples for One State? Rereading the History of Zionism*. Although the book was written before October 7, the professor later told Middle East Eye[62] he would not have "changed a theoretical line" if he had published it after the Hamas-led attack on Israel and the subsequent war on Gaza. "Perhaps I would have specified that 7 October is a confirmation of my fears," he clarified. Sand had this to say about the One-State solution: "We can only move towards a political organization of the two peoples in a federation or confederation. Otherwise, there will

---

Mouvements no. 3–4, 2004. To read the document: file:///C:/Users/USER/Downloads/depasser-le-sionisme.pdf

59 See Roger Copple, "Christians, Muslims, and Jews for a Secular One-State Solution in Palestine-Israel," The International Movement for a Just World (JUST), May 28, 2024.

60 They present themselves as "Christians mobilizing against the weaponization of our theology and our tax dollars by Christian Zionists to perpetrate the genocide of the Palestinian people." Christians, they say, "have a responsibility to use our voices as powerfully as possible for the cause of peace and justice."

61 Shlomo Sand is also the author of the best-seller book in English *The Invention of the Jewish People* (Verso, 2009), originally published in Hebrew (Resling, 2008) as *Matai ve'eich humtsa ha'am hayehudi?* (When and How Was the Jewish People Invented?). This book has generated a heated controversy, not least because, according to Sand's critics, it presents "dubious theories" regarding Jewish identity as historical facts. One such provocative theory espoused by Sand is the hypothesis that Ashkenazi Jews are descended from Khazars, who purportedly converted to Judaism in the early Middle Ages. Khazars are a multi-ethnic conglomerate of mostly Turkic peoples who formed a semi-nomadic khanate in and around the northern and central Caucasus and the Pontic–Caspian steppe. The hypothesis also postulated that after the collapse of their empire, the Khazars fled to Eastern Europe and made up a large part of the Jews there. (Source: Wikipedia)

62 Hassina Mechaï, "Israeli academic Shlomo Sand: 'Jews and Palestinians will have to live together'," *Middle East Eye,* August 22, 2024.

always be more disasters like 7 October and its consequences in Gaza," and he further cautioned: "Before reaching this historic compromise between the two peoples, we will experience other disasters that will make this political solution indispensable."

In a previous interview[63] Sand answered the question "You are no longer in favor of the two-state solution?" by saying:

> Eight hundred and fifty thousand Israelis, including six ministers, live in the West Bank, and these people will not be torn from the place where they live. Two million Arabs are integrated into Israel. I do not see how we can be separated. I am in favor of a kind of federation such as that advocated by Menachem Begin. People on the left bristle at the name of Begin, who is less of an extremist than Netanyahu! In his speech to the Knesset in 1977, he declared that Israel, in order not to become Rhodesia (which practiced radical apartheid), had to integrate the Arabs of Judea, Samaria and Gaza, offering them the possibility of acquiring Israeli nationality, and even land in Israel. He did not aim for a binational state, but a democratic one, which would lead to an "original cultural mix."

The proposal has sparked fear among the Israeli right and rejection from the left. He concluded the interview by declaring:

> I am not "for" a binational state, I say that we have no other solution. There is no future here for my grandchildren without the Palestinians. So I am for a federation, a confederation, whatever ... We must recognize the tragedy of 1948, and partially correct the injustice suffered. It is a painful process but we have no choice.

---

63 Vincent Remy, "Shlomo Sand, historien israélien: 'Je ne suis pas "pour" un État binational mais on n'a pas d'autre solution" ("Shlomo Sand, Israeli historian: 'I am not "for" a binational state but we have no other solution'"), *Télérama,* January 5, 2024.

CHAPTER EIGHT

A NEW GLOBAL ORDER IN THE MAKING?

"For the Romans I set no boundaries of time and space;
I have granted them empire without end."
—PUBLIUS VERGILIUS MARO[1]

"If the United Nations once admits that international disputes
can be settled by using force, then we will have destroyed the
foundation of the organization and our best hope of establishing a
world order."
—DWIGHT D. EISENHOWER

In the Beginning Was Westphalia

In my abovementioned book, which I wrote in the wake of the 2014 Gaza war, also known as Operation Protective Edge, I posited that:

- The end of the Cold War had the effect of making two major international realities more evident: the consecration of the position of the United States of America as the dominant world power, due to its military, political, economic and technological weight; and the shift of

---

1 Publius Vergilius Maro, usually called Virgil or Vergil in English, was an ancient Roman poet of the Augustan period. He composed three of the most famous poems in Latin literature: the *Eclogues* (or *Bucolics*), the *Georgics,* and the epic *Aeneid.* The 12-book Latin poem tells the story of Aeneas, son of the goddess Venus, a royal refugee from war-torn Troy, and a legendary ancestor of the emperor, as he is driven by fate to Italy, where he is to settle and where, centuries later, his descendant Romulus is to build Rome. The epigraph, where Jupiter addresses the Romans, is from the first book: Aeneid I, 278–79, of the poem.

the global economic and commercial center of gravity from the Old Continent to the Pacific region as a result, in particular, of the prodigious development achieved by the Chinese dragon. And despite its relative decline caused by the economic and financial crisis of 2007/2008, the United States, being precisely a nation that is both Atlantic and Indo-Pacific, will continue to play a leading role during the 21st century.

- The vicissitudes of the "Arab Spring," the politico-military maneuvers in the East and South China Sea, and the developments of the Ukrainian crisis, far from constituting epiphenomena of turbulent current affairs, are in fact the most telling manifestations of a geostrategic upheaval in a globalized world entering a phase of accelerated reconfiguration. Obviously, this development, which is gradually taking the form of a multipolar world, is not to the taste of those in favor of the perpetuation of Western domination of the world, more than ever symbolized by the power of the American leader.

- The history of the 21st century, particularly its first half, seems to revolve around two contradictory struggles. The first will consist of attempts by secondary powers to form coalitions to try to contain the hegemonism of the United States. The second will encompass preventive actions on the part of this country aimed at preventing the formation of such coalitions that could endanger its strategic interests in the world.

- Regardless of the real sponsors of September 11 attacks and their true motives, this historic event provided the United States with the opportunity to implement its strategy of domination over a Muslim world considered—despite its present state of asthenia—as a potential adversary that must be continually weakened, while exploiting its significant natural resources, especially its energy. Since the invasions of Afghanistan in 2001 and Iraq in 2003, a new "Sykes-Picot" seems to be taking shape in the region. But while the secret Franco-British agreements of 1916 aimed to "facilitate the creation of a State or a Confederation of Arab States," the current process aims to dismantle existing States. This strategy of "mass disintegration" would allow the United States to achieve a triple objective: guaranteeing the preservation of its strategic interests in the region; strengthening the position of its Israeli ally, thereby ensuring its survival as a Jewish state; and redirecting most of U.S. efforts and resources toward the most important region of the world: the Pacific region.

Since then, and fundamentally, the U.S. geostrategic vision has not changed one iota, as clearly evidenced by the October 2022 Biden-Harris Administration's National Security Strategy.[2] Indeed, the document states that

> The Strategy is rooted in our national interests: to protect the security of the American people, to expand economic opportunity, and to realize and defend the democratic values at the heart of the American way of life. In pursuit of these objectives, we will: Invest in the underlying sources and tools of American power and influence; build the strongest possible coalition of nations to enhance our collective influence to shape the global strategic environment and to solve shared challenges; and modernize and strengthen our military so it is equipped for the era of strategic competition.

It also stresses that

> The most pressing strategic challenges we face as we pursue a free, open, prosperous, and secure world are from powers that layer authoritarian governance with a revisionist foreign policy. We will effectively compete with the People's Republic of China, which is the only competitor with both the intent and, increasingly,

---

2 To read the document: https://bidenwhitehouse.archives.gov/briefing-room/statements-releases/2022/10/12/fact-sheet-the-biden-harris-administrations-national-security-strategy/

the capability to reshape the international order, while constraining a dangerous Russia.

With regard to the Middle East region, the U.S. envisions "A more integrated Middle East that empowers our allies and partners" and advances "regional peace and prosperity, while reducing the resource demands the region makes on the United States over the long term."

What has crucially changed, however, is the very world the U.S. has relentlessly striven to dominate since the end of WWII, and even more so after the collapse of the Soviet Union, which, as history will record, was only a temporary "freezing" of the Cold War.

The outbreak of the Ukraine War in 2022 and, to a greater degree, the ongoing round of the War on Gaza, have brought Israel, Ukraine, and the West closer to each other,[3] and by the same token have further distanced them from the rest of the world, all the while accelerating the transition to a multipolar global order.

At this point, it is both appropriate and warranted to emphasize, with John Ikenberry once again, that "the world's most powerful state has begun to sabotage the order it created. A hostile and revisionist power has indeed arrived on the scene, but it sits in the Oval Office, the beating heart of the Free world."

The French Academy dictionary defines order as "an arrangement, a regular layout of things in relation to one another; a necessary relationship which regulates the organization of a whole into its parts." In reality, the notions of order and disorder are part of a practical, ethical, political, even mythical and religious discourse. From a philosophical point of view, according to Professor Bertrand Piettre,[4] these two notions seem to be more normative than descriptive and have more value than reality. Thus, the term "order" is understood at least in two contradictory senses:

---

3 Ukraine's President Volodymyr Zelensky has spoken strongly in favor of Israel after the surprise assault by Hamas on October 7, 2023. He called on world leaders to show solidarity and unity in supporting Israel and condemning the "terrorist attack." Zelensky, who is also Jewish, said that Israel had an unquestionable right to defend itself from attacks by Hamas and controversially compared it to Russia's invasion and occupation of Ukraine, saying Hamas and Moscow were "the same evil, and the only difference is that there is a terrorist organization that attacked Israel, and here is a terrorist state that attacked Ukraine." Israeli reports also said that Zelensky wanted to make a solidarity visit to Israel but was told "now is not the time."

4 Bertrand Piettre, "Ordre et désordre: Le point de vue philosophique" (Order and disorder: The philosophical point of view), 1995.

either order is thought of as finalized, as carrying out a purpose, pursuing a direction, thence making sense; disorder is then defined by the absence of an intelligent design. Or, order is thought of as a stable or recurring structure and, thereby, recognizable and locatable, as a constant and necessary arrangement; but as such, it can appear totally devoid of finality and purpose. Disorder, then, is not thought of as what is devoid of a finality, but as what appears to be devoid of necessity. These two meanings, he further explains, refer to two philosophically different visions of the world: finalist or mechanist, and their combination, in a play of contingency and necessity, produces the diversity of the material and living world that we know.

In the realm of international relations, order is commonly understood to mean the set of rules and institutions that govern relations between the key players in the international environment. Such an order is distinguished from chaos, or random relationships, by a certain degree of stability in terms of structure and organization.

Perhaps one of the best studies ever done on this topic is the one published by the Rand Corporation in 2016 under the title "Understanding the Current International Order."[5] The main aim of this study was to understand the workings of the existing international order, assess current challenges and threats to the order, and accordingly, recommend future policies deemed sound to U.S. decisionmakers.

The report says that in the modern era the foundation of the international order was built on the bedrock principles of the Westphalian system, which reflected fairly conservative conceptions of order while relying on pure balance-of-power politics in order to uphold the sovereign equality and territorial inviolability of States.

This Westphalian system led to the development of the territorial integrity norm, considered to this day as a cardinal norm against outright aggression toward neighbors with the aim of seizing their lands, resources or citizens, which was once a common practice in world politics. Thus defined in its main elements, this system has continued to prevail, especially since the Concert of Europe, also known as the Vienna Congress system, which from 1815 to 1914 established a whole series of principles, rules and practices that greatly contributed, after the

5 RAND Corporation, *Understanding the Current International Order*, 2016. This study was sponsored by the Office of the United States Secretary of Defense's Office of Net Assessment and conducted within the International Security and Defense Policy Center of the RAND National Defense Research Institute.

Napoleonic wars, to maintaining a balance between European powers and shielding the Old Continent from a new all-out conflict. It stood fast until the outbreak of World War I.

At the close of the horrific hostilities of the Great War, U.S. President Woodrow Wilson spent several months of 1919 in Europe, working closely with British Prime Minister David Lloyd George, French Prime Minister Georges Clemenceau, and other leaders to build a more peaceful postwar order. Together, they brought to life the League of Nations. Unfortunately, the League was dealt an early and deadly blow when the U.S. Senate rejected U.S. membership in it, refusing to participate in an international legal system that it deemed would encroach on the country's sovereignty. The League's failure to provide an effective response to the nationalism and militarism in Europe and Asia during the 1930s further damaged its credibility and precipitated its demise. Yet, this innovative burst of order-building left an important imprint on global affairs and was akin to a general dress rehearsal for the international architecture, later decided by world plenipotentiaries gathered in San Francisco in 1945, to take shape as the United Nations Organization.

In sum, even if it took different forms in practice, the Westphalian order continued to be a permanent feature of the relations between the great world powers during all the aforementioned periods, thus allowing, to the greatest possible extent, the prevalence of structured relations designed to forswear territorial conquest and curtail any global disorder susceptible of generating wars or large-scale violence in their midst.

The RAND report indicates that since 1945, the United States, which was the greatest beneficiary of the restored peace, has pursued its global interests through the creation and maintenance of international economic institutions, bilateral and regional security organizations, and liberal political norms and standards. These ordering mechanisms are often collectively referred to as the "international order." However, in recent years, rising powers have begun to challenge the sustainability and legitimacy of some aspects of this order, which is clearly seen by the U.S. as a major challenge to its global leadership and vital strategic interests. Three broad categories of potential risks and threats likely to jeopardize this order have thus been identified by the writers of the report:

- some leading states consider that many components of the existing order are designed to restrict their power and perpetuate American hegemony;

- volatility due to failed states or economic crises;
- shifting domestic politics at a time of slow growth and growing inequality.

Two years before the publication of this study, Henry Kissinger, the veteran of American diplomacy credited with having officially introduced "Realpolitik" (realistic foreign policy based on the calculation of forces and the national interest) into the White House while serving as Secretary of State under Richard Nixon's administration, had further explored the theme of world order in a landmark book so titled.[6]

From the outset, Mr. Kissinger asserts that no truly global "world order" has ever existed. The order as defined by our times was devised in Western Europe four centuries ago, on the occasion of a peace conference held in Westphalia "without the involvement or even the awareness of most other continents or civilizations." This conference, it should be remembered, followed a century of sectarian conflict and political upheavals across Central Europe, which ended up provoking the Thirty Years' War (1618–1648), an appalling and pointless "total war" where a quarter of the population of Central Europe died from combat, disease, and starvation.

The negotiators of this peace of Westphalia did not think of laying the foundations of a system applicable to the whole world. How could they have thought to do so when then, as always before, every other civilization or geographic region, seeing itself as the center of the world and viewing its principles and values as universally relevant, defined its own conception of order? In the absence of possibilities for prolonged interaction and of any framework for measuring the respective power of the different regions, Henry Kissinger rightly observed, each of these regions viewed its own order as unique and defined the others as "barbarians" which were "governed in a manner incomprehensible to the established system, and irrelevant to its designs except as a threat."

Subsequently, thanks to Western colonial expansion, the Westphalian system spread around the world and imposed the structure of a state-based international order, while failing, of course, to apply the concepts of sovereignty to its colonies and colonized peoples. It is these same principles and other Westphalian ideas that were put forward when the colonized peoples began to demand their independence. Sovereign state, national independence, national interest, noninterference in

---

6 Henry Kissinger, *World Order* (New York: Penguin Press, 2014).

domestic affairs and respect for international law and human rights have thus asserted themselves as effective arguments against the colonizers during armed or political struggles, both to regain independence and, afterwards, to protect the newly formed states in the 1950s and 1960s, in particular.

At the end of his reflection combining historical analysis and geo-political prospective, Kissinger draws important conclusions about the current international order and asks essential questions about its future. The universal relevance of the Westphalian system, he said, derived from its procedural nature that is value-neutral, which made its rules accessible to any country. Its weakness had been the flip side of its strength: designed by states exhausted from the bloodletting they inflicted on each other, it offered no sense of direction; it proposed methods of allocating and preserving power, without indicating how to generate its legitimacy.

More fundamentally, Kissinger argued that in building a world order, a key question inevitably concerns the substance of its unifying principles, which represents a cardinal distinction between Western and non-Western approaches to order. Quite aptly, he pointed out that since the Renaissance, the West has widely adopted the idea that the real world is external to the observer, that knowledge consists in recording and classifying data with the greatest possible precision, and that the success of a foreign policy depends on the assessment of existing realities and trends. Therefore, the "Peace of Westphalia" embodied a judgment of reality and more particularly of realities of power and territory—in the form of a concept of a secular order supplanting the demands of religion.

In contrast, other great contemporary civilizations conceived of reality as internal to the observer and defined by psychological, philosophical or religious convictions. Consequently, Kissinger was of the opinion that sooner or later, any international order must face the consequences of two trends that compromise its cohesion: either a redefinition of legitimacy or a significant shift in the balance of power. In such circumstances, upheavals could emerge, the essence of which being that

> while they are usually underpinned by force, their overriding thrust is psychological. Those under assault are challenged to defend not only their territory, but the basic assumptions of their way of life, their moral right to exist and to act in a manner that until the challenge, had been treated as beyond question.

Like many other thinkers, political scientists and strategists, especially Westerners, the American statesman considered that the multifaceted developments underway in the world are fraught with threats and risks that could lead to a sharp rise in tensions, and chaos threatens

> side by side with unprecedented interdependence: in the spread of weapons of mass destruction, the disintegration of states, the impact of environmental depredations, the persistence of genocidal practices, and the spread of new technologies threatening to drive conflict beyond human control or comprehension.

This is the main reason why he thought that our age is insistently engaged in an obstinate search, sometimes almost desperately, for a concept of world order, and not without expressing his concern, which takes on the appearance of a warning. In our time, he said,

> a reconstruction of the international system is the ultimate challenge to government. And in the event of failure, the penalty will be not so much a major war between States (though in some regions this is not foreclosed) as an evolution into spheres of influence identified with particular domestic structures and forms of governance, for example the Westphalian model as against the radical Islamist version

with the risk that "at its edges each sphere would be tempted to test its strength against other entities of order deemed illegitimate."

The major conclusion of this scholarly book which concerns us in the context of our theme is this: "The mystery to be overcome is one all peoples share: how divergent historical experiences and values can be shaped into a common order."

Worldviews and World Orders: The "Individual and Secular" vs. the "Collective and Sacred"

All civilizations try to balance themselves between the individual and the collective, between the temporal and the spiritual, and between this-worldliness and otherworldliness. Shifts between the relative importance given to the one at the expense of the others is what gives the different civilizations their distinctive identity and coloring; and critical disjunctions in human history occur when the individual paradigm is overturned or tilted toward the collective, or vice versa.

In modern Western societies, especially within the Anglosphere, it is an indisputable fact that since the Renaissance, which was at the origin of the Enlightenment movement and thought, there has been a gradual and probably decisive and irreversible shift away from the collective and the sacred toward the individual and the secular.

This being the case, in the self-image of Western or Westernized societies, the individual is ennobled and endowed with the power and tools to determine, alone, the course of his personal development and fulfillment as well as those of society, through the idiom—which is then erected into absolute dogma—of individual (civil) rights and the practice of a democracy based on laws and rules. The primacy of the individual over collective rights thus gradually paved the way for the dismantling of the post-war welfare state, making the dividing line between the public and private domains increasingly blurred, and providing wide-open avenues to an unbridled individualism.

In the following paragraphs, I shall attempt to explain why and how the 500-year long global dominance of the "Western civilization" is coming to an end—a fate first and most significantly epitomized and signaled by the West's self-immolation during the bloodbath of the two Western civil wars, also known as the two World Wars it ignited in a span of only 30 years and led to the loss of 100 million lives. One good way of doing so is by surveying the writings of seven authors who have had a profound influence on Western Man's thinking, and seven other authors who have predicted and warned against an impending twilight of this Western predominance. Indeed, what we take to be the ethical, social, economic, and ideological bedrock of Western thought has, far and away, been laid down in seven landmark references put forward since the beginning of the European Renaissance and the Age of the Enlightenment.

Thus, in his 1513 book *The Prince,* Italian Niccolò Machiavelli described methods—including through deliberate deceit, hypocrisy and perjury—that an aspiring prince can use to acquire the throne, or an existing prince can resort to in order to maintain his reign. English Pastor Thomas Robert Malthus claimed in his 1798 "Essay on the Principle of Population" that population tends to grow faster than the food supply. He also posited that the planet would be unable to support more than one billion inhabitants and advocated therefore for a limitation on the number of poor people as a better controlling device. English biologist Charles Darwin's 1859 seminal book *The Origin of Species* promoted a theory of evolution by natural selection through the notion of "survival of the fittest," thus profoundly challenging Victorian-era ideas about the role of humans in the universe. English philosopher/sociologist Herbert Spencer's 1864 *Principles of Biology* transferred Darwin's theory from the realm of nature to society. He believed that the strongest or fittest would and should dominate the poor and the weak who should ultimately disappear. This meant that certain races—in particular European Protestant individuals and nations—were entitled to dominate others because of their "superiority" in the natural order. German Karl Marx's 1867 *Capital* is the foundational theoretical text in materialist philosophy, economics and politics. Belief in some of its teachings led to communism and caused millions of deaths in the utopian hope of bringing about an egalitarian society. In his most celebrated book *Thus Spoke Zarathustra* (1883–1885) German philosopher Friedrich Nietzsche elaborated on ideas like the eternal recurrence of the same, the death of God, and the prophecy of the "Übermensch" (Overman), that is the ideal superior man of the future who could rise above conventional Christian morality to create and impose his own values. Finally, Austrian Sigmund Freud's theories, although subject to a lot of criticism, were enormously influential. His best-known 1930 book, *Civilization and Its Discontents,* analyzes what he sees as the fundamental tensions between civilization and the individual. The primary friction, he asserts, stems from the fact that the immutable individual's quest for instinctive freedom (notably desires for sex) are at odds with what is best for society (civilization) as a whole, which is why laws are created to prohibit killing, rape, and adultery, and implement severe punishments if they are broken. The result is an ongoing feeling of discontent among the citizens of that civilization.

Beyond shadow of a doubt, Western Man's mindset, worldview, and behavior have been considerably influenced by the presuppositions of the "seven deadly sins" embodied in this literature—materialism, individualism, scientism, unbridled pursuit of profit, nationalism, racial supremacy—led to such calamities for the world as excessive will to power, wars, colonization, imperialism, and eventually civilizational decadence and the decline of the Western world.

As a result of this irreversible process, especially following the moral wreckage and colossal human and material cost of the Great War, prominent thinkers and philosophers started to voice their concern about the coming demise of the West. Chief among those are seven authors whose books argue that while it is true that the West is in decline, there's still time to mitigate it or even to reverse it and preserve it for posterity. Those books are: Oswald Spengler's *The Decline of the West* (1926); Arnold Toynbee's *Civilization on Trial* (1958); Eric Voegelin's *Order and History* (1956–1987); Francis Fukuyama's *The End of History and the Last Man* (1992); Samuel Huntington's *The Clash of Civilizations and the Remaking of World Order* (1996); Niall Ferguson's *Civilization: The West and the Rest* (2012); and Michel Onfray's *Décadence: Vie et mort du judéo-christianisme.*[7] Emmanuel Todd's recently published book *La Défaite de l'Occident*[8] equally deserves to be added to this selective collection.

Another stated or implied common feature of these books is the belief that "Western Christian civilization" has to be defended anew both from internal decay and threats arising externally, mainly Islam, or even worse, an alliance of "Islamic" and "Sinic (Chinese)" civilizations. This fear of Islam is by no means new; it's deep-rooted in the Western psyche. Today, however, it is being exacerbated to such an unprecedented extent that the debate on the resurgence of Islam has become, more often than not, inextricably intertwined with the talk about the decline of the Western civilization.

Already, back in 1940, when there was no question as yet of the so-called Islamist or Islamic threat, and even less so of a "clash of civilizations" that plague our current world, then French Colonel Charles de Gaulle—although on full combat against Nazi Germany's Wehrmacht—gave the following response to his chaplain who questioned him about the situation on the battlefield and rumors of an armistice:

> Mr. Chaplain, this war is only one episode in a clash
> of peoples and civilizations. It will be long. And when
> the clash with China, this very great people, arises
> ... what will we be and what will we do? But I have
> confidence. The last word will be given to the highest
> and most disinterested civilization, ours, the Christian

---

7 Michel Onfray, *Décadence: Vie et mort du judéo-christianisme* (*Decadence: Life and Death of Judeo-Christianity*) (Flammarion, 2017).

8 Emmanuel Todd, *La Défaite de l'Occident* (*The Defeat of the West*) (Gallimard, 2024).

civilization ... But the greatest and most immediate danger can come from the Muslim transversal, which ranges from Tangier to the Indies. If it were to come under Russian communist obedience, or what would be worse, Chinese, we are doomed. And believe me, Mr. Chaplain, there will no longer be a possible Battle of Poitiers.[9]

The same refrain was famously repeated by none other than Samuel Huntington in his no less celebrated book,[10] written in response to his former student Francis Fukuyama's 1992 highly controversial best-seller[11] in which, following the collapse of communism leading to a metamorphosis of world politics, Fukuyama addressed a question that has for time immemorial engaged the minds of great philosophers and thinkers: Is there a direction to the history of mankind? And if it is directional, to what end is it moving?

Fukuyama argues that a remarkable consensus concerning the legitimacy of "liberal democracy" as a system of government has emerged throughout the world. Thus, liberal democracy may constitute the "end point of mankind's ideological evolution," and the "final form of government"; and as such constituted the "end of history." The other great question that would then follow is: Can political and economic liberty and equality characterizing the state of affairs at the presumed "end of history" bring about a stable society in which man may be said to be, at last, completely satisfied? Or will the spiritual condition of this "last man" in history, "deprived of outlets for his striving for mastery," inevitably lead him to plunge himself and the world into the chaos and bloodshed of history? For Prof. Joelle M. Abi-Rached, "The ongoing genocide in Gaza reveals that the contest over political legitimacy, human rights, and state sovereignty was always far from settled—that history's conflicts

9 Quoted in Marc Ferro, *De Gaulle expliqué aujourd'hui* (*De Gaulle Explained Today*) (Paris: Éditions du Seuil, 2010). The Battle of Poitiers, also called the Battle of Tours, occurred in France on October 10, 732. It resulted in victory of the Frankish and Aquitainian forces led by Charles Martel over the Umayyad forces led by the governor of al-Andalus (Muslim-ruled Spain and Portugal) Abd al-Rahman al-Ghafiqi. The issue of the battle was a decisive factor in curtailing the spread of Islam in Western Europe.

10 Samuel P. Huntington, *The Clash of Civilizations and the Remaking of World Order* (Simon & Schuster, 1996).

11 Francis Fukuyama, *The End of History and the Last Man* (New York: The Free Press, 1992).

over power, identity, and justice will persist until the claims of humanity reach 'the last man.'"[12]

With regard to Huntington, it is important, first of all, to clarify, as has Richard Bulliet,[13] professor of history at the prestigious Columbia University, that the phrase "Clash of Civilizations" was not invented by Huntington; it was most probably coined, for the first time, by Basil Mathews in his 1926 book titled *Young Islam on Trek: A Study in the Clash of Civilizations*.[14] Yet, by wielding the "clash of civilizations" phraseology at a propitious moment, the Harvard professor significantly, shrewdly but maliciously shifted the discourse of Middle East confrontation that had been dominated by nationalist and Cold War rhetoric since the days of Gamal Abdel Nasser in the 1950s and 1960s. Bulliet rightly observed that this new formulation "took on almost cosmic proportions: the Islamic religion, or more precisely the world Muslim community that professes that religion, versus contemporary Western culture, with its Christian, Jewish, and secular humanist shadings."[15]

Huntington also wrote that:

> Islam and China embody great cultural traditions very different from and in their eyes infinitely superior to that of the West. The power and assertiveness of both in relation to the West are increasing, and the conflicts between their values and interests and those of the West are multiplying and becoming more intense ... Underlying the differences on specific issues is the fundamental question of the role these civilizations will play relative to the West in shaping the future of the world. Will the global institutions, the distribution of power, and the politics and economies of nations in the twenty-first century primarily reflect Western values and interests or will they be shaped primarily by those of Islam and China? ... Islamic and Sinic

---

12 Joelle M. Abi Rashed, "Gaza and the End of History," *Boston Review,* Summer 2025.

13 Richard Bulliet, *The Case for Islamo-Christian Civilization* (Columbia University Press, New York, 2004).

14 Basil Mathews, *Young Islam on Trek: A Study in the Clash of Civilizations* (Friendship Press, New York, 1926). Mathews was an American Protestant missionary. He worked as a secretary in the World's Alliance of YMCAs.

15 Richard Bulliet, op cit.

societies which see the West as their antagonist thus
have reason to cooperate with each other against the
West ... This cooperation occurs on a variety of issues,
including human rights, economics, and most notably
the efforts by societies in both civilizations to develop
their military capabilities, particularly weapons of
mass destruction and the missiles for delivering them,
so as to counter the conventional military superiority
of the West.

More recently, in his latest book,[16] French historian and Sinologist
Emmanuel Lincot retraces the geopolitical stakes of Sino-Muslim relations. He believes that, at the dawn of the new century, China and the
Muslim world intend to put an end to a world dominated by the West
through the "ghastly prospect" of a multifaceted alliance between them.
Such an alliance obviously encompasses the revitalization of the mythical and once greatest trade route in history—the Silk Road—that linked
and mutually enriched the two civilizations for centuries, before it was
eclipsed by the Western-dominated maritime trade. The contemporary
Chinese "Belt and Road Initiative," which aims to develop both land
and maritime corridors, is the main means to achieve such a strategic
objective.

On closer inspection, we may argue that throughout the Western
colonial period, the Cold War and until after *"Les Trente Glorieuses"*
(The Glorious Thirty),[17] the West was somewhat indifferent if not condescending to Islam as a religion. The overwrought fear of Islam has followed the demise of social democracy in the West, especially since the
events of "May 68," and the decay of progressive and socially-centered
movements in the Third World. The Iranian revolution of 1979, itself
begotten by this historical development, and the attacks of September 11,

---

16 Emmanuel Lincot, *Chine et Terres d'islam: un millénaire de
géopolitique* (*China and the Lands of Islam: A Millennium of Geopolitics*)
(Presses Universitaires de France, 2021).

17 "The Glorious Thirty" is a term coined by French Jean Fourastié in his
book, *Les Trente Glorieuses, ou la Révolution invisible de 1946 à 1975* (The
Glorious Thirty, or the Invisible Revolution from 1946 to 1975) to characterize a
thirty-year period of great economic growth in France, as well as in the West in
general) following the end of World War II. This same period was also marked
by a "Baby Boom" in most of the world, particularly in the United States and
Canada in North America and France and Austria in Europe.

2001 radically changed the geostrategic situation in the eyes of Western countries. Islam is increasingly at the center of their concerns today and a rampant Islamophobia has naturally and dangerously ensued.

As Mr. Allawi so rightly put it in his insightful book, *The Crisis of Islamic Civilization,*[18] Islam's religion, cultures, civilization, nations and peoples have become the subject of meticulous scrutiny by a wide array of analysts, "from the most thoughtful to the most incendiary, from the most illustrious to the most obscure, from the most sympathetic to the most bigoted."

If truth be said, for centuries Islamic civilization has often been shaken by powerful opposing currents. The crusades, the Mongol invasion, Western colonization and imperialism, and today, the intense globalization movement have been the most striking ones. It has just as often bent under their blows but has never broken. Far from it; its contribution to universal civilization and to the construction of the "old" and "new" worlds is undeniable.

The chronicle of this role, especially during the period of the Ottoman Empire, has been the subject of a remarkable book: *God's Shadow: The Ottoman Sultan Who Shaped the Modern World,* written by Alan Mikhail, professor of history and chair of the Department of History at Yale University.[19] In the introduction to his narrative, presenting a new and holistic picture of the last five centuries and demonstrating Islam's constituent role in the forming of some of the most fundamental aspects of the history of Europe, the Americas, and the United States, Mikhail declares that:

> If we do not place Islam at the center of our grasp
> of world history, we will never understand why the
> Moor-slayers (Matamoros)[20] are memorialized on the
> Texas-Mexico border or, more generally, why we have
> blindly, and repeatedly, narrated histories that miss
> major features of our shared past.

---

18 Ali A. Allawi, *The Crisis of Islamic Civilization* (Yale University Press, 2009).

19 Alan Mikhail, *God's Shadow: The Ottoman Sultan Who Shaped the Modern World* (New York: W.W. Norton & Co., 2020).

20 "Matamoros" is the name of a city located in the northeastern Mexican state of Tamaulipas across the border from Brownsville, Texas, in the United States. It was coined by Catholic Spaniards for whom it was the duty of every Christian soldier to be a Moor-slayer.

Richard Bulliet, before Mikhail, made a similar observation, saying: "The past and future of the West cannot be fully comprehended without appreciation of the twinned relationship it has had with Islam over some fourteen centuries. The same is true of the Islamic world." He went as far as to speak of an "Islamo-Christian Civilization," a term never used heretofore, and went on to make another fundamental remark:

> The question confronting the United States is whether the tragedy of September 11 should be an occasion for indulging in the Islamophobia embodied in slogans like "Clash of Civilizations" or an occasion for affirming the principle of inclusion that represents the best in the American tradition ... "Clash of Civilizations" must be retired from public discourse before the people who like to use it actually begin to believe it.

International law or a "rules-based international order"?

On March 8, 1992, the *New York Times* published excerpts from the Pentagon's draft of the Defense Planning Guidance for the Fiscal Years 1994–1999. This important piece of archive addressed the "fundamentally new situation which has been created by the collapse of the Soviet Union, the disintegration of the internal as well as the external empire, and the discrediting of Communism as an ideology with global pretensions and influence." The new international environment, it was explained, has "also been shaped by the victory of the United States and its coalition allies over Iraqi aggression—the first post-cold-war conflict and a defining event in U.S. global leadership."

The drafters of this "Guidance" stated that the United States' first objective should be "to prevent the re-emergence of a new rival, either on the territory of the former Soviet Union or elsewhere, that poses a threat on the order of that posed formerly by the Soviet Union." This is a dominant consideration underlying the new regional defense strategy and "requires that we endeavor to prevent any hostile power from dominating a region whose resources would, under consolidated control, be sufficient to generate global power. These regions include Western Europe, East Asia, the territory of the former Soviet Union, and Southwest Asia." And the second objective is "to address sources of regional conflict and instability in such a way as to promote increasing respect for international law, limit international violence, and encourage the spread of democratic forms of government and open economic systems." They also acknowledged that while the U.S. cannot become the world's "policeman," by assuming responsibility for righting every wrong, the U.S. will "retain the pre-eminent responsibility for addressing selectively those wrongs which threaten not only our interests, but those of our allies or friends, or which could seriously unsettle international relations." They furthermore determined the various types of U.S. interests involved in such instances as being: access to vital raw materials, primarily Persian Gulf oil; proliferation of weapons of mass destruction and ballistic missiles; threats to U.S. citizens from terrorism or regional or local conflict; and threats to U.S. society from narcotics trafficking.

As a matter of fact, during the whole decade of the 1990s, as the tumultuous twentieth century shuddered toward its close, the global geopolitical landscape was overwhelmingly dominated by a much-heated American internal debate about a big question: will America strive to dominate the world, or lead it?

This topic was the object of an influential book, *The Choice: Global Domination or Global Leadership*,[21] written by Zbigniew Brzezinski, former National Security Advisor under President Jimmy Carter. In it, he reminded Americans that their might should not be confused with omnipotence, and that their well-being and the world's are entwined. He explained that panicky preoccupation with "solitary American security, an obsessively narrow focus on terrorism, and indifference to the concerns of a politically restless humanity neither enhance American security nor comport with the world's real need for American leadership." The conclusion Brzezinski then quite logically drew was that "unless it can harmonize its overwhelming power with its seductive but also unsettling social appeal, America could find itself alone and under assault in a setting of intensifying global chaos."

Such a conclusion was all the more logical, accurate and timely as America—and the world with it—swiftly found themselves at the turn of the new millennium in an unprecedented state of disarray in the wake of the 2001 September 11th attacks. These led, among other epochal events, to the American blunders of the invasions of Afghanistan and Iraq in 2001 and 2003 respectively, from whose adverse consequences the world at large is still suffering.

---

21 Zbigniew Brzezinski, *The Choice: Global Domination or Global Leadership* (New York: Basic Books, 2004).

It is equally worthwhile to recall that when G. W. Bush took office in 2000, he brought with him Vice President Dick Cheney, Secretary of Defense Donald Rumsfeld, and Deputy Secretary of Defense Paul Wolfowitz, all of whom had served together in Ronald Reagan's and G. H. W. Bush's administrations. In 1992, while he was in the Defense Department, Wolfowitz—long recognized as the intellectual force behind a radical neoconservative fringe of the Republican Party—was asked to write the first draft of a new National Security Strategy, a document entitled "The Defense Planning Guidance."[22] The most controversial elements of that strategy were that the United States: should dramatically increase its defense spending; be willing to take preemptive military action; and be willing to use military force unilaterally, with or without allies.

Out of power during the Clinton administration, Wolfowitz and his colleagues presided over the creation, in 1997, of the Neoconservative think tank, "Project for a New American Century" (PNAC), which was placed under the chairmanship of William Kristol, the "Godfather" of American neoconservatism. Once it was brought back into power within Bush, Jr.'s administration in 2000, Wolfowitz's team became engaged in shaping a neoconservative U.S. foreign policy, whose main principles were laid down in a defining document titled "Rebuilding America's Defenses: Strategy, Forces and Resources for a New Century."[23] This 90-page document was written in September of 2000, a full year before the 9/11 attacks.

Interestingly enough, in its section V entitled "Creating Tomorrow's Dominant Force," it stated that "the process of transformation, even if it brings revolutionary change, is likely to be a long one, absent some catastrophic and catalyzing event—like a new Pearl Harbor." One year later, that event would indeed happen, and two decades later, the most important question of "what really happened on September 11, 2001?" remains unanswered. Was it the result of a needed conspiracy to execute a premeditated plan? Or was it a mere coincidence exploited by believers in conspiracy theories? Only time will tell. However, what History has already recorded for sure is that this catastrophic event brought about equally catastrophic consequences, both intended and unintended, for

---

22 See this document which has been declassified under authority of the Interagency Security classification Appeal Panel: https://www.archives.gov/files/declassification/iscap/pdf/2008-003-docs1-12.pdf

23 Read the document here: https://cryptome.org/rad.htm

America itself, for the Arab and Islamic world, and for the rest of the world as well.

In hindsight, Brzezinski's 2004 assessment and expectations represented something of an unexpected 180-degree turn compared to his previous well-known ideological and geostrategic attitude and writings. In effect, only seven years before, he had written a hugely authoritative book, *The Grand Chessboard: American Primacy and its Geostrategic Imperatives,*[24] in which he outlined a strategy entirely based on the oft-cited phrase of Sir Halford J. Mackinder, who is generally considered the founding father of geopolitics: "Who rules Eastern Europe rules the continental heart; who rules the continental heart rules the world-island; who rules the world-island rules the world."[25] Here, Brzezinski argued that the last decade of the twentieth century had witnessed a tectonic shift in world affairs: "For the first time, a non-Eurasian power rose not only to the position of a key arbiter of relations among the states of Eurasia, but also to the position of the dominant global power.

> The defeat and fall of the Soviet Union completed the rapid rise of a northern hemisphere power, the United States, as the sole and, indeed, the first truly global power. Eurasia, however, retains its geopolitical importance. Not only does its western periphery— Europe—still hold much of the world's political and economic power, but its eastern region—Asia—has recently become a center of vital economic growth and growing political influence.

That said, the ability of the United States to effectively and sustainably exercise global primacy will depend entirely on how it manages its complex relationships with the powers of this region, and particularly on the absolute imperative of "preventing the emergence of a dominant and antagonistic Eurasian power."

In a language strongly reminiscent of that of Niccolò Machiavelli's *The Prince,* Brzezinski first specifies that in the blunt terminology of past empires, the three great geostrategic imperatives would be summarized

---

24 Zbigniew Brzezinski, *The Grand Chessboard: American Primacy and its Geostrategic Imperatives* (New York: Basic Books, 1997).

25 Halford J. Mackinder, *Democratic Ideals and Reality* (New York: Holt, 1919).

as follows: "Avoid collusion with vassals and maintain them in the state of dependence justified by their security; cultivate the docility of protected subjects; prevent barbarians from forming offensive alliances." He then advocates, on this basis, a strategy of unilateral domination, which had been called for before him by neoconservative ideologues and would later be adopted as a line of conduct during the terms of George W. Bush.

The essential point to keep in mind, Brzezinski says—giving sense to current events in Ukraine—is that

> Russia cannot be in Europe without Ukraine being there as well, while Ukraine can be in Europe without Russia being there ... Ukraine, a new and important space on the Eurasian chessboard, is a geopolitical pivot because its very existence as an independent country helps to transform Russia. Without Ukraine, Russia ceases to be a Eurasian empire. Russia without Ukraine can still strive for imperial status, but it would then become a predominantly Asian imperial state ... However, if Moscow regains control over Ukraine, with its 52 million people and major resources as well as its access to the Black Sea, Russia automatically again regains the wherewithal to become a powerful imperial state spanning Europe and Asia. Ukraine's loss of independence would have immediate consequences for Central Europe, transforming Poland into the geopolitical pivot on the eastern frontier of a united Europe.

In the final analysis, and contrary to Brzezinski's "updated" wishes and predictions, America failed to become either the guarantor of its own and the world's security or the promoter of the global common good. Far from it. What the United States effectively did is what all states normally do, as Lord Palmerston once famously proclaimed[26]—most probably

---

26 Twice UK Prime Minister (1855–58 and 1859–65) Lord Palmerston, also known as Henry John Temple, said before Parliament in 1848: "Therefore I say that it is a narrow policy to suppose that this country or that is to be marked out as the eternal ally or the perpetual enemy of England. We have no eternal allies, and we have no perpetual enemies. Our interests are eternal and perpetual, and those interests it is our duty to follow."

having in mind the United States precisely—that's to say, pursue their interests.

And while Brzezinski seemed to make amends in this respect, many other scholars and ideologues were advocating for an American empire. Renowned economist Deepak Lal for one, also in 2004, wrote a controversial book, *In Praise of Empires: Globalization and Order,*[27] in which he laid out a historical and cross-civilizational examination of the role empires have played to provide the order required for peace and prosperity, and how this imperial role "has come to be thrust on the United States." Expressing wish fulfillment for America mirroring Virgil's hope for Rome, Lal argued that

> if the U.S. public does not recognize the imperial burden that history has thrust upon it, or is unwilling to bear it, the world will continue to muddle along as it has for the past century—with hesitant advances, punctuated by various alarms and by periods of backsliding in the wholly beneficial processes of globalization. Perhaps, if the United States is unwilling to shoulder the imperial burden of maintaining the global pax, we will have to wait for one or other of the emerging imperial states—China and India—to do so in the future.

Till then, he concluded, "we may be fated to live with the ancient Chinese curse, 'May you live in interesting times.'"

To be sure, since its founding, the United States has consistently pursued a grand strategy focused on acquiring and maintaining preeminent power over various rivals, first on the North American continent, then in the Western hemisphere, and finally globally. During the Cold War, this strategy was manifested in the form of "containment," which provided a unifying vision of how the United States could protect its systemic primacy as well as its security, ensure the safety of its allies, and eventually enable the defeat of its adversary, the Soviet Union. This is exactly what a 2015 Council on Foreign Affairs (CFR) report stated.[28]

---

27 Deepak Lal, *In Praise of Empires: Globalization and Order* (New York: Palgrave Macmillan, 2004).

28 Robert D. Black will and Ashley J. Tellis, *Revising U.S. Grand Strategy Toward China,* Council Special Report no. 72, Council on Foreign Affairs, March 2015.

Unlike the March 1992 "Guidance" which rarely, if ever, mentions China as being a rival or a foe, CFR's President, Richard Haas—who has written the foreword part of this report—concurs with the authors' conclusion according to which "Of all the nations—and in most conceivable scenarios—China is and will remain the most significant competitor to the United States for decades to come."

Said omission of China in previous similar literature is also explained in the report by the fact that "the American effort to 'integrate' China into the liberal international order has now generated new threats to U.S. primacy in Asia—and could eventually result in consequential challenge to American power globally."

In reality, behind those openly expressed fears and criticism lies an undisclosed threat that perhaps supersedes all others. That is the fact that Beijing's domestic policies that have succeeded in transforming China from an impoverished nation into a world superpower in a relatively short period of time—more precisely thanks to the reforms implemented by Deng Xiaoping since 1978, after Mao Zedong's death in 1976—have been performed within a paradigm that does not fully comply with the conventional fundamental Western liberal values and recipes. Those policies are thought to have contributed to an "economic miracle" distinctively characterized by an eightfold growth in gross national product over two decades. This prompted Joshua Cooper Ramo in 2004 to coin the term "Beijing Consensus,"[29] a moniker that nods to the "Washington Consensus" whose set of political and economic development prescriptions severely impacted the socio-economic situation of so many developing countries, especially in Latin America in the late 1980s.[30]

Hence, the overarching argument for China's ideological threat to the West in general and the United States in particular is that China's prodigious and rapid growth is providing an attractive alternative development model for the Global South, thereby signaling a challenge to American soft power. Stefan Halper argued in his 2010 book, *The*

---

29 Joshua Cooper Ramo, "The Beijing Consensus," The Foreign Policy Centre, 2004. Later on, in 2016, Ramo explained that the Beijing Consensus shows not that "every nation will follow China's development model, but that it legitimizes the notion of particularity as opposed to the universality of a Washington model." See Maurits Elen, "Interview: Joshua Cooper Ramo," *The Diplomat,* August 2016.

30 See Jhana Gottlieb, "The Beijing Consensus: A Threat of Our Own Creation," Center for International Maritime Security, April 22, 2017.

Beijing Consensus: Legitimizing Authoritarianism in Our Time,[31] that the "net effect of these developments is to reduce Western and particularly American influence on the global stage—along both economic and ideational axes."

In the face of the challenge represented by the meteoric growth of the Chinese economy and its military power, Washington thus needs "a new grand strategy that centers on balancing the rise of Chinese power rather than continuing to assist its ascendancy." This strategy, the report goes on to say, cannot be built on a bedrock of containment, as was the earlier effort to limit Soviet power, because of the current realities of globalization. And short of a "fundamental collapse of the Chinese state [that] would free Washington from the obligation of systematically balancing Beijing," even the alternative of a "modest Chinese stumble would not eliminate the dangers presented to the United States in Asia and beyond" and would constitute a serious threat to the U.S.-dominated international order.

The "Chinese challenge" continues unabated to haunt the American security establishment—which is largely autonomous and operates behind a wall of secrecy—lending additional credence and great contemporary relevance to the prescient views put forward by French scholar and politician Alain Peyreffitte in his 1973 essay concerning the likely shocking impact of an awakening of China.[32] Indeed, in 2021 the Atlantic Council published a paper titled "Global Strategy 2021: An Allied Strategy for China."[33] It was prepared in collaboration with policy planning officials and strategy experts from ten "leading democracies."[34]

---

31 Stefan Hapler, *The Beijing Consensus: Legitimizing Authoritarianism in Our Time* (New York: Basic Books, 2010).

32 Alain Peyreffitte, *Quand la Chine s'éveillera. . . le monde tremblera* (*When China Awakens. . . the World Will Tremble*) (Paris: Fayard, 1973). The essay's main thesis is that given the size and growth of the Chinese population, it will inevitably end up imposing itself on the rest of the world as soon as it masters sufficient technology, and that "Today's China only makes sense if we put it in perspective with yesterday's China." As for the title, it comes from a phrase attributed to Napoléon I: "Let China sleep, because when China awakens the whole world will tremble." Napoléon would have uttered this sentence in 1816 in Saint Helena after reading *Voyage en Chine et en Tartarie* (*Journey to China and Tartary*) written by Lord George Macartney, Great Britain's first envoy to China.

33 To read the Strategy: https://www.atlanticcouncil.org/global-strategy-2021-an-allied-strategy-for-china/

34 United States, Italy, Japan, Germany, Australia, India, France, Canada, UK, and South Korea.

Its foreword was written by none other than Joseph S. Nye, who coined the term "soft power" in the late 1980s, before it circled the globe and came into widespread usage following an article he wrote in 1990 in *Foreign Policy* magazine.[35]

The strategy states that

> China is the foremost geopolitical threat to the rules-based international system since the end of the Cold War, and the return of great-power rivalry will likely shape the global order for decades to come. Likeminded allies and partners need to take deliberate and coordinated action to strengthen themselves and counter the threat China poses, even as they seek longer-term cooperation with Beijing.

The Free World, the concluding remarks read, has "an impressive record of accomplishment in defeating challenges from autocratic great-power rivals and constructing a rules-based system," and by pursuing this strategy "with sufficient political will, resilience, and solidarity," they can "once again outlast an autocratic competitor and provide the world with future peace, prosperity, and freedom."

In contrast to other similar previous papers, one sentence is repeated time and again in this strategy, namely "the rules-based system." It has since become the alpha and omega of American—and British—officials, academics, and media pundits.

For example, as recounted by John Dugard in a particularly insightful study, *The Choice Before Us: International Law Or A "Rules-Based International Order,"*[36] President Biden published an op-ed[37] about

---

35 Joseph S. Nye, "Soft Power," *Foreign Policy* no. 80 (1990): "These trends suggest a second, more attractive way of exercising power than traditional means. A state may achieve the outcomes it prefers in world politics because other states want to follow it or have agreed to a situation that produces such effects. In this sense, it is just as important to set the agenda and structure the situations in world politics as to get others to change in particular cases. This second aspect of power—which occurs when one country gets other countries to want what it wants—might be called co-optive or soft power in contrast with the hard or command power of ordering others to do what it wants."

36 John Dugard, "The choice before us: International law or a 'rules-based international order'?" *Leiden Journal of International Law* 36, no. 2 (June 2023), pp. 223–232.

37 Joe R. Biden Jr., "How the US Is Willing to Help Ukraine," *The New*

Ukraine in the *New York Times* in which he declared that Russia's action in Ukraine "could mark the end of the rules-based international order and open the door to aggression elsewhere, with catastrophic consequences the world over."[38] There is no mention of international law. Later, in a press conference at the conclusion of the June 2022 NATO Summit Meeting in Madrid, he warned both Russia and China that the democracies of the world would "defend the rules-based order" (RBO). Again, there is no mention of international law. On October 12, 2022 the U.S. president published a National Security Strategy which makes repeated reference to the RBO as the "foundation of global peace and prosperity," with only passing reference to international law.[39]

So, what is this RBO "creature" that American political leaders have increasingly invoked since the end of the Cold War instead of international law? Is it a harmless synonym for international law, as suggested by European leaders? Or is it something else, a system meant to replace international law, which has governed the behavior of states for over 500 years?

The RBO may be seen as the United States' alternative to international law, an order that encapsulates international law as interpreted by the United States to accord with its national interests, "a chimera, meaning whatever the U.S. and its followers want it to mean at any given time."[40] Premised on "the United States' own willingness to ignore, evade or rewrite the rules whenever they seem inconvenient,"[41] the RBO

York Times, International Edition, June 2, 2022.

38 The White House Briefing Room, "Remarks by President Biden in Press Conference (Madrid, Spain)," The White House, June 30, 2022. https://bidenwhitehouse.archives.gov/briefing-room/speeches-remarks/2022/06/30/remarks-by-president-biden-in-press-conference-madrid-spain/

39 The White House, *National Security Strategy,* October 2022. https://bidenwhitehouse.archives.gov/wp-content/uploads/2022/10/Biden-Harris-Administrations-National-Security-Strategy-10.2022.pdf

40 See further: Richard Falk, "'Rule-Based-International-Order': A New Metaphor For U.S. Geopolitical Primacy – OpEd," *Eurasia Review,* June 1, 2021   (https://www.eurasiareview.com/01062021-rule-based-international-order-a-new-metaphor-for-us-geopolitical-primacy-oped/); and Grenville Cross, "Rules-based order: Hypocrisy masquerading as principle," *China Daily,* May 3, 2022 (https://www.chinadailyhk.com/hk/article/269896#Rules-based-order:-Hypocrisy-masquerading-as-principle-2022-05-02).

41 S. Walt, "China Wants a 'Rules Based International Order' Too," *Foreign Policy,* March 31, 2021. https://www.belfercenter.org/publication/china-wants-rules-based-international-order-too

See also Ali Tuygan, "The Rules-based International Order," *Diplomatic*

is seen to be broad, open to political manipulation and double standards, and "seems to allow for special rules in special—sui generis—cases."[42]

According to Dugard and many other scholars who have studied this subject, the rationale behind the reference by Washington to the RBO rather than to international law is that the U.S. is not a party to a number of important multilateral treaties and other legal instruments that constitute the backbone of international law as it is commonly known, including some fundamental legal instruments governing international humanitarian law.[43]

And as it relates to the War on Gaza, the rationale is that the United States is unwilling to hold some states, such as Israel, accountable for violations of international law. They are "treated as sui generis cases in which the national interest precludes accountability." This exceptionalism in respect of Israel was spelled out by the United States in its joint declaration with Israel on the occasion of President Biden's visit to Israel in July 2022,[44] which reaffirms "the unbreakable bonds between our two countries and the enduring commitment of the United States to Israel's security" and the determination of the two states "to combat all efforts to boycott or de-legitimize Israel, to deny its right to self-defense, or to single it out in any forum, including at the United Nations or the International Criminal Court."

This commitment explains the consistent refusal of the United States to hold Israel accountable for its repeated violations of humanitarian law, support the prosecution of perpetrators of international crimes before the International Criminal Court, condemn its assaults on Gaza, insist that Israel prosecute killers of a U.S. national (journalist Shireen

---

Opinion, May 10, 2021. https://www.diplomaticopinion.com/2021/05/10/the-rules-based-international-order/

42 Stefan Talmon, "Rules-based Order v. International Law?," *GPIL - German Practice in International Law,* January 20, 2019. https://www.gpil.jura.uni-bonn.de/2019/01/rules-based-order-v-international-law

43 Among others: the 1977 Protocols to the Geneva Conventions on the Laws of War, the 1982 UN Convention on the Law of the Sea, the 1989 Rights of the Child Convention, the 1997 Anti-Personnel Mine Ban Convention, the 1998 Rome Statute of the International Criminal Court, the 2006 Convention of the Rights of Persons with Disabilities, and the 2008 Convention on Cluster Munitions.

44 The White House Briefing Room, "The Jerusalem US-Israel Strategic Partnership Joint Declaration," The White House, July 14, 2022. https://bidenwhitehouse.archives.gov/briefing-room/statements-releases/2022/07/14/the-jerusalem-u-s-israel-strategic-partnership-joint-declaration/

Abu Akleh), criticize its violation of human rights as established by both
the Human Rights Council and the General Assembly, accept that Israel
applies a policy of apartheid in the Occupied Palestinian Territory,[45] and
oppose its annexation of East Jerusalem. And, of course, there is the
refusal of the United States to acknowledge the existence of Israel's
nuclear arsenal or allow any discussion of it in the context of nuclear
proliferation in the Middle East.[46] Such measures on behalf of Israel
are possibly seen as consistent with the rules-based international order
(RBO) even if they violate basic rules of international law.

The RBO has been routinely criticized by Russia and China. Thus,
in 2020 Sergey Lavrov, the Russian foreign minister, declared that the
West advocated a "West-centric rules-based order as an alternative to
international law with the purpose of replacing international law with
non-consensual methods for resolving international disputes by bypassing international law."[47] He further explained that the RBO was coined to
"camouflage a striving to invent rules depending on changes in the political situation so as to be able to put pressure on disagreeable States and
even on allies." And again, on May 25, 2022 Lavrov, on the occasion of
Africa Day, read out a statement by President Putin in which he declared
in the context of Russia's action in Ukraine that:

> The main problem is that a small group of U.S.-led
> Western countries keeps trying to impose the concept
> of a rules-based world order on the international com-
> munity. They use this banner to promote, without any
> hesitation, a unipolar model of the world order where
> there are "exceptional" countries and everyone else
> who must obey the "club of the chosen.[48]

---

45 B. Samuels, "The US State Department Rejects Amnesty's Apartheid
Claim against Israel," *Haaretz,* February 1, 2022.

46 Victor Gilinsky and Henry Sokolski, "Biden Should End U.S. Hypocrisy
on Israeli Nukes," *Foreign Policy,* February 19, 2022.

47 Cited in Alexander N. Vylegzhanin et al., "The Term 'Rules-Based
Order in International Legal Discourse'," *Moscow Journal of International Law*
35 (July 2021).

48 Kester Kenn Klomegah, "Russia Renews its Support to Mark Africa
Day," *Modern Diplomacy,* May 27, 2022. https://www.moderndiplomacy.
eu/2022/05/27/russia-renews-its-support-to-mark-africa-day/

As for China, its foreign minister Wang Yi stated in 2021, at a virtual debate of the UN Security Council on the theme of multilateralism, that "International rules must be based on international law and must be written by all. They are not a patent or privilege of a few. They must be applicable to all countries and there should be no room for exceptionalism or double standards."[49]

The "Global South": From Fence-Sitter to Arbiter?

The existing world order is at an inflection point, and the times ahead will likely be radically different from those experienced in our lifetimes and will determine the course of decades to come. The last similar epochal circumstances in recent history occurred between 1930 and 1945 and between 1999 and 2008. In both periods a confluence of peculiar political, economic, social, and cultural conditions led to fundamental shifts in world order; and in both instances such conditions paved the way for American leadership, or more accurately, its global primacy.[50]

In the currently changing global strategic environment, opposition to and disapproval of the RBO—due to its incompatibility with international law as enshrined in the UN charter, multilateral treaties, and customary rules—are not exclusive to a resurging Russia and a rising China. They also have been and still are being voiced by an increasing number of emerging countries of a more assertive Global South determined to play its legitimate part and have a say in the governance of world affairs.

Moreover, the West's—and especially the U.S.'s—support for Israel's genocide in Gaza, in blatant violation of international and humanitarian law, when combined with condemnation and imposition of immediate and unprecedented sanctions on Russia following its invasion of Ukraine, proves that the RBO talk is sheer hypocrisy, thereby immensely complicating the West's position in the battle of narratives and global influence it is engaging with Russia and China.

---

49 State Councilor and Foreign Minister Wang Yi, "Remarks by State Councilor and Foreign Minister Wang Yi at the United Nations Security Council High-level Meeting on the Theme 'Maintenance of International Peace and Security: Upholding Multilateralism and the United Nations-centered International System'," Ministry of Foreign Affairs of the People's Republic of China, May 8, 2021. https://www.fmprc.gov.cn/mfa_eng/wjdt_665385/zyjh_665391/202105/t20210508_9170544.html

50 See Ray Dalio, *Principles for Dealing with the Changing World Order: Why Nations Succeed and Fail* (Simon & Schuster, 2021).

As I referred to earlier, the essential narrative of the West is built into the U.S. national security strategy, the core idea of which is that China and Russia are implacable foes that are "attempting to erode American security and prosperity" and are determined "to make economies less free and less fair," and "to control information and data to repress their societies and expand their influence."

The irony, as remarked by Prof. Jeffrey Sachs—who has served as adviser to three UN Secretaries-General, and is currently serving as a Sustainable Development Goals (SDGs) Advocate under Secretary-General António Guterres—is that

> since 1980 the U.S. has been in at least 15 overseas wars of choice (Afghanistan, Iraq, Libya, Panama, Serbia, Syria, and Yemen just to name a few), while China has been in none, and Russia only in one (Syria) beyond the former Soviet Union. The U.S. has military bases in 85 countries, China in 3, and Russia in 1 (Syria) beyond the former Soviet Union.[51]

The same irony is also manifested in the West's unconvincing mantra that it is opposing dictatorships and championing freedom, human rights and democracy around the world. No wonder the Global South sees hypocrisy in the U.S.'s framing of its hostility to and competition with such countries as China, Russia, Iran and North Korea—regularly singled out in successive National Security Strategies and lumped together in an "Axis of Upheaval"[52]—as a battle between democracy and autocracy. How else can one explain the fact that Washington continues to support many "undemocratic" and even "dictatorial" regimes and governments, selectively providing them with multifaceted aid and assistance?

Indeed, according to Freedom House, as of fiscal year 2015 the U.S. government has been providing military assistance to 36 of the 49 nations the NGO counts as dictatorships, a percentage of 73%! In 2021, this proportion had not changed since 35 out of 50 continued to receive

---

51 Jeffrey Sachs, "The West's False Narrative about Russia and China," *Othernews*, August 22, 2022. https://www.jeffsachs.org/newspaper-articles/h29g9k7l7fymxp39yhzwxc5f72ancr

52 Andrea Kendall-Taylor and Richard Fontaine, "The Axis of Upheaval: How America's Adversaries Are Uniting to Overturn the Global Order," Center for a New American Security, April 23, 2024.

such aid. Worst still, Freedom House informed[53] that during the same period, as COVID-19 spread,

> governments across the democratic spectrum repeatedly resorted to excessive surveillance, discriminatory restrictions on freedoms like movement and assembly and arbitrary or violent enforcement of such restrictions by police and non-state actors. Waves of false and misleading information, generated deliberately by political leaders in some cases, flooded many countries' communication system, obscuring reliable data and jeopardizing lives.

These withering blows marked the 15th consecutive decline in global freedom, the NGO lamented.

An answer to this large and troubling question of the U.S. relations with authoritarian countries was given in a thoroughly researched study[54] published by the Carnegie Endowment for International Peace in 2023. The paper reached three overarching conclusions:

First, Biden's policy with regard to authoritarian countries represents, on the whole, more continuity with than change from most previous U.S. Presidents, reflecting deep structures of interest that have shaped U.S. relations with these countries for decades.

Second, security issues are the dominant driver of U.S. relations with authoritarian countries—for both positive and negative relations—and span a wide range of security concerns, including competition with China and Russia, terrorism, and regional instability. Economic interests—such as energy investments, critical minerals, arms sales, or ensuring U.S. market access—also play a role in spurring positive U.S. relations with some authoritarian states though overall they are far less important than security concerns. Therefore, when the United States has a clear security interest in maintaining friendly relations with an authoritarian country, concerns about democracy are usually on the back burner, if not absent entirely.

---

53 Sarah Repucci and Amy Slipowitz, "Freedom in the World: Democracy under Siege," Freedom in the World 2021, Freedom House.
54 Thomas Carothers and Benjamin Feldman, "Examining U.S. Relations With Authoritarian Countries," The Carnegie Endowment for International Peace, December 13, 2023.

Third, the trends going forward appear to be mixed. With U.S.-China and U.S.-Russia tensions continuing to escalate, "the United States will have more reasons to put aside its concerns about democracy and human rights in some authoritarian countries as it tries to convince them to move closer to its camp. It will also be motivated to turn a cold shoulder to other countries that align themselves with its rivals."

The Carnegie study points to the fact that many people in U.S. policy circles debate the wisdom of the administration's trade-offs between its stated interest in supporting democracy globally versus countervailing interests that lead it to maintain close ties with some autocrats. But these debates are often confined to a few high-profile cases and rarely draw from a broader understanding of the overall landscape of U.S. relations with authoritarian regimes and the trajectory of such relations across recent decades. The authors of the paper conclude by saying that Washington's policy "produces justifiable charges of hypocrisy among observers around the world who see a U.S. administration apply the principle and deliver generous doses of self-righteous rhetoric in one country and then completely ignore democracy and rights issues in another."

With regard to the Ukraine war, the West's narrative is that it is a brutal and unprovoked attack by Vladimir Putin in his quest to recreate the Russian empire. Yet the real story of what caused the crisis is the Western promise to the reformist President Mikhail Gorbachev that NATO would not enlarge to the east. "Not one inch eastward"[55] was the assurance given by U.S. Secretary of State James Baker to Gorbachev on February 9, 1990. What has followed, however, is a wave of aggrandizements that concerned former members of the defunct Warsaw Pact and two Scandinavian nations as of late: three in 1999, seven in 2004, two in 2009, one in 2017 and 2020, and one in 2023 (Finland) and 2024 (Sweden), in addition to the 2008 commitment to incorporate Georgia and Ukraine—two countries in the immediate vicinity of Russia. Since the Alliance was created in 1949, its membership has thus grown from the 12 founding members to today's 32 members.

All this despite early warnings emanating from very experienced U.S. diplomats. In fact, on February 5, 1997, diplomat-historian George Kennan did not mince words in arguing that "expanding NATO would be the most fateful error in American policy in the entire post-cold war

---

55 To read the related declassified document: https://nsarchive.gwu.edu/briefing-book/russia-programs/2017-12-12/nato-expansion-what-gorbachev-heard-western-leaders-early

era. Such a decision may be expected … to impel Russian foreign policy in directions decidedly not to our liking."[56] And one year later, on February 1, William Burns—then U.S. ambassador in Moscow and now CIA Director—sent a confidential cable to Washington D.C., which he titled "Nyet Means Nyet: Russia's NATO Enlargements Redlines." The main part of that famous cable read:

> Ukraine and Georgia's NATO aspirations not only touch a raw nerve in Russia, they engender serious concerns about the consequences for stability in the region. Not only does Russia perceive encirclement, and efforts to undermine Russia's influence in the region, but it also fears unpredictable and uncontrolled consequences which would seriously affect Russian security interests. Experts tell us that Russia is particularly worried that the strong divisions in Ukraine over NATO membership, with much of the ethnic-Russian community against membership, could lead to a major split, involving violence or at worst, civil war. In that eventuality, Russia would have to decide whether to intervene; a decision Russia does not want to have to face.[57]

President Valdimir Putin also sent strong messages to the West at least on three occasions: in his speech at the Munich Security Conference in 2007 where he denounced the U.S.-led unipolar order; through his war against Georgia, at the end of which Tbilisi lost Abkhazia and South Ossetia in 2008; and finally with the annexation of Crimea in 2014. Retrospectively, one may conclude that those messages have been inadequately understood, to put it mildly.

Back in 2022, John Mearsheimer said in this regard that "My argument is that the West, especially the United States, is principally responsible for this disaster. But no American policymaker is going to acknowledge that line of argument. So they will say the Russians are responsible."[58] More recently, he reiterated this same conviction

---

56 George F. Kennan, "A Fateful Error," *The New York Times*, February 5, 1997.

57 This document was revealed by *Wikileaks:* https://wikileaks.org/plusd/cables/08MOSCOW265_a.html\

58 Cited in Isaac Chotiner, "Why John Mearsheimer Blames the U.S. for

in a conference titled "The Causes and Consequences of the Ukraine Crisis."[59]

For all these main reasons and others, Jeffrey Sachs was perfectly right to conclude that "Europe should reflect on the fact that the non-enlargement of NATO and the implementation of the Minsk II agreements would have averted this awful war in Ukraine," and that "It's past time that the U.S. recognized the true sources of security: internal social cohesion and responsible cooperation with the rest of the world, rather than the illusion of hegemony." With such a revised foreign policy, he added, the U.S. and its allies would avoid war with China and Russia, and enable the world to face its myriad environment, energy, food and social crises.[60]

Sachs's good advice is precisely what China in particular has been advocating and applying through a series of eye-catching initiatives aimed at increasing its power and boosting its diplomatic clout and global prestige to fulfil President Xi Jinping's "Chinese Dream" vision, all the while countering Western hegemony.

On that account, Beijing launched the "Belt and Road Initiative" (BRI) in 2013, the "Community of Shared Future of Mankind" in 2015, the "Global Development Initiative" (GDI) in 2021, and the "Global Security Initiative" (GSI) in 2022. Moreover, in light of President Biden's "Democracy vs. Authoritarianism" narrative and ahead of the second Summit for Democracy,[61] President Xi Jinping announced the "Global Civilization Initiative" (GCI).[62] At the Communist Party of China's "Dialogue with World Political Parties High-level Meeting," he said that the initiative will allow nations worldwide to adopt a new type of modernization and development and assist them in having a firm hold on their future development and progress.[63] He also declared that China wants other nations to uphold the principle of equality, have an

the Crisis in Ukraine," *The New Yorker,* March 1, 2022.

59 Video available at: https://youtu.be/JrMiSQAGOS4

60 Jeffrey Sachs, "The West's False Narrative about Russia and China," Op Cit.

61 See United States Department of State's Presentation of the Summit at: https://2021-2025.state.gov/summit-for-democracy-2023

62 Kashif Anwar, "Xi Jinping's Global Civilization Initiative," April 22, 2023.

63 "Full text of Xi Jinping's keynote address at the CPC in Dialogue with World Political Parties High-level Meeting," *Xinhua,* March 16, 2023: https://english.news.cn/20230316/31e80d5da3cd48bea63694cee5156d47/c.html?utm_source=substack&utm_medium=email

open mindset, refrain from imposing their values and models, and build a global network for inter-civilizational dialogue and cooperation.

As a result of this frantic battle of narratives, today more than ever the Global South is being courted by both sides, hence finding itself in a historically favorable position to pursue its own interests, which for too long have been cynically disregarded by the world's too often condescending great powers. And the answer to the important question of the direction in which the majority of the Global South's countries and public opinion will be tipped seems to be embodied in the compelling fact that bold actions and initiatives are being undertaken together with China and Russia, not with the West.

Among other significant common undertakings that signal a new age of international relations ushering the world into a multipolar global order is the creation of the BRICS group in 2009 and the "Group of Friends in Defense of the Charter of the United Nations" in 2021.

Named after its five founding members (Brazil, Russia, India, China and South Africa), the BRICS group is a collective of emerging economies eager to sustain and improve their economic trajectory. The four fundamental values and principles that underpin this non-Western grouping are: economic development, multilateralism, global governance reform, and solidarity.

The inclusion of Egypt, Ethiopia, Iran, and the United Arab Emirates in the 16th BRICS Summit in Kazan, Russia, in October 2024 formally marked its expansion. During that Summit, convened under the theme "Strengthening Multilateralism for Just Global Development and Security," the leaders of the member states commended the Russian chairship for hosting an "Outreach"/ BRICS Plus" Dialogue with the participation of emerging developing countries from Africa, Asia, Europe, Latin America, and Middle East under the motto: "BRICS and Global South: Building a Better World Together." Almost three dozen more countries—including NATO member Türkiye, close U.S. partners Thailand and Mexico, and Indonesia, the world's largest Muslim country—have applied to join the henceforth BRICS+.

The group now dwarfs the Western G7, both demographically (46% of the world's population, compared with the G7's 8.8%) and economically (35% of global GDP, compared to the G7's 30%). It also has the potential "to serve as a catalyst for a long-overdue revamping of global governance so that it better reflects twenty-first-century realities."[64]

---

64 Brahma Chellany, "The BRICS Effect," *Project Syndicate,* October 18,

As for the "Group of Friends of the Charter of the United Nations" (GoF), so far composed of 18 member states,[65] it concurs that

> one of the key elements for ensuring the realization of the three pillars of the Organization of the United Nations and of the yearnings of its peoples, as well as of a peaceful and prosperous world and a just and equitable world order, is ensuring precisely, compliance with and strict adherence to, the purposes and principles enshrined in the Charter, for it is the consolidation of relations and cooperation among States that will ensure peace, security, stability and development to the international community as a whole."

It, however, considers that multilateralism, which is at the core of the Charter, is currently under an unprecedented attack, which, in turn, threatens global peace and security.

The GoF members also reject the attempt to establish a RBO. On the occasion of the first meeting of national coordinators of the GoF held in Tehran, Iran, on November 5, 2022, the participants reiterated their "serious concern" at continued attempts aimed at replacing the tenets enshrined in the UN Charter, which have been agreed upon by the entire international community for conducting their international relations, with a "so-called 'rules-based order,' that remains unclear, that has "not been discussed or accepted by the wide membership," and that has the "potential, among others, to undermine the rule of law at the international level." Further, they called for the redoubling of efforts toward "democratization of international relations," the "strengthening of multilateralism and of a multipolar system," while expressing their "categorical rejection of all unilateral coercive measures, including those applied as tools for political or economic and financial pressure against any country, in particular against developing countries."

It is worth recalling that the GoF's initial creation came shortly after the U.S. and a number of its allies and partners supported the

---

2024.

65 Algeria, Belarus, Bolivia, China, Cuba, the Democratic People's Republic of Korea, Equatorial Guinea, Eritrea, the Islamic Republic of Iran, the Lao People's Democratic Republic, Mali, Nicaragua, the State of Palestine, the Russian Federation, Saint Vincent and the Grenadines, Syria, Venezuela, and Zimbabwe.

increasingly nonsensical presidential claims of Juan Guaidó, head of the opposition-controlled National Assembly in Venezuela, in defiance of President Nicolás Maduro, who stood accused of engineering his win at the elections, and that the group's recurrent calls for additional membership come amid renewed great power competition between the U.S. and its top rivals, China and Russia.[66]

In 2023, just a few months before the wreckage of international and humanitarian law in the mass killing fields of Gaza, *Foreign Affairs* magazine's executives devoted much of the May/June issue[67] to the topic of the state of world order. On that occasion, several policymakers and scholars from Africa, Latin America, and South and Southeast Asia were invited to explore the dangers, as well as the new opportunities, that the war in Ukraine and the broader return of great-power conflict present for their respective countries and regions. The overarching conclusion of the different contributors was that Russia's war in Ukraine has drawn Western allies together, but it has not unified the world's democracies in the way U.S. President Joe Biden might have hoped for when the war started. Further, the unfolding events highlighted just how different much of the rest of the world sees not only the war but also the broader global landscape.

Voicing the point of view of Africans, South African Professor Tim Murithi[68] pointed out that many African countries declined to take a strong stand against Moscow, and more and more among them in the continent and elsewhere in the Global South are refusing to align with either the West or the East, "declining to defend the so-called liberal order but also refusing to seek to upend it as Russia and China have done." The reason for that, Murithi argues, is that the rules-based international order has not served the African interests. On the contrary, it has preserved a status quo in which major world powers, be they Western or Eastern, have maintained their positions of dominance over the Global South, relegated African governments to "little more than bystanders in their own affairs," and ignored their longstanding calls for the UN Security Council to be reformed and the broader international system to be reconfigured on more equitable terms. If the West wants Africa to stand up

---

66 Tom O'Connor, "China, Russia, Iran, North Korea and More Join Forces 'in Defense' of U.N.," December 3, 2021.

67 "The Nonaligned world: The West, the Rest, and the New Global Disorder," *Foreign Affairs,* May/June 2023.

68 Tim Murithi, "Order of Oppression: Africa's Quest for an International System."

for the international order, he said, then "it must allow that order to be remade so that it is based on more than the idea of might makes right."

For Brazilian Professor Matias Spektor,[69] developing countries are increasingly seeking to avoid costly entanglements with the major powers, trying to keep all their options open for maximum flexibility; they are pursuing a strategy of hedging because they see the future distribution of global power as uncertain and wish to avoid commitments that will be hard to discharge. They hedge not only to gain material concessions but also to raise their status, and they embrace multipolarity as an opportunity to move up in the international order. If the United States wants to remain first among the great powers in a multipolar world, Professor Spektor concludes, it "must meet the Global South on its own terms."

For her part, Nirupama Rao,[70] India's Foreign Secretary from 2009 to 2011 and former ambassador to China and the United States, believes that India has "limited patience for U.S. and European narratives which are both myopic and hypocritical," and although Europe and Washington may be right that Russia is violating human rights in Ukraine, "Western powers have carried out similar violent, unjust, and undemocratic interventions—from Vietnam to Iraq." New Delhi is therefore uninterested in Western calls for Russia's isolation. To strengthen itself and address the world's shared challenges, Rao added, "India has the right to work with everyone." This perspective isn't unique to her country, and much of the Global South is wary of being dragged into siding with the U.S. against China and Russia. Developing countries, she rightly observes, are

> understandably more concerned about their climate vulnerability, their access to advanced technology and capital, and their need for better infrastructure, health care, and education systems. They see increasing global instability—political and financial alike—as a threat to tackling such challenges. And they have watched rich and powerful states disregard those views and preferences in pursuit of their geopolitical interests.

69 Matias Spektor, "In Defense of the Fence Sitters: What the West Gets Wrong About Hedging."

70 Nirupama Rao, "The Upside of Rivalry: India's Great-Power Opportunity."

That's why Rao goes on to say, India "wants to make sure the voices of these poorer states are heard in international debates" and is positioning itself as "a heartland of global South—a bridging presence that stands for multilateralism."

In a remarkably balanced piece he wrote in the same *Foreign Affairs* issue, former UK Secretary of State for Foreign and Commonwealth Affairs David Miliband concurred with the views and legitimate demands of the "fence-sitting" Global South. It is to be hoped that Miliband's fellow Western citizens will listen carefully to his message and, more importantly, heed his wise advice, because as he rightly highlighted in the subtitle of his contribution,[71] what is also at stake in the present historical juncture is no less than "the survival of the West."

---

71 David Miliband, "The World Beyond Ukraine: The Survival of the West and the Demands of the Rest."

CONCLUSION

THE END OF EMPATHY, GENOCIDE, AND THE LAST WESTERN MAN

"The death of human empathy is one of the earliest and most telling signs of a culture about to fall into barbarism."
—HANNAH ARENDT

"The old world is dying, and the new world struggles to be born; now is the time of monsters."
—ANTONIO GRAMSCI

"The man who wants to govern men must, more than ever, have the soul of an apostle and the entrails of a father."
—MALEK BENNABI[1]

A Dystopian "Brave New World" Made Real

It's now possible to reflect more fully on Israel's genocide of the people of Gaza. My earlier reflection, which I laid out in a series of articles[2] beginning a year ago, addresses a war that from its outbreak on October 7, 2023, seemed in many respects to be fundamentally different from all previous Israeli military expeditions against the Palestinian population. This contrast convinced me to call it *"the war to end all Gaza wars."* I had also predicted that this war would have long-lasting and far-reaching consequences given its potential to reshape the entire Middle East, to further exacerbate international tensions, and to possibly provoke a conflagration that could spread beyond a part of the world

---

1 Malek Bennabi, *L'Afro-Asiatisme: Conclusions sur la Conférence de Bandoeng* (Le Caire, Imprimerie Misr S.A.E, 1956).
2 These articles are accessible through the author page for Amir Nour at *GlobalResearch*. https://www.globalresearch.ca/author/amir-nour

that has experienced more than its share of humiliation for more than a century.

Since a series of momentous events appears to confirm the accuracy of my argument, far from taking satisfaction, I will repeat what I anticipated in the introduction. Gaza is almost completely destroyed and its population is undergoing an unprecedented genocide.[3] Up until its final days, the departing U.S. administration supported the Israeli slaughter with all means possible. President Joe Biden's "parting gift"[4] to Israel of $8 billion[5] in weapons sales was another step toward its establishing a "Greater Israel," which will extend beyond the borders of Gaza and the West Bank to incorporate chunks of Lebanon and Syria. Paid for with rivers of blood, this is another giant step toward the realization of the Zionist dream.

In support of this objective, eight Israeli lawmakers recently sent a letter to Minister of Defense Israel Katz calling for their coalition government to intensify the siege of the already strangulated Gaza concentration camp. Claiming the IDF's present strategy was not adequate to defeat Hamas, the letter demanded that the IDF use sieges, infrastructure destruction, and the killing of anyone without a white flag to purge northern Gaza of its residents, while insisting this policy should be used in other parts of the enclave.[6]

In the eyes of incoming U.S. President Donald Trump such collective punishment wasn't severe enough. As if Palestinians could possibly be brutalized more than the "crime of crimes" they've been subjected to for over a year, the President-elect threatened Hamas that it would have

---

3 On January 26, 2024, the International Court of Justice found that a plausible case can be made that Israel is committing genocide in Gaza; on November 21, 2024, the International Criminal Court issued arrest warrants for Israeli Prime Minister Benjamin Netanyahu and former Israeli Defense Minister Yoav Gallant for crimes against humanity and war crimes; on December 5, 2024, Amnesty International issued a 296-page report detailing Israel's genocide in Gaza; and on December 19, 2024, Human Rights Watch issued a 179-page report detailing Israel's genocide in Gaza. See John J. Mearsheimer, "The Moral Bankruptcy of the West," *John's Substack,* December 24, 2024.

4 Chris Hedges, "Genocide: The New Normal," *The Chris Hedges Report,* January 6, 2025.

5 This amount is to be added to $17.9 billion in military aid to Israel provided from October 2023 to October 2024, on top of $3.8 billion the U.S. gives to Israel annually. In sum, it is an absolute record for a single fiscal year.

6 Noa Shpigel, "Israeli Lawmakers Call on Military to Destroy Food, Water and Power Sources in Gaza," *Haaretz,* January 3, 2025.

"hell to pay" if the hostages were not released by the time he assumed office on January 20, 2025. Those responsible, he warned, "will be hit harder than anybody has been hit in the long and storied history of the United States of America." Benjamin Netanyahu thanked Trump for his "strong support."

The entire Middle East is in a state of chaos as the flames of war have expanded to Lebanon, Yemen, Iraq, Syria and Iran. It seems that the Western Zionist plans to break up the Arab-Muslim world through a new "Sykes-Picot" are in full swing. More than ever before, we must remind ourselves of both former Israeli senior official and journalist Oded Yinon's 1982 plan entitled "A Strategy for Israel in the 1980s" and former U.S. commander of NATO forces General Wesley Clark's revelation about the five-year plan devised by the White House after the 9/11 strikes to attack, in addition to Afghanistan, seven majority-Muslim countries.

Indeed, on August 12, 2025, Netanyahu told news channel i24 that he feels "very attached" to the vision of a "Greater Israel," which includes the occupied Palestinian territories, as well as parts of Egypt, Jordan, Syria, Lebanon, Iraq, and Saudi Arabia. He further said he considers himself on a "historic and spiritual mission that generations of Jews that dreamt of coming here and generations of Jews who will come after us."[7]

On the global stage, violence since the end of the Cold War is at an all-time high. According to the Norwegian Peace Research Institute, Oslo,[8] there have never been so many armed conflicts across the globe as in 2023: 59 state-based and 75 non-state conflicts were recorded in 34 countries, many instigated and/or fueled by Western powers in Africa and the Middle East, the highest number of conflicts since the data collection starting point in 1946. Furthermore, President-elect Donald Trump has broached an expansionist agenda targeting Panama, Greenland, and even Canada for potential acquisition, including by means of annexation. As of January 2024, the "Doomsday Clock," which warns of the risk of nuclear war, is set at 90 seconds to midnight, its most dangerous setting since the Cuban missile crisis of October 1962.

---

7 Watch Netanyahu's interview on the i24NEWS English YouTube channel: https://youtu.be/u8xhaxo2JJY

8 Siri Aas Rustad, *Conflict Trends: A Global Overview, 1946–2023,* Peace Research Institute Oslo (PRIO) Paper, 2024.

Ringing the alarm, UN Secretary-General António Guterres fore-warned the Security Council of the horrific trajectory in which events seemed to be proceeding:

> Almost eight decades after the incineration of Hiroshima and Nagasaki, nuclear weapons represent a clear danger to global peace and security, growing in power, range and stealth. States possessing them are absent from the negotiating table, and some statements have raised the prospect of unleashing nuclear hell.[9]

To Pope Francis possession of these weapons is "immoral"; the Hibakusha, survivors of Hiroshima and Nagasaki, advocate for a world free of these weapons; and for Hollywood, where *Oppenheimer* brought the harsh reality of nuclear doomsday to vivid life, this "nuclear madness" must end. In the words of Guterres, "Humanity cannot survive a sequel to *Oppenheimer*."

Clearly, these calls are struggling to resonate with the great powers. Recently, former Russian President Dmitry Medvedev, currently the deputy chairman of the Security Council of Russia, and President Putin warned that provocations by Ukraine and its allies could result in nuclear war.[10] Their warnings came shortly after President Biden gave the green light for Ukraine to employ U.S.-made ATACMS long-range missiles to hit a Russian weapons facility in Bryansk Oblast. Moscow perceives this provocation to be a response to North Korea's sending of thousands of soldiers to Russia.

In fact, these developments reflect a global upheaval, a tidal wave of change nurtured by increasing divisions within and between nations: West vs. East, Collective West vs. Global South, left vs. right, black vs. white, men vs. women, old vs. young, modernity vs. tradition, skeptics vs. believers, religion versus spirituality, fake news vs. real news, and the list goes on and on. Our age is also one of extreme polarization where self-styled "strongmen" are rising to power in an increasing number of

---

9 António Guterres, "Nuclear Warfare Risk at Highest Point in Decades, Secretary-General Warns Security Council, Urging Largest Arsenal Holders to Find Way Back to Negotiating Table," United Nations, March 18, 2024.

10 Hugh Cameron, "Putin Ally Warns the West Risks 'Nuclear Catastrophe'," *Newsweek,* September 26, 2024.

countries to become a central feature of global politics,[11] where stark opinions and radical views thrive, in the midst of dizzying advances in science and technology and an unprecedented information overload. As a result, in the collision between the establishment's propaganda and the skepticism of the so-called conspiracy theorists—once tolerated as harmless cranks but now considered in light of their increasing appearance of cogency as dangerous "new heretics"[12] whose views must be removed from public view—nuanced debate is lost and confusion reigns supreme.

In the West in general and the United States in particular, for at least two decades now many NGOs, thinkers, political scientists and social activists have been warning that the expanding social inequality and steady erosion of democratic institutions would inevitably lead to populism, authoritarian states, and more generally to what Stanford University's Larry Diamond calls "democratic recession."[13]

Moreover, the Russo-Ukrainian conflict, which is clearly turning to Moscow's advantage, and, even more so, the war against Palestine, have accentuated the crystallization of some political and geopolitical dynamics that have been at work for several decades now. In particular, the gradual questioning of the power of the Western powers and the international system they established since 1945 have had the palpable effect of pushing the world into an accelerated phase of "de-Westernization," that is, the irreversible erosion of the values, power, and influence of the "Global North." For the first time in five centuries, "Western powers are no longer in a position to impose their demands on the rest of the world, neither militarily nor politically or culturally, (and) for the first time in human history, the peoples seem in a situation to take their destiny into their own hands."[14] This, at the very moment when the emerging powers

---

11 Gideon Rachman, *The Age of the Strongman: How the Cult of the Leader Threatens Democracy Around the World* (London: The Bodley Head, 2022).

12 Andy Thomas, *The New Heretics: Understanding the Conspiracy Theories Polarizing the World* (London: Watkins, 2021).

13 Read his latest assessments where he depicts the current state of democracy in the world, why it started to retreat in 2006, and how to renew its momentum: Larry Diamond, "Democracy's Arc: From Resurgent to Imperiled," *Journal of Democracy* 33, no. 1 (January 2022), pp. 163–79; and Larry Diamond, "Power, Performance, and Legitimacy," *Journal of Democracy* 35, no. 2 (April 2024), pp. 5–22.

14 Didier Billion and Christophe Ventura, *Désoccidentalisation: Repenser l'ordre du monde* (Editions Agone, 2023).

of the "Global South" are asserting themselves on the world stage and seeking to shake up the old balances.

When all is said and done, is it not permissible to ask: are we not living in a "Brave New World," almost exactly as the Russian Yevgeny Zamyatin and the Britons Aldous Huxley and George Orwell foresaw in the last century? And isn't it possible that such concepts as modernity, secularism, development, and progress are no more than long-held utopian views, and that the political impasses and economic shocks impacting our societies, as well as the irreparably damaged environment, corroborate the bleakest views of a long list of thinkers, starting with the nineteenth-century critics who condemned modern capitalism as "a heartless machine for economic growth, or the enrichment of the few, which works against such fundamentally human aspirations as stability, community and a better future?"[15]

Nihilism, Genocide, and the Fate of Western Civilization

Perhaps one of the major unintended consequences of the war on Gaza is that it is providing a likely convincing answer to Francis Fukuyama's "old/new" question which, surprisingly, has not been sufficiently highlighted either by the proponents of the "end of history" thesis or by its opponents. To return to this: Can political and economic liberty and equality characterizing the state of affairs at the presumed "end of history" bring about a stable society in which man may be said to be, at last, completely satisfied? Or, will the spiritual condition of the "last man" in history, "deprived of outlets for his striving for mastery," inevitably lead him to plunge himself and the world into the chaos and bloodshed of history?

In truth, the debate on this fascinating question of moral and political philosophy—can man reasonably enjoy unrestrained freedom in the name of his individual rights and is such unbounded freedom compatible with his responsibilities toward society and nature?—has taken place before, in particular a century ago, under the auspices of two of the greatest philosophers of all time: Russian Fyodor Dostoevsky and German Friedrich Nietzsche, who continue to be influential today. They both argued against modern rationalism, strongly believing its corrosive influence would have severe implications for civilization and eventually

---

15 Pankaj Mishra, *Age of Anger: A History of the Present* (Farrar, Straus and Giroux, 2017).

destroy all moral, religious, and metaphysical convictions, thereby precipitating the greatest crisis in human history. But while agreeing on the diagnosis of the "disease" of modernity, they diverged on the "cure," offering two diametrically opposed paths forward: Nietzsche points to a path "beyond God," while Dostoevsky offers a solution pointing man "back to God."

Arguably, this divergence is exactly what is happening within Western governments and societies with regard to the situation in Gaza in general and the acquiescence to the genocide Israel is perpetrating, more specifically. Indeed, against an emerging global consensus in favor of the Palestinian cause, the U.S. continues to arm Israel; the UK insists it remains a "staunch ally" of Israel; diplomatically and militarily, Germany continues to support Israel; and France has declared that Netanyahu enjoys immunity because Israel is not a signatory to the ICC (International Criminal Court). France's declaration not only is a betrayal of its past support for the Rome Statute of the ICC, which it helped to negotiate in 1998 and whose spurious charges directed against Russian President Vladimir Putin it supported, but also weakens the institution's global standing.

Israeli American professor of Holocaust and Genocide Studies at Brown University Omer Bartov says Israel's war on Gaza combines "genocidal actions, ethnic cleansing and annexation of the Gaza Strip." He warns that impunity for Israel would endanger the entire edifice of international law. This is "a total moral, ethical failure by the very countries that claim to be the main protectors of civil rights, democracy, human rights around the world." What's more, the Palestinian occupied territories have become the perfect laboratory for the Israeli military-techno complex: from

> constant surveillance, home demolitions and indefi-
> nite incarceration, to the hi-tech devices that drive the
> "Start-up Nation," Israel has become a global leader
> in spying technology and defense hardware: the oc-
> cupation is the ideal marketing tool, and Palestine the
> proving ground.[16]

---

16 Antony Loewenstein, *The Palestine Laboratory: How Israel exports the Technology of Occupation Around the World* (Verso, 2023).

Likewise, *The Guardian's* Nesrine Malik observed that Israel's destruction of Gaza is "just a part of life [that] seems to say: yes, this is the world we live in now. Get used to it." The cheapening of Palestinian life involves

> separating our lives from theirs, separating legal and moral worlds into two—one in which we exist and deserve freedom from hunger, fear and persecution, and a second in which others have demonstrated some quality that shows they are not owed the same. Once you are taught to cease to identify with others on the basis of their humanity, the work of necropolitics[17] is complete.

Malik emphasizes that the sanctity of human life is what separates us from barbarism. She concludes by saying: "the end result [of barbarism] is a world in which when the call comes to aid people in need, no one will be capable of heeding it."[18]

German-American political philosopher Hannah Arendt once famously wrote: "The death of human empathy is one of the earliest and most telling signs of a culture about to fall into barbarism." In the United States, Barack Obama admitted during his 2008 campaign for the presidential election that: "our lack of empathy is America's essential deficit," far more concerning than its federal deficit. And in the United Kingdom, a 2018 YouGov survey[19] found that 51% of respondents in that country are said to be concerned that empathy is on the wane, with 51% of the persons surveyed believing that Britons' ability to sense, understand and share the feelings of others and put themselves in others' shoes has declined, versus only 12% who thought it had increased.

---

17 Achille Mbembe, *Necropolitics* (Duke University Press, 2019). In this essay Mbembe theorizes the genealogy of the contemporary world, a world plagued by ever-increasing inequality, militarization, enmity, and terror as well as by a resurgence of racist, fascist, and nationalist forces determined to exclude and kill.

18 Read Nesrine Malik's following articles in *The Guardian:* "A new terror has entered the Gaza war: that it is ushering in an age of total immorality," July 28, 2024; "The lesson of Israel's unfathomably cruel war: Ours is still a world where might is right," October 28, 2024; "A consensus is emerging: Israel is committing genocide in Gaza. Where is the action?," December 23, 2024.

19 *The Week* staff, "Is Britain experiencing an 'empathy crisis'?," October 4, 2018.

Such predicament is anything but a novel phenomenon, as documented by Christopher Powell in his book *Barbaric Civilization: A Critical Sociology of Genocide*,[20] in which he dealt with the central issues of "Why have the largest mass murders in human history taken place in the past hundred years?" and "Why have European colonizers so often denied the humanity of the colonized?"

A case in point here is the motherland of Nietzsche and Arendt—Germany, whether imperial, Nazi, or federal. From the 1884–85 Berlin Conference during which European states arrogated themselves the "right" to carve up the African continent, to the genocides it soon afterward committed in Namibia and Tanzania, all the way through to the crimes against humanity of WWII, Germany's racial philosophy taught that Aryans were the master race and that some other races were *Untermensch* (sub-humans). This philosophy then translated into a policy of ruthless persecution of all the populations which were controlled or subjugated (Jews, Blacks, Slavs, Gypsies, people with disabilities, Jehovah's witnesses, etc.) through eugenics, sterilization, euthanasia, and forced labor in dozens of thousands of incarceration sites, of which over 1,000 were concentration camps. As for today's federal Germany, its total lack of empathy toward Palestinians is equaled only by its unconditional and multifaceted support for Israel. Chancellors Angela Merkel and Olaf Scholz went as far as to declare repeatedly this support has the force of a "raison d'État" (Staats-raison), in other words, "an unacknowledged transgression of the law in the name of a higher security imperative."[21] This situation prompted Indian writer and activist Arundhati Roy to say: "Who would have imagined that we would live to see the day when German police would arrest Jewish citizens for protesting against Israel and Zionism and accuse them of anti-Semitism?"[22]

As has been discussed before, if the West's antagonism with China is today essentially of an economic nature and will tomorrow concern the conditions under which to manage world affairs politically, the quarrel between the Collective West on the one hand, and the Russian and Islamic spheres on the other, lie first and foremost in

---

20 Christopher Powell, *Barbaric Civilization: A Critical Sociology of Genocide* (McGill-Queen's University Press, 2011).

21 Enzo Traverso, *Gaza devant l'histoire* (*Gaza Before history*) (Lux Editeur, 2024).

22 Arundhati Roy, "No Propaganda on Earth Can Hide the Wound That Is Palestine: Arundhati Roy's PEN Pinter Prize Acceptance Speech," *The Wire*, October 11, 2024.

fundamental and longstanding cultural divergences, if not contrasting worldviews altogether. In the short term, if Western nations genuinely want to understand the Islamic psyche so they can devise policies that respect the Arab-Muslim world, they would benefit from meditating deeply on the ideas expressed by Robert Nicholson in an editorial about America's 2021 withdrawal from Afghanistan. Using an evocative title for his piece, "The Unconquerable Islamic World,"[23] Nicholson argued that despite its investment of "trillions of dollars, tens of thousands of lives, and two decades of warfare," the West failed to comprehend that here, "politics lies downstream of culture, and culture downstream of religion." Its "blindness [was] driven by a noble desire to see humans as equal, interchangeable beings for whom faith and culture are 'accidents of birth.' But these accidents are non-negotiable truths for hundreds of millions of people who would rather die than concede them."

Nicholson's thesis shares Samuel Huntington's view that Islamic societies belong to a distinctive civilization that resists the forceful imposition of foreign values. Indeed, in *The Clash of Civilizations* Huntington argues that

> The West won the world not by the superiority of its ideas or values or religion (to which few members of other civilizations were converted) but rather by its superiority in applying organized violence. Westerners often forget this fact; non-Westerners never do.

He also warned that

> to preserve Western civilization in the face of declining Western power, it is in the interest of the United States and European countries ... to recognize that Western intervention in the affairs of other civilizations is probably the single most dangerous source of instability and potential global conflict in a multi-civilizational world.

Huntington is right, non-Westerners do remember, and so must the Palestinians. That's precisely the reason why, in his recently published

---

23 Robert Nicholson, "The Unconquerable Islamic World," *The Wall Street Journal,* August 19, 2021.

memoirs,[24] former Algerian foreign minister Ahmed Taleb-Ibrahimi—citing his own father Sheikh Bachir Ibrahimi who had delineated fronts where anti-colonial struggle should take place, labeling them the "3 M's," namely the Military, the Missionaries and the Merchants—considers that a fourth "M," the front of Memory, is also a front in the struggle against Zionism. To this end, he appealed to Algerian and all Muslim youth to establish a museum dedicated to the memory of the Palestinian Nakba (Catastrophe). Similar to *Yad Vashem,* Israel's Holocaust Museum, such an institution, he says, would recall, with great educational value, the horrors of the dark periods of human history and bring art and culture back into line with ethics and morality. Among other contemporary museums that embody Taleb-Ibrahimi's vision are museums of the indigenous peoples of the Americas, the House of Slaves on Senegal's Gorée Island and the Atomic Bomb Museum in Nagasaki.

In the case of Gaza, one of the best illustrations of the impact of the Islamic faith on its followers, is undoubtedly that provided by Nour Jarada, a psychologist working with "Médecins du Monde France." Speaking of daily life in an enclave punctuated by war, she writes:

> No one knows what the future holds. But what I do know is that oppressions always end one day. As the poet Abu al-Qasim al-Shabi wrote: "If the people ever want to live, destiny will respond." And as God promises in the Qur'an: "With difficulty there is indeed ease!" Despite all that we endure, we cling to our strength and resilience. Every day, we put aside our pain to take on our roles and reach out to those around us. Helping those the world has forgotten gives our lives meaning and purpose. Yet, I have also discovered a resilience in myself that I never imagined I possessed. I have endured fear, displacement, loss, grief, tears, and unimaginable sorrow. I have faced it all patiently, even when I had no choice. Through it all, I have been carried by my unwavering faith, a conviction that there is a reason for everything, even if only God knows it. We believe in God. Every trial

---

24 Ahmed Taleb-Ibrahimi, *Mémoires d'un Algérien, tome 4: Craintes et espérances (1988–2019)* [*Memoirs of an Algerian, volume 4: Fears and hopes (1988–2019)*] (Algiers: Casbah Editions, 2024).

we face carries with it a wisdom that our minds cannot comprehend. We commit our hearts to God, even
when the trial seems beyond our human capacity. This
faith has driven me to persevere, to keep working, to
fight, and to support those around me.[25]

History will repeat itself once more. And what happened in
Afghanistan will sooner or later happen in the Middle East, though the
manner and circumstances will possess their own character.

Towards an "Ecumenical" Era?

As Nicholson says, the Western world's focus "must be on curing
the spiritual sickness that blinded us in the first place, recovering our
own sense of civilizational self and reorienting our priorities accordingly." His reflection recalls 14th-century Arab philosopher/historian
Abd ar-Raḥmān Ibn Khaldun whose *Muqaddimah,* or *Prolegomena*
(Introduction), states:

> Sometimes, when the empire is in the last period of
> its existence, it (suddenly) deploys enough force to
> make people believe that its decadence has stopped;
> but it is only the last glimmer of a candle wick that
> is about to stop burning. When a lamp is about to go
> out, it suddenly gives off a burst of light which makes
> one suppose that it is turning on again, when it's the
> opposite that happens.

Broadly speaking, there are three main categories of analysts in the
West who now attempt to mitigate its malfeasance throughout history,
whether it be for the past crimes of slavery, genocide, and colonization,
or for the current aggressions against other peoples and the illegal ex-
ploitation of their riches, as is notably the case with the Palestinian tragedy. There are those who recognize the malefactors and their ill deeds and
call for forgiveness and redemption,[26] those who admit some of the worst

---

25 Nour Z. Jarada, "Journal d'une Gazaouie: 'Nous sommes morts de
toutes les morts possibles'" (Diary of a Gazan: "We died every possible death"),
Liberation, December 31, 2024.

26 Among others: French authors Emmanuel Todd who, in his book *The
defeat of the West* (2024), devoted a whole postscript under the title "American

crimes committed by the West while seeking to promote some of its other "positive accomplishments" that might help ameliorate its crimes and
absolve the culprits,[27] and those who purely and simply mythologize and
glorify the victimizers while placing blame on the victims and making
them feel guilty about their victimhood.[28]

But now, in the face of growing domestic and global awareness
of the West's past crimes brought about as the suffering in Gaza sheds
a blinding light on its abominations and exposes the liars—politicians,
pundits and press—that promote and defend it, bringing enlightenment
to an aghast global public with regard to events both contemporary and
historical, is there, indeed, a way to envision a change in course?

Malek Bennabi, an Algerian Muslim then living under the yoke
of French colonialism, may have formulated the best advice to the West
and to world leaders. Having observed the crisis of Western civilization,
its culmination in a dead end, and the loss of the motivations for its
existence, he stated that "The new civilization must be neither a civilization of a proud continent nor that of a selfish people, but of a humanity
pooling all its potentialities."[29]

And while recognizing the transformative power of the European
fact in the world, he called on Europe—[the West, in today's jargon]—to
integrate itself into the global conscience that its civilization has created. To that end, he saw the task of "Afro-Asianism" [the Global South]
as lying in "helping Western man to reach this dimension to which its

---

nihilism: The proof by Gaza"; Didier Fassin who wrote a book, *The strange
defeat: The consent to the crushing of Gaza* (2024); and François Martin who
wrote an essay devoted to "The time of Fractures: The West versus the Rest of
the World" (2024).

27 Among others: French author Gilles Kepel who describes the attacks
of October 7, 2023 as a "pogrom raid" that has produced "The upheaval of the
world" (2024), and British political commentator Douglas Murray who, in his
2022 book titled *The War on the West: How to Prevail in the Age of Unreason*,
believes that "in recent years there is a cultural war being waged remorselessly
against all the roots of the Western tradition and against everything good that the
Western tradition has produced."

28 Like British Prof. Nigel Biggar whose 2023 book *Colonialism: A
Moral Reckoning* is considered by many as outrageous, and French Jean-
François Colosimo for whom the Russian, Ottoman, Persian, Chinese and Indian
empires of the 19th century are back and rising up against "The West, world
enemy no. 1."

29 Malek Bennabi, *Les conditions de la renaissance* (*The conditions for
renaissance*) (Algiers: Editions En-Nahdha, 1949).

conscience has not yet arrived." Bennabi then expressed his conviction that history will continue to be made with Western input:

> For good as for evil, its choice still has a global impor-
> tance ... We must not let Europe [the West] fall back on
> its axis, withdraw from the world to sulk at humanity
> which it can no longer dominate. It is necessary to
> show [the West] that its security does not depend on
> power, but on the development of its conscience in the
> dimension of others and of its genius in harmony with
> current trends and a higher human interest.

And because he believed that one cannot "engage in the ecumeni-cal era[30] with the complexes bequeathed by colonialism," he pleaded for the universal exigence according to which:

> A great pity for oneself and for all that is human must
> inspire those who govern, knowing that under the
> greatest perversion there is always a possibility of
> redemption, and under the appearance of force there
> is always a great weakness that sums up human weak-
> nesses. Power increasingly requires the highest moral
> qualities.

Accordingly, Bennabi declared: "The man who wants to govern men must, more than ever, have the soul of an apostle and the entrails of a father."

Is this the ultimate trajectory to be hoped for from the West? Or will it sink into nihilism, barbarism and disarray as its grip on global power is inevitably wrested from it?

---

30 As early as 1956, Bennabi spoke of the realization of a "great human mutation" whereby "mankind, which had crossed with the Neolithic the first level of its history by rising to the level of civilizations, must now move to the second level of its history by rising to the level of the civilization of the ecumenical man."

POSTSCRIPT

YAHYA AL-SINWAR'S WILL [1]

"I am Yahya, the son of a refugee who turned exile into a temporary homeland and turned a dream into an eternal battle. As I write these words, I recall every moment that has passed in my life: from my childhood in the alleys, to the long years of imprisonment, to every drop of blood that was shed on the soil of this land.

"I was born in Khan Yunis camp in 1962, at a time when Palestine was a torn memory and forgotten maps on the tables of politicians. I am the man whose life was woven between fire and ashes, and who realized early on that life under occupation meant nothing but permanent imprisonment. I knew from a young age that life in this land is not ordinary, and that whoever is born here must carry an unbreakable weapon in their heart and be aware that the road to freedom is long.

"My will to you starts here, from that child who threw the first stone at the occupier and learned that stones are the first words we utter in the face of a world that stands silent in the face of our wound.

"I learned in the streets of Gaza that a person is not measured by the years of their life, but by what they give to their homeland. This was my life: prisons and battles, pain and hope. I entered prison for the first time in 1988, and was sentenced to life imprisonment, but I did not know fear. In those dark cells, I saw in every wall a window to the distant horizon, and in every bar a light illuminating the path to freedom. In prison, I learned that patience is not just a virtue, but rather a weapon, a bitter weapon, like drinking the sea drop by drop.

"My will to you: do not fear prisons, for they are only part of our long journey toward freedom. Prison taught me that freedom is not just a stolen right, but rather an idea born of pain and refined with patience. When I was released in the 'Loyalty of the Free' prisoner exchange deal in 2011, I did not emerge the same; I emerged stronger and so did my

---

1 This exclusive document was sent to the author exclusively by Palestinian sources, and published, for the first time, by the author in Arabic on October 20, 2024, and subsequently translated into English and French.

244

belief that what we are doing is not just a passing struggle, but rather our destiny, one that we carry until the last drop of our blood.

"My will to you is that you continue to cling to the gun, to the dignity that cannot be compromised, and to the dream that does not die. The enemy wants us to abandon resistance, to turn our issue into an endless negotiation. But I say to you: do not negotiate over what is rightfully yours. They fear your steadfastness more than they fear your weapons. Resistance is not just a weapon we carry, but rather it is our love for Palestine in every breath we take, it is our will to remain, despite the siege and aggression.

"My will to you is that you remain loyal to the blood of the martyrs, to those who departed and left us this path full of thorns. They are the ones who paved the path of freedom for us with their blood, so do not waste those sacrifices in the calculations of politicians and the games of diplomacy. We are here to continue what the first generation started, and we will not deviate from this path no matter the cost. Gaza was and will remain the capital of steadfastness, and the heart of Palestine that never stops beating, even if the world closes in around us.

"When I took over the leadership of Hamas in Gaza in 2017, it was not just a transfer of power, but rather a continuation of a resistance that began with stones and continued with rifles. Every day, I felt the pain of my people under the siege, and I knew that every step we take toward freedom comes at a price. But I tell you: the cost of surrender is much greater.

"Therefore, hold on firmly to the land as roots cling to the soil, for no wind can uproot a people who have chosen to live. In the Battle of Al-Aqsa Flood, I was not the leader of a group or movement, but the voice of every Palestinian dreaming of liberation. I was guided by my belief that resistance is not just an option, but a duty. I wanted this battle to be a new chapter in the book of Palestinian struggle, where the factions unite and everyone stands in one trench against an enemy that has never differentiated between a child and an old man, or between a stone and a tree.

"The Al-Aqsa flood was a battle of spirit before it was a battle of bodies, and of will before a battle of weapons. What I have left behind is not a personal legacy, but a collective one, for every Palestinian who dreamed of freedom, for every mother who carried her son on her shoulder as a martyr, for every father who wept bitterly for his daughter who was killed by a treacherous bullet.

"My final will to you is to always remember that resistance is not in vain, nor is it a bullet fired, but a life that we live with honor and dignity. Prison and siege taught me that the battle is long, and that the road is difficult, but I also learned that peoples who refuse to surrender create miracles with their own hands. Do not expect the world to do you justice, for I have lived and witnessed how the world remains silent in the face of our pain. Do not wait for fairness, but be the fairness. Carry the dream of Palestine in your hearts, and make every wound a weapon, and every tear a source of hope.

"This is my will to you: do not lay down your weapons, do not throw away your stones, do not forget your martyrs, and do not compromise on a dream that is rightfully yours.

"We are here to stay, in our land, in our hearts, and in the future of our children.

"I entrust you with Palestine, the land I loved until death, and the dream I carried on my shoulders like a mountain that never bends.

"If I fall, do not fall with me, but carry for me a banner that never falls, and make my blood a bridge for a generation that will rise from our ashes stronger. Do not forget that the homeland is not a story to be told, but a reality to be lived, and that with every martyr a thousand more resistance fighters are born from the womb of this land.

"If the flood returns and I am not among you, know that I was the first drop in the waves of freedom, and that I lived to see you continue the journey.

"Be a thorn in their throat, a flood that knows no retreat, and do not rest until the world acknowledges that we are the rightful owners, and that we are not just numbers in the news bulletins."

INDEX